WITHDRAWN

Blogosphere

Blogosphere

The New Political Arena

Michael Keren

LEXINGTON BOOKS

A division of
ROWMAN & LITTLEFIELD PUBLISHERS, INC.
Lanham • Boulder • New York • Toronto • Plymouth, UK

LEXINGTON BOOKS

A division of Rowman & Littlefield Publishers, Inc.
A wholly owned subsidary of The Rowman & Littlefield Publishing Group, Inc.
4501 Forbes Boulevard, Suite 200
Lanham, MD 20706

Estover Road
Plymouth PL6 7PY
United Kingdom

British Library Cataloguing in Publication Information Available

Library of Congress Cataloging-in-Publication Data

Library of Congress Control Number: 2006932839

ISBN-13: 978-0-7391-1671-5 (cloth : alk. paper)
ISBN-10: 0-7391-1671-1 (cloth : alk. paper)
ISBN-13: 978-0-7391-1672-2 (pbk. : alk. paper)
ISBN-10: 0-7391-1672-X (pbk. : alk. paper)

Printed in the United States of America

♾™ The paper used in this publication meets the minimum requirements of American
National Standard for Information Sciences—Permanence of Paper for Printed Library
Materials, ANSI/NISO Z39.48–1992.

Contents

Acknowledgments

I would like to express my gratitude to the Canada Research Chairs Program and the University of Calgary for granting me a Canada Research Chair in Communication, Culture and Civil Society, which allowed me to work on this study in the highly professional setting of the University of Calgary. I am particularly grateful to Professors Stephen Randall, Dean of the Faculty of Social Sciences and Kathleen Scherf, Dean of the Faculty of Communication and Culture, for their help and friendship.

I benefited from my encounter with many colleagues to whom I am indebted, especially David Bercuson, John Ferris, David Mitchell, Barbara Schneider, and David Taras who read various chapters of the manuscript and provided me with useful comments. Special thanks are due to Susanna Egan of the University of British Columbia whose comments and encouragement were invaluable. I am also grateful to Aaron Ben-Zeev of Haifa University, Craig Howes of the University of Hawaii, Brian Roberts of the University of Huddersfield, Joel Migdal of the University of Washington and Shlomo Shoham of Tel-Aviv University for their inspiring insights on central themes of this study.

I would like to thank my research assistants Aiden Buckland, Julia Brotea and Victoria Guglietti who guided me through blogosphere and Cynthia Little who edited and formatted the manuscript.

Finally, I would like to thank the publishers who granted me permission to incorporate in this book material I published in the following articles:

"Blogging and the Politics of Melancholy." *Canadian Journal of Communication* 29.1 (2004): 5-23.

"Narrative and Image in the Commemoration of War: The Blog of LT Smash." *Journal of Strategic and Military Studies* 7.3 (Spring 2005).

"Online Life Writing: One Israeli's Search for Sanity" *Auto/biography 13.3* (December 2005): 187-205. Edward Arnold (Publishers) Ltd. <www.hodderarnoldjournals.com>

"How Canadians Blog" *In How Canadians Communicate* David Taras and Maria Bakardkieva eds., University of Calgary Press, 2006.

Calgary, February 2006

Chapter 1

Emancipation and Melancholy

April 10, 2003, 2:30 p.m. The American-led coalition seems to be victorious in the Iraq war. Yesterday, armored and infantry units entered Baghdad and television stations across the world carried images of a statue of Sadam Hussein in the Iraqi capital being demolished. While the screening of such images as part of the psychological war conducted against the collapsing Iraqi regime was encouraged, American officials warned that the war was not over yet. This was confusing and neither the morning radio and television broadcasts nor the offline and online editions of the newspapers helped to reduce the confusion. Blogosphere, however, is never confused.

Blogosphere, the aggregation of millions of online diaries known as "blogs," is naturally preoccupied today with the war. I am looking at the neo-conservative "Little Green Footballs,"[1] (subsequently deemed "Best International Blog" in a Washington Post poll). At 10:52 a.m. Charles Johnson, the blogger, posted a cartoon by John Cole of the *Durham Herald-Sun* titled "Oh, you poor people!" The cartoon shows a group of anti-war demonstrators facing rejoicing Iraqis yet murmuring in sadness: "Oh you poor people ... the pain you must be feeling."

When I began writing these two paragraphs, 45 comments on the cartoon had already been posted by other bloggers. This has climbed to 74 posts and their number will reach 121 by the end of the day. It is clear to me that this book will never keep up with the phenomenon it is studying. Understanding blogosphere is like chasing a running rabbit. Just following the comments on this one cartoon by 121 anonymous diarists who direct me to their own blogs, and to many other Websites they recommend, is a never-ending affair.

At 10:54, two minutes after the *Herald-Sun* cartoon had been posted, "tom

@ work" labeled it "brilliant." Tom is an online diarist whose time at work is apparently devoted to reading others' online diaries and updating his own, for he himself has just posted a Fox News item on the war. This item is accompanied by a comment on the spelling of "Fox News" by "Veronikka."[2] A quick visit to Veronikka's blog reveals that she has not posted an entry since yesterday because, in her words, "I'm not doing well, that's why postings have been really light this past week. When I stop being so damn near death, I'll try to get around to writing something."

Although I do not know Veronikka, and do not even know if she is a woman, a man, a child or a virtual figure invented by a group of Web-designers, I feel an urge to check why she is near death and am relieved to find out she is not in a life-threatening situation. I also take a look at her self-description: "Age: 23. Location: Mesa, Arizona Umm...that's it so far. I don't know what else to add. I'll think of something later." Over two years of blogging, before her blog disappeared from the World Wide Web for ever, Veronikka had, however, lots of information to add. At one point, she answered a questionnaire floating around in cyberspace and shared the answers with the world:

> Last car ride: Driving to work.
> Last food consumed: Chicken/balsamic vinegar/feta cheese/ spinach.
> Last time showered: Last night.
> Last trip to the bathroom: Sometime this morning, during my morning routine.
> What are you wearing now—Dress shoes, dress pants, dress shirt. It's work.
> Socks: Panty hose. Again, I'm at work.
> After this—work. That's what I should be doing now, but I am not. I am a bad, bad person.
> Talking to—No one. If I were talking to someone, why would I be filling this out? Or is this supposed to be asking about online people? I don't talk to online people, so N/A I guess.
> Do you think you are hot: Cute, yes. Hot, no. Angelina Jolie is hot, I am very very far from hot.

These responses point to some of the recurrent themes found in online diaries, especially the focus on the routine aspects of a person's life: eating, taking a shower, going to the bathroom, putting on a dress, etc. They also highlight the common perception of many diarists of their life as worthless. Angelina Jolie is "hot," while the diarist is anything but Angelina Jolie. More than once, Veronikka defines herself as "stupid." On February 25 she speaks of her urge to "make something." She decides to build a bed and even consults the instructions appearing in *Metropolitan Home*, but ultimately realizes she cannot do it. On another occasion, she has an urge to paint but settles for what she calls a "girlie magazine" instead.

Veronikka's life-story is filled with missed opportunities but this does not make the story, or for that matter the life, worthless. The more entries in the diary, the more an online identity emerges for us to love, hate, envy, pity, trust, mistrust, be interested in, learn something from, get attracted to, be curious about, or simply ignore. Veronikka is no George Eliot, Virginia Wolf, Indira

Ghandi, Simone de Beauvoir or Xevira Hollander, but over time she stops making statements like "I don't know what else to add."

On February 28, 2003, for instance, she feels "intensely cute" in the morning and "officially retarded" in the evening. In between, she gets into a political mood and posts the thoughts of one of her favorite bloggers, James Lileks, who is also a columnist for the *Minneapolis Star-Tribune*, about the tyrants of the twentieth century (who seem to him divorced from human nature). She promotes the columnist's statements in her blog because she finds him impressive "whether he's talking about politics or shopping at Target." In March 2003, she provides her own political comments on the coming war in Iraq and becomes one of the many bloggers, located between the "intensely cute" and "officially retarded," whose Websites are frequented every day by thousands of Web surfers all over the world.

When anti-war demonstrations in the world's capitals caused unease among supporters of the war, they were able to turn to Veronikka's diary, which not only served as a search engine sorting out relevant media stories and images but allowed them to feel like they were drinking coffee in her living room in the company of comrades sharing similar views. All they had to do was to link their own blog to "Veronikka" and relax. On March 2 at 11 a.m. she wrote that anti-war activists who went to Iraq to serve as human shields "should be fucking shot." At 11:55 a.m. she decided that actor Viggo Mortensen's anti-war statements sounded like "the crap some self-absorbed junior high kid would write on LiveJournal."

On March 5 at 12:30, after two earlier entries, on margaritas and peanut butter, and on a suicide bombing in Israel, she posted a newspaper photo of three demonstrators in schoolgirl outfits and asked: "Do the kind of chicks to whose political opinions you would listen dress up in schoolgirl outfits in public?" The next day, she posted a newspaper report on an anti-war march turned ugly, accompanied by her comment that peace protesters were not the "lovey dovey peaceniks they pass themselves off to be." On March 24, she posted pictures of demonstrators, pointing out the repulsive appearance of some of them like "the chicken-strutting bitch in the black t-shirt."

Turning back to "Little Green Footballs," the comments on the *Durham Herald-Sun* cartoon continue to flow in. Immediately after "tom @ work" announced his view of the cartoon as brilliant, "Zulubaby" found it "fabulous," "Clutch" complained the demonstrators sketched in the cartoon looked way too clean and intelligent, "Jeff" found "a deep message" in the picture, and "J.I Joe" called it "classic." In no time, the comments begin to mix with bigotry and hate speech. With every additional comment, the writers cuddle in each other's bosom and the language becomes self-serving and defiant toward the outside world. Here is a sample:

'Peace' Pricks doing their best to display their complete lack of sanity.
I am having the time of my life laughing at all the lefties today! I hope it never ends. I hope the whole world joins me!

Fuck the left-o-fascists.

You jews juz don't get it do you?

I've had a similar experience with a Leftie yesterday.

I think you are right that there is something psychotic about these people.

OK—True enough. When it comes to killing vast numbers of people, Saddam is bush league compared to the Communists.

What's the difference between San Francisco and Baghdad? One is full of anti-American socialists and the other is in the Middle East.

Liberal (Left) Fascists will use lies, distortions and commit criminal acts to shape the political landscape in a democratic society.

What do the French and our American soldiers have in common? Neither of them has bathed in three weeks.

As I observe the formation of this virtual community, I am aware that hundreds of other such communities are forming at the same time on the World Wide Web, with the bigotry not confined to one side of the political debate. Shortly after midnight, Aaron Trauring, a peace activist writing in "Stand Down: The Left-Right Blog opposing an Invasion of Iraq,"[3] expresses his despair over talking to "know nothings," apparently referring to bloggers who express opposing views to his. He writes that "anyone with a bit of heart can't help but feeling joy for the Iraqi people now that Saddam has been overthrown. But anyone with a bit of heart must also feel great sadness for the tens of thousands Iraqi dead and untold numbers injured and maimed for life."

Responses to this entry pour in for two nights and a day.

1:09 a.m. "Johnson" thinks that the problem with the war-lovers, especially the non-thinking ones, is that they think in simplistic infantile terms of black and white.

1:41 a.m. "Kynn" posts an assurance that a quick victory does not repudiate anything the anti-war movement stood for.

2:06 a.m. "unseller' asks where Trauring's figures are coming from. Twenty minutes later "Kynn" answers that we may never know.

3:54 a.m. "Vin Carreo" expresses his worries that Iran or North Korea may be next in line for an American attack.

5:47 a.m. "Buermann" calls the Bush government "colonial."

7:49 a.m. "Donald Johnston" shifts the discourse towards a familiar pattern: soul searching. "I don't think we on the left should gloss over some of our own overheated predictions that proved wrong," he writes. A blogger nicknamed "aronst," however, is not sure "why anyone in the anti-war crowd is beating his breast just yet." And "Johnson" redefines the goal of the anti-war movement: "to stop America, its predatory capitalism, its imperialism, its exploitation of other peoples and their resources, etc."

During the night, a blogger named "Dave" proposes some practical steps to be taken by the anti-war movement, such as moving the protests from the streets to Capitol Hill, but, as is often the case in soul-searching sessions, is being ignored. At 8:20 a.m. he files the following complaint:

This is the third time I have suggested a specific positive action which opponents of the war can take, now that the war that shouldn't have happened is nearly won. This is also the third time the suggestion has been completely ignored. Refusal to discuss specific alternative policies has been a consistent feature of this blog. This silence, amid the clamor of insults, accusations, paranoid whinery, and outright bigotry, speaks volumes about how little the denizens of this place really care about the real suffering of real people in the real world. Are you all so low and pathetic that you can't e[v]en FANTASIZE about doing something good or positive?

Dave's question is a good starting point for a discussion of blogosphere. What are we experiencing here—a new political arena in which serious concerns about "the real suffering of real people in the real world" are communicated and acted upon or rather a gathering place for the "low and pathetic"? In order to answer this question, which is at the core of this study, let me begin with some definitions and conceptualizations.

A New Medium

Blogs, short for "Weblogs," are online diaries with links to Websites of presumed interest such as traditional media outlets or other blogs. They came into being in the mid 1990s when Web designers put up personal journals at their home pages and linked to each other. In 1999, a company named Pyra introduced software that enabled people who were not skilled in Web design to create and manage their own blogs, and the phenomenon burgeoned. Today, millions of blogs have emerged from all five continents.[4]

Blogs came to public attention during the September 11, 2001 attacks on New York and Washington when they provided first-hand images and personal perspectives on the traumatic events, informing disoriented audiences about the shaky world around them. During the Iraq war of March-April 2003, many bloggers turned into alternate journalists by sorting out information from other media and providing commentary. Although this "do it yourself journalism" was criticized for being produced by people who mostly did not leave their computers, it became clear that a new medium of information gathering and sharing had emerged.

Blogs are receiving substantial attention in the mainstream media. In a *Newsweek* article in 2002, Steven Levy coined the term "blog-osphere"[5] to denote the alternate universe created by the aggregation of hundreds of thousands of blogs, tying the creation of this universe to the desire among ordinary folk to speak out after September 11. In a United Press International publication, James C. Bennett predicted that the "weblog, a sort of amalgam of commentary, diary and reference, may be to the Anglosphere's traditional modes of power what the printing press was to the medieval church and its intellectual monopoly 500 years ago."[6] In the *Ottawa Citizen*, David Warren referred to blogs as a revolution in journalism, listing many occasions when bloggers drew public attention to mistakes by the mainstream media. In several such instances, bloggers exposed misquotations by journalists through links to original transcripts; they forced one newspaper to retract a story about a meeting between American and British officials, which in fact had not taken place, and showed that a journalist's report from "behind Iraqi lines" could not have been accurate because the town he reported from had been occupied by the US Army at the time.[7]

On several occasions, blogs seemed to have direct political impact, as in late 2002 when bloggers linking to a C-span video clip of allegedly racist comments (made by then US senate majority leader Trent Lott at a birthday party) kept the story alive until Lott was forced to resign. The resignation in June 2003 of New York Times' executive editor Howell Raines and managing editor Gerald Boyle over the Jason Blair scandal was also attributed to continual pressure by bloggers. In the 2003 US race for the democratic presidential nomination, several candidates—Howard Dean, Dick Gephardt, John Kerry and others—made use of the blog format in their Internet campaigns. And when in September 2004, CBS's Dan Rather produced, on *60 Minutes,* documents apparently showing that George W. Bush received preferential treatment during his years in the Texas Air National Guard, it was bloggers who exposed the falseness of the documents. Such achievements convinced mainstream media to devote substantial attention to bloggers' political comments.

A major story that caught the media's attention during the Iraq War was that of a blogger known as "Salam Pax," a 29-year-old Iraqi living in a Baghdad suburb. His two week silence at the end of March 2003, when the Iraqi capital came under heavy American bombing, became a major news story, as did his return to cyberspace (and later his recruitment by *The Guardian*). During that war, news organizations became alarmed when writers ranging "from American naval officers to biological-warfare specialists and women soldiers posting their entries on the Internet from tents in the desert"[8] bypassed them, and when some of their own journalists, embedded in the field with US military forces, posted their reports in blogs. As Ted Landphair puts it, if the Spanish-American War was the newspaper war, World War II the radio war, and the war in Vietnam the television war, the Iraq War is the Internet war.[9]

The burgeoning of the phenomenon, and the growing attention given by the mainstream media to this new medium, raises questions about the politics of blogosphere. What are the political implications of the exposure of large numbers of people to an unprecedented amount of news selected for them by trusted virtual figures? Can the view of the press as a watchdog of democracy be applied to blogosphere despite the lack of journalistic standards and traditions among bloggers? How does the blurring of the private/public divide, while intensifying the digital divide, affect global political discourse? And how do value structures emerging in blogosphere differ from those prevailing in offline communities?

It is not easy to answer these questions because of methodological difficulties inherent in the study of blogs; it is hard to apply common research methods to this new medium. Generalizations about blogs on the basis of random sampling, for example, are impossible to make in the absence of a clear, stable, finite universe of blogs to be sampled. Online diaries come and go, and communities of bloggers are mostly formed ad hoc. Websites such as Diarist.net or LiveJournal bring diarists together, but many other blogs float freely in cyberspace.

Studies in which traditional sampling techniques are used to make general statements about the gender or socio-economic composure of bloggers are therefore false, especially since the phenomenon studied is located in virtual reality. While research on such subjects as the politics of newspapers deals with individuals and institutions whose identity can in principle be traced, here we know little about the producers of blogs besides their nicknames. The person presented in the diary may be in part or in full a fictional character, and for all practical purposes ought to be treated as such. Therefore, any statement about the nature and politics of blogging does not necessarily apply to an identifiable group of offline actors. Moreover, the tendency of bloggers to classify blogs by categories such as "politics," "society," "feminism," "sex," etc., is misleading, and self-reflective writings on the nature of the phenomenon suffer from acute self-aggrandizement.

A useful approach to blogging can be found in life writing research, which derives theoretical and historical statements from autobiographical works, whose unique character is acknowledged, and whose range incorporates both real and fictional writings. It is assumed that a systematic analysis of Winston Churchill's autobiography, for instance, may generate important insights into the political world even though it does not constitute a sample of leaders' autobiographies. It is similarly assumed that a systematic analysis of George and Weedon Grossmith's novel *The Diary of a Nobody* may generate important hypotheses on political life in Victorian England despite the unique nature of this fictional diary.

Applying life-writing methods to blogosphere is quite natural because blogging is a form of life writing. Tristine Rainer has assigned life writing genres into any number of divisions including autobiographies, memoirs, confessions, spiritual quests, meditations, personal essays, travelogs, autobiographical short-stories and novels; portraits, complaints, conceptual writings, works of humor, and family histories.[10] As blogging encompasses all these genres, we can view its development within the tradition of life writing.

Since ancient times, individuals have had the urge to develop their unique voice but the voices in novels, published diaries, autobiographies, etc. are mostly of people who have achieved public prominence. Others were doomed, as Rainer puts it, to "singing in the shower."[11] The World Wide Web gave anyone with access to a computer the opportunity to develop a unique voice. In the past, the private lives of individuals may have been the subject of village or town gossip, and some private diaries received public attention as reflections of particular eras, such as the American civil War, but most private lives did not reach the public domain. Blogging, on the other hand, denotes a transition from earlier genres, such as the autobiographical novel, written mainly by few incumbents of the bourgeoisie who had the time, money and access to publishers.

Blogs allow individuals from all strata of society to pronounce their private thoughts, feelings, desires, and deeds. This is often seen by bloggers as a sign of emancipation, that is, liberation from the authority of parents, peers, governments, institutions, or publishers who, in the past, decided about which life-story was worthy of print and which not. As blogger Rebecca Blood announced: "Let us use our weblogs to define ourselves individually as we move forward together as a community, joined by our shared commitment to self-expression, free speech, and the vigorous exchange of ideas."[12]

Blogging and Emancipation

In her book on subjectivity, identity, and the body, Sidonie Smith made a link between autobiography and emancipation, stressing the present change from a human rights regime based on traditional liberal values, which emerged in the patriarchal world of the enlightenment, to one based on a new subjectivity. The book begins with an attack on "the tyranny of the arid 'I.'"[13] Traditionally, Smith maintains, autobiography had been the story of a universal "I" obscuring through a gray and shapeless mist everything colorful that lay within its vision.

This refers of course to the enlightenment model of Rational Man, a model ignoring subjective differences and proposing an abstraction that is both universal and exclusionary at the same time. Although politically the enlightenment self is aggressively individualistic in its desires and liberal in its philosophical perspective, Smith writes, "the individual self could endure as a concept of human beingness only if, despite the specificities of individual experience, despite the multiplication of differences among people, the legend continued to bear universal marks."[14]

The universal individual of the enlightenment seems to Smith arid because it excludes everything that is colorful, that is, everything that becomes identified culturally as "other, exotic, unruly, irrational, uncivilized, regional, or paradoxically unnatural."[15] To secure the universality of the self, she contends, cultural practices set various normative limits of race, gender, sexuality, and class identifications. One of these practices was autobiography, which consolidated its status as one of the West's master discourses and in which the distinction between center and periphery had been set:

> Autobiographies told of public and professional achievements, of individual triumphs in strenuous adventures. They chronicled private journeys of the soul toward God. They chronicled stages of intellectual development, the evolution of consciousness. They charted a progressive narrative of individual destiny, from origin through environment and education to achievement.[16]

While this genre promoted a unified vision of the universal subject, it also served those formerly excluded from the vision:

> However problematic its strategies, autobiographical writing has played and continues to play a role in emancipatory politics. Autobiographical practices

become occasions for restaging subjectivity, and autobiographical strategies become occasions for the staging of resistance ... Purposeful, bold, contentious, the autobiographical manifesto contests the old inscriptions, the old histories, the old politics, the ancien régime, by working to dislodge the hold of the universal subject through an expressly political collocation of a new 'I.'[17]

Blogosphere may be conceptualized as the arena in which the newly emancipated individuals, the "colorful" to use Smith's expression, are defining their particularistic identities vis à vis an *ancien régime* consisting of traditional politics and the mainstream media. The inclusion of millions of formerly silent voices in the communication flow in society has not been lost on scholars who did not wait for empirical evidence to announce the rebirth of the "public sphere," whose rise and fall was described by Jürgen Habermas.

To Habermas, the public sphere is the discursive arena of civil groups demanding freedom of expression, due process, constitutionalism and other democratic rights. He associates these groups with the bourgeoisie living within the absolutist regimes of early modern Europe. According to Habermas, the liberalization of the market since the High Middle Ages brought about the crystallization of "civil society" as a private realm, a process enhanced by the rise of forums bringing individuals together, such as the coffee house and literary salon, where they engaged in issues beyond those sanctioned by economic patrons, church patriarchs and state leaders. Habermas lamented the loss of these forums with the rise of the mass media in the late nineteenth century.[18]

The channels opened by the Internet to individual self-expression have raised hopes for a reinvigoration of a public sphere worn off in an age of centralized mass media. As noted by Jenkins and Thorburn: "The current diversification of communication channels... is politically important because it expands the range of voices that can be heard in a national debate, ensuring that no one voice can speak with unquestioned authority."[19]

Many discussions have been held on the pros and cons of Internet use as a way to revitalize citizen-based democracy.[20] The various views of the Internet as enhancing democracy were divided by Lincoln Dahlberg into three "camps": a communitarian camp, which stresses the possibility of the Internet as enhancing communal spirit and values, a liberal-individualistic camp, which sees the Internet as assisting the expression of individual interests, and a deliberative camp, which promotes the Internet as the means for an expansion of the public sphere of rational–critical citizen discourse. Dahlberg is optimistic about the prospect of online deliberative democracy, believing that under appropriate structural management of the discourse, the Internet may become a means to expand the public sphere.[21]

In one of the first studies of blogs, Torill Mortensen and Jill Walker consider the Internet, by nature of its giving individuals the means to write their private thoughts for the world to see, as a rebirth of the public sphere. Mortensen and Walker agree that in the modern world of mass media, private persons have largely lost the means to participate in public discourse. On television, for instance, the private, individual view no longer has any real potential for influence; it has been made part of the public show. Blogs, however, revive the early nineteenth century salon or coffee house where private concerns could be discussed and consequently turned into public issues. They see the blog as being like the salon: a buffer zone between the private and public spheres. A blog expresses the attitudes and convictions of its writer while being in the public domain, and raising questions that may be of public interest. The blog connects the public arena with that of individuals.[22]

It must be remembered, however, that the individual of the twenty-first century is very different from the idealized *bürger* of the coffee houses and literary salons of early modern Europe. Just imagine what the bourgeois actor of Habermas's public sphere went through in the last 200 years—being mobilized by grand ideologies, crushed under the wheels of overwhelming technologies, and subdued by huge bureaucratic structures.

Ideology, technology, and bureaucracy transformed the life of individuals as they went through the world wars, the rise and fall of totalitarianism, the Holocaust, the atomic bomb, de-colonization, the cold war, and so forth. In those 200 years, the coffee houses were filled with shining-eyed revolutionaries promising people a redemptive future while unknowingly turning them into slaves of the gigantic power structures of Fascism, Communism, and Capitalism. The literary salons were replaced by the new meeting places of the industrial revolution: factories and railway cars; bars and jazz clubs; laboratories and bomb shelters; shopping centers and office buildings. The universal ideals proposed by the enlightenment were often discarded and the bourgeoisie was seen as "public enemy number 1" by almost every social movement and political philosophy.

Thus, before we rejoice over the rebirth of an imagined bourgeois public sphere, we must be sensitized to the modes of expression that developed as a result of the changes and their effects on the actors in that sphere, over the last 200 years. And before we indulge in the new autobiographical discourse just because it involves liberation from the exclusionary practices of the past, and the apparent assertion of an exciting, all-inclusive, new version of enlightenment, we must observe the actual political norms emerging in it. This is important because as the arena in which millions are redefining their identities, blogosphere is also the arena in which new political modes, norms, and forms of action and inaction are emerging.

The Politics of Blogosphere

Blogosphere is an important arena from a political perspective for here, individuals undergoing the transformation from the bourgeois householder to the multicultural world citizen not only comment on public affairs, as they do in Internet forums or chatrooms, but also exhibit their real or imagined private lives and thus may be seen as negotiating the nature and boundaries of the new public sphere. A study of blogs is an important step in the construction of an updated political philosophy whose emphasis on the private/public divide was traditionally affected by an abstract notion of the individual, and lack of means to penetrate his or her private sphere or lack of incentive to do so because it was considered irrelevant. Today, with individuals in all continents presenting their life stories for us to follow on a daily, sometimes hourly basis, it becomes impossible to ignore these stories as a component of the public domain.

In what follows, I characterize the public domain emerging in blogosphere, but first a word of caution is needed. Blogs are often voyeuristic, gossipy, and creepy. They appear authentic while they are not, and they portray lives we may not necessarily approve of. Laurie Mcneill admits to her difficulty to avoid a snobbish attitude towards them. She mentions the uncomfortable feeling that learning too much about people's daily lives invokes, lives that involve nothing particularly extraordinary except the diarists' own sense of importance. She admits her tendency to bring her book culture values to bear on texts not meant to be read this way, and her feelings of dismay that result from a literary and aesthetic arrogance.

This confession helps as a warning to avoid applying the wrong criteria to the study of blogs. In Mcneill's words:

> Bypassing the commercial, aesthetic, or political interests that dictate access to traditional print media, and that decide whose life stories deserve to be told, online diaries can be read as assertions of identity, and arguments for the importance of an individual's life. Even as their authors retain a degree of anonymity, these texts make very personal connections to a reading audience that recognizes and confirms these individual life assertion.[23]

In this study, I analyze online diaries which assert a handful of early twenty-first century identities: a cyberspace celebrity, a devout feminist, an Iranian student seeking freedom, an Israeli woman seeking political sanity, a Canadian baby boomer, an American soldier on a war ship, a showbiz star on the rise, an Indian mother of a sick child, and an African man writing about hunger, war, and misery. I analyze the characters (whether fictional or real) that emerge from these diaries in an attempt to assess the political implications of their newly acquired emancipation.

These online diaries are not a sample of the millions of diaries out there, and the issue areas they discuss are not an exhaustive list of the areas discussed in blogs. These are personal diaries written by individuals of different ages and genders, in different geographic locations, but which are marked by a friendly design and writing style, a personal perspective (i.e., not written by a political party or commercial enterprise), and a degree of acceptance in blogosphere.[24] These online diaries, however, are instructive to the observer of the early twenty-first century world. They allow us to examine some of the political values emerging in the public sphere as a result of the blurring of the private/public divide, and highlight the nature of blogosphere, the virtual public arena of the early twenty-first century challenging the traditional world of media and politics.

This new arena can be characterized by a unique combination of the fresh

voice of emancipation and a deep sense of withdrawal and rejection. The World
Wide Web has an emancipating effect but it does not replicate the emancipation
from Church doctrine that occurred during the fifteenth to seventeenth centuries.
That emancipation gave rise to the model of the enlightened individual who is:

> curious about the world, confident in his own judgments, skeptical of orthodox-
> ies, rebellious against authority, responsible for his own beliefs and actions, en-
> amored of the classical past but even more committed to a greater future, proud
> of his humanity, conscious of his distinctiveness from nature, aware of his artis-
> tic powers as individual creator, assured of his intellectual capacity to compre-
> hend and control nature, and altogether less dependent on an omnipotent God.[25]

While many bloggers may be enlightened individuals, this study, observing
them in their role as online actors, proposes an updated ideal type of the blogosphere resident not as enlightened but as melancholic.

Melancholy, the "unappeasable attachment to an ungrievable loss,"[26] has
been identified since ancient times as a medical and psychological condition. It
has also long been a symbolic motif of art as well as a familiar literary theme,
notably in Cervantes's *Don Quixote.*[27] In "Mourning and Melancholia," Sigmund Freud defined the distinguishing mental features of melancholy as pro-
foundly painful dejection, abrogation of interest in the outside world, loss of the
capacity to love, inhibition of all activity, and a lowering of self-regarding feelings "to a degree that finds utterance in self-reproaches and self-revilings, and
culminates in a delusional expectation of punishment."[28]

Freud distinguished melancholy from mourning by the fall in self-esteem it
involves and by the fact that the loss felt by the melancholic may not be real but
imagined, which accounts for the ambivalence surrounding that condition. The
inhibition of the melancholic, he wrote, "seems puzzling to us because we cannot see what it is that absorbs him so entirely."[29] Not always does melancholy
puzzle us as melancholics may simply be seen as people who come close to self-
knowledge, but what remains puzzling is their need to speak extensively about
their condition to others:

> [I]t must strike us that after all the melancholiac's behaviour is not in every way
> the same as that of one who is normally devoured by remorse and self-reproach.
> Shame before others, which would characterize this condition above every-
> thing, is lacking in him, or at least there is little sign of it. One could almost say
> that the opposite trait of insistent talking about himself and pleasure in the con-
> sequent exposure of himself predominates in the melancholiac.[30]

Melancholy is not only a psychological condition but can also be seen as a
form of social withdrawal stemming from the loss of a solid normative base,
especially the solid base provided by the universalized "I" of the enlightenment.
In *Melancholy Dialectics* Max Pensky introduced a sociology of melancholy
based on two major characteristics of the melancholic: solitude and the inability
to act. Since its pre-Socratic origin, Pensky explains, melancholy has been
closely associated with solitude stemming not only from the melancholic's sad

temperament but also from insight into the structure of the real. "Melancholy isolates; conversely, the enforced isolation from social institutions and practices produces both melancholic sadness and the alienation necessary to gain a critical insight into the structure of society itself."[31]

This critical insight is not, as in the case of the enlightened person, constructive and active but destructive and passive. Pensky argues after Robert Merton that melancholy constitutes a specific form of rebellion: the despair and hopelessness of the melancholic arise from the concrete or imagined condition of utter helplessness in the face of a social order experienced as oppressive or stifling. From this perspective:

> melancholia is a retreat from and a total rejection of society, due not only to the repressive function of social norms but also to the total effect of society, which the melancholic experiences as suffocating. The melancholic's rebellion is therefore a passive one. Under the conviction, whether justified or not, that all avenues toward effective action have been closed off, the melancholic rebel recedes into a resigned interiority, brooding over the very conditions of the impossibility of action themselves.[32]

In his *Critique of Information* Scott Lash characterized the melancholic from a political perspective. In the past, he wrote, politics was embedded in the good life—one had to be a man of substance to be a citizen. The melancholic, on the other hand, unlike Aristotle's virtuous and noble man, is a person not of the mean but of the extremes. Melancholics are not virtuous but vicious, and they are inactive:

> "The politics of speed, of melancholy, of indifference, is a politics of the outcasts, of the wild zones. The melancholic leads not the good life, but the bad life ... This is not a politics of those living in the margins as undecidables or unclassifiables, but of people living on the other side of the margins, abjected or extruded into the wild zones".[33]

A literary prototype of the melancholic can be found in Dostoevsky's *Notes From Underground* whose protagonist represents the reversal of the rational, enlightened citizen. While that citizen is marked by a readiness to compromise with fellow beings and serve the community, Dostoevsky's Underground Man feels aversion toward other human beings and society. He lives his life in a corner, in a mouse-hole, and knows that this is a form of existence a serious person could never aspire to change. He also knows that only fools can expect to avenge the punches they take from a hostile environment—be it the political system, or the mass media, and the like. Thus, he accepts his hyper-conscious existence in the mouse-hole: "There, in its nasty, stinking, underground home our insulted, crushed and ridiculed mouse promptly becomes absorbed in cold, malignant and, above all, everlasting spite."[34]

Yet, Underground Man has a voice. He keeps writing the notes, although he does not know why. His main explanation is that he writes them because he is bored. Anyone who found himself confined underground for 40 years, he says, would look for something to do. He does not wish to be hampered by any restrictions in compiling his notes; he just wishes to jot things down as he remembers them:

> What precisely is my object in writing? If it is not for the public, then after all, why should I not simply recall these incidents in my own mind without putting them down on paper? Quite so; but yet it is somehow more dignified on paper. There is something more impressive in it; I will be able to criticize myself better and improve my style. Besides, perhaps I will really get relief from writing."[35]

This is not to say that any of the millions of bloggers is necessarily "absorbed in cold, malignant, and, above all, everlasting spite." Bloggers can be found in all occupations, social strata, and spheres of life. Journalists who in addition to their work in the established media write a blog, university professors who feel the urge to disseminate their thoughts beyond the classroom, politicians hoping to gain public support, performers seeking attention, teenagers writing their diaries online because of the availability of the medium, and ordinary citizens writing blogs as a way to experiment with the freedom of expression granted them by this medium, as a hobby, as a boredom remover, or to have their "day in court," do not go underground. To the contrary, many of them gain social status, even celebrity, in the real world. Prominent bloggers like Andrew Sullivan, Mickey Kaus, Wonkette, Megnut, Hugh Hewitt, Rebecca Blood, and others are invited to speak at conferences, publish know-how books, turn their blogs into commercial enterprises, and so forth.

But the politics of blogosphere is marked by melancholy. This argument is clearly inconsistent with the self-indulgence of many bloggers in their new emancipation; in conference panels I attended on blogging, I was probably the only melancholic in the room. But an analysis of a political process led by any advance guard cannot be based on the way it depicts itself but on the norms apparent in its thought and action, and those emerging in blogosphere are often norms of withdrawal, not of enlightenment. Moreover, melancholy has been shown by Freud to turn into mania, so it should not surprise us that those exerting withdrawal from political action may express in a conference room "joy, triumph, exultation."[36]

The politics of blogosphere is melancholic not because it lacks joy, triumph, and exultation but because when these emotions, like any other feelings, thoughts, or activities are present, their relation to real life is incidental. Blogosphere involves journalism without journalists, affection without substance, community without social base, politics without commitment. It replaces action by talk, truth by chatter, obligation by gesture, and reality by illusion.

Millions of individuals write their lives while giving up on living them, if only because of the long hours they spend at their computers. Spending time at the computer is also part of life but it turns life writing into a cyclical exercise: writing about writing, reporting about reporting. Bloggers assert an individuality that gets lost in the need for approval by others, for it requires quite an effort to get one's blog posted on other bloggers' lists of favorites. They speak the truth without clear standards about what speaking truth on the Internet means, do good and refrain from evil in virtual reality, and often turn into political activists without leaving home. At times, blogosphere is praised by its residents as an agent of political change, as when Howard Dean, running for the democratic party's nomination to the US presidency in 2004, made use of bloggers to mobilize young supporters and raise a substantial amount of money, clicked in by Internet users. Dean lost, however, big time, once ballots rather than nicknames were counted.

Blogosphere and Civil Society

The withdrawal and rejection identified with melancholy, I would like to argue, is not a personal quality of bloggers but a systemic attribute of blogosphere. Bloggers do not live in mouse holes—they live everywhere—but the energy released from their keyboards at any given moment creates the hyper-conscious existence described by Dostoevsky. Blogosphere consists of a gigantic network of virtual exchanges exceeding the boundaries of political reality and the inhibitions of civil society.

In "Civilization and its Discontents," Freud defines individual liberty as primordial, and civilization as a restraining force. The urge for freedom is therefore directed against particular forms and demands of civilization, or against civilization altogether, he says.[37] The unrestrained nature of online writing and the unbounded political exchange in cyberspace can be seen as such freedom and the fact that many bloggers are prominent social actors only reinforces the transformation from a politics epitomized by boundaries and inhibitions to one marked by melancholic existence.

In recent decades, lots of scholarly effort has been invested in the renewal of Aristotle's notion of civil society, defined as a relatively autonomous sphere of political activity in which citizens do not act only as subjects of the state but think, talk, assemble, and act in matters that are of public importance. The freedom granted by civil society from absolute state control was seen as dependent on a public discourse that recognizes boundaries. A polity with a flourishing civil society is one composed of autonomous citizens who are conscious of their own rights as well as of the rights of others. They have actual interests whose pursuit requires cooperation and they believe in reason as the means to negotiate these interests. Consequently, they engage in a more or less rational exchange of ideas within a framework of social obligation and political responsibility.[38]

This notion of civil society stands in contrast to melancholic politics as it emerges in blogosphere. The latter is filled with nicknames rather than people, a fetishism of ideas rather than a presentation of interests, solipsistic discourse rather than an orderly exchange, and a lack of clear frameworks of social obligation and political responsibility.

The following chapters, analyzing early twenty-first century characters as they come into view online, draw a model of blogosphere as the political arena in which emancipation meets melancholy. These bloggers assert the new freedoms offered them by digital technology, tell their private life stories in cyberspace, and become part of a new political reality in which private concerns, whether or not responded to by other bloggers, become part of the public domain. As we have seen, this public domain is hard to grasp because of the rowdy flow of information in an endless number of links that makes this communication network seem more like a mythological sea creature than an orderly political entity. However, as we follow these blogs in their specific cultural and political contexts, they exhibit components not of civil exchange but of melancholic existence, which seems to increasingly denote the age we live in.

Here are people living in different continents and countries, representing varying modes of social and political belonging, whose life stories become commonplace, and who still remain on the margins. Their blogs display political passivity, trivialization of political issues, and disenchantment stemming from gaps between illusions over power acquired online and political reality. They show a preference for meditation over dialogue, form fake communal relations and blur the distinction between personal narrative and public image. They often crave fame and celebrity and when they do not achieve them but rather get punched by individuals or institutions, find refuge in verbal fetishism. Even when dealing with great hardships in the real world, which many of them do, they encourage delusion in the face of such hardships. It may be paradoxical that these variables of melancholy and withdrawal are detected in blogs written by the vanguard of the new emancipation of the early twenty-first century but this paradox is immanent in the new age we live in.

Blogosphere, turning into an important political forum if only because so many voters, subjects, opinion leaders, and consumers of political information visit it in their millions, has broken some of the monopolies that constrained the public sphere in the past. It has overcome the hegemonic voice of the rich and powerful and allowed anybody with access to the Internet to have a voice. It has opened up the mainstream media to voices from the margins, at least on one side of the digital divide, and formed a complex network of opinion sharing in which personal trust, rather than institutional reputation, becomes the source of opinion formation. It has made political discourse interactive and abolished etiquettes that have previously served as means to silence legitimate voices on the edges. It has allowed private or group needs (e.g., health needs) to become matters of public concern and to expand the range of issues that require political attention. It has also allowed civil groups to form, mobilize, interact, gain financial and emotional support, and be heard beyond national and geographic boundaries. It has become a place of breeding and residence for the contemporary global citizen.

This explains some of the features emerging on the global political scene. Blogosphere is of course only one dimension of that scene, but it is not without real, i.e., offline, political implications. The fact that so many global citizens solve the world's problems online, reduce political issues to their verbal dimensions, talk mainly to themselves, abandon standards of civil responsibility, and form online communities whose members may disappear from the Net at any given moment, may account for some of the symptoms of melancholy we encounter in the real world: a general feeling of helplessness and disenchantment over the ability of individuals to bring about social change; apathy and disgust toward politics enduring in an age of increased democratization; widespread resort to escapist and delusional substitutes for problem solving (such as rock concerts substituting for the rescue of the dying African continent), greater tolerance for idiosyncratic, extremist, or simply void political rhetoric (such as leaders' "apologies" in the face of ongoing genocide), and withdrawal of some to urban and global terrorism—the strongest expression of resentment. When the global citizen who has been promised a world marked by individualism, egalitarianism, and economic prosperity discovers that this promise, like so many previous ones, has little effect on his or her real destiny, withdrawal into various facets of the mouse hole can be expected. I will return to this contention after my analysis of the online diaries, situated at the meeting point between emancipation and melancholy.

Notes

1. http://www.littlegreenfootballs.com/
2. http://www.livejournal.com/allpics.bml?user=veronikka (this blog has been deleted and purged).
3. http://www.nowarblog.org/
4. On August 5, 2005 the *New York Times*' editorial included the following data from "Technocraty," a Website that indexes blogs. At that time, nearly 80,000 new blogs were created every day. There were 14.2. million in existence, 55% of which remain active. Some 900,000 new blog postings are added every day. Blogosphere doubles its size every 5 months. If the expansion continues at this rate, says the editorial, every person who has Internet access will be a blogger before long, if not an actual reader of blogs.
5. Steven Levy, "Living in the Blog-osphere." *Newsweek* 26 August 2002.
6. James C. Bennett, "Anglosphere: The New Reformation?" United Press International, <http://www.upi.com/view.cfm?StoryID=28122001-050733-7164r> (29 Dec. 2001).
7. David Warren, "Truth Serum." *Ottawa Citizen*, 8 June 2003.
8. Lack Grimson and Sarah Baxter, "Dramatic War Stories Flow in Internet Diaries," *Calgary Herald*, 31 March 2003.
9. Ted Landphair, "Online Journal Writing Opens Up Iraq War to Various Perspectives, Opinions," *VOA News.Com*, 30 March 2003.
10. Tristine Rainer, *Your Life as Story: Discovering the 'New Autobiography' and Writing Memoir as Literature* (New York: Putnam, 1998).
11. Rainer, *Your Life as Story: Discovering the 'New Autobiography' and Writing Memoir as Literature*, 125.

12. Rebecca Blood, *The Weblog Handbook: Practical Advice on Creating and Maintaining your Blog* (Cambridge, Mass.: Perseus 2002), 164.

13. Sidonie Smith, *Subjectivity, Identity, and the Body: Women's Autobiographical Practices in the Twentieth Century* (Bloomington, IN: Indiana University Press, 1993), 3.

14. Smith, *Subjectivity, Identity, and the Body: Women's Autobiographical Practices in the Twentieth Century,* 8–9.

15. Sidonie, *Subjectivity, Identity, and the Body: Women's Autobiographical Practices in the Twentieth Century,* 9–10.

16. Smith, *Subjectivity, Identity, and the Body: Women's Autobiographical Practices in the Twentieth Century,* 18–9.

17. Smith, *Subjectivity, Identity, and the Body: Women's Autobiographical Practices in the Twentieth Century,* 156–7.

18. Jürgen Habermas, *The Structural Transformation of the Public Sphere* 1992.

19. Henry Jenkins and David Thorburn, "Introduction: The Digital Revolution, the Informed Citizen, and the Culture of Democracy" in *Democracy and the New Media,* eds Henry Jenkins and David Thorburn (Cambridge, MA: MIT Press 2003), 2.

20. See Howard Rheingold, *The Virtual Community: Homesteading on the Electronic Frontier* (Cambridge, MA: MIT Press 2002); James E. Katz and Ronald E. Rice, *Social Consequences of Internet Use: Access, Involvement, and Interaction* (Cambridge, MA: MIT Press 2002).

21. Lincoln Dahlberg, "The Internet and Democratic Discourse: Exploring the Prospects of Online Deliberative Forums Extending the Public Sphere," *Information, Communication & Society* 4 (2001): 615–33.

22. Torill Mortenses and Jill Walker, "Blogging Thoughts: Personal Publication as an Online Research Tool," in *Researching ICTs in Context*, ed. Andrew Morrison (Oslo: InterMedia Report, 2002), 249–72.

23. Laurie Mcneill, "Teaching an Old Genre New Tricks: The Diary on the Internet," *Biography* 26 (Winter 2003): 26.

24. Jason Kottke's blog, discussed in chapter 1, has accumulated according to "technorati" 7078 links from 5506 different sources. Kottke also made headlines in the mainstream media, such as the *New Yorker* and the *Washington Post*, as had his girlfriend, Meg Hourihan, a co-founder of "Blogger", one of the first versions of blogging software. "Technocrati" counted 941 Websites that created 1091 links to Meg's blog, discussed in chapter 2. "Marn's Big Adventure," discussed in chapter 3, received several awards from such sites as "Diarist.net" and "Weblog" (where the award was based on no less than 366,187 votes cast over ten days). "Not a Fish," discussed in chapter 4, had 375 links from 257 distinct sources and received "the most egregious omission award" based on 63,000 votes cast on a site named "Weblog" over ten days. "Citizen Smash", discussed in chapter 5, received 1538 links from 1112 distinct sources. *Forbes*' online magazine recognized it as the best political blog. It is also listed in the political Weblogs section of the "Internet Public Library." Pamela Ribon's blog, discussed in chapter 6, has attracted 616 links from 536 sources, and earned several awards from diarist.net. "Iranian girl", discussed in chapter 7, ceased to exist, for reasons explained later, after a relatively short time, but had gained 156 links from 150 different online sources during its appearance on the Web, and attracted considerable attention in mainstream media in the West. "A Mother in India," discussed in chapter 8, has been chosen from blogs appearing in "Schizophrenia.com," a Website listed in many mental health related sources in Canada, the United States, and Britain. Finally, "On Lesotho," run by Rethabile Ma-

silo, discussed in chapter 9, is included in various African Webrings (portals citing blogs of a similar location or other characteristics) and on the blogroll of many other African bloggers.

25. David Tarnas, *The Passion of the Western Mind* (New York: Ballantine, 1991), 282.
26. Rebecca Comay, "Perverse History: Fetishism and Dialectic in Walter Benjamin." *Research in Phenomenology* 29 (1999): 51.
27. See Lynn Enterline, *The Tears of Narcissus: Melanc holia and Masculinity in Early Modern Writing* (Stanford, CA.: Stanford University Press, 1995); Teresa Scott Soufas, *Melancholy and the Secular Mind in Spanish Golden Age Literature* (Columbia MO: University of Missouri Press, 1990).
28. Sigmund Freud, "Mourning and Melancholia." *Collected Papers*, Joan Riviere trans. (London: Hogarth, 1971), 153.
29. Freud, Mourning and Melancholia, 155.
30. Freud, Mourning and Melancholia, 157.
31. Max Pensky, *Melancholy Dialectics: Walter Benjamin and the Play of Mourning* (Amherst, MA: University of Massachusetts Press, 1993), 33.
32. Pensky, *Melancholy Dialectics: Walter Benjamin and the Play of Mourning*, 34.
33. Scott Lash, *Critique of Information* (London: Sage, 2002), 139.
34. Fyodor Dostoevsky, *Notes from Underground and The Grand Inquisitor* (New York: Dutton, 1960), 10.
35. Dostoevsky, *Notes from Underground and The Grand Inquisitor*, 36.
36. Freud, "Mourning and Melancholia," 164.
37. Sigmund Freud, "Civilization and its Discontents," in *Civilization, Society and Religion* (London: Penguin, 1985).
38. See Michael Keren, *The Citizen's Voice: Politics and Literature in the Twentieth Century* (Calgary: University of Calgary Press, 2003).

Chapter 2

Cyberspace Celebrity

Jason Kottke is the poster child of the new emancipation. The blogger's skills as a Web designer allowed him even before the introduction of more accessible blogging software to employ the freedoms of self-expression, a point that was not lost on the many Internet surfers piously following his diary on a daily basis. The young Web designer has achieved a degree of celebrity in cyberspace comparable to the celebrity of Ronald Reagan, Jesse Ventura, Arnold Schwarzenegger, or Britney Spears in the "real world."

And, as in their case, his celebrity has led to a very special version of individual freedom. The exposure of his private life to hundreds of thousands of Internet surfers to admire allows him to express independent and innovative ideas, exhibit idiosyncratic behavior, lead fashions and trends, and shape the attitudes of many. Yet, an observation of hundreds of entries published in this blog since 1998 reveals a similar phenomenon to the one often found in celebrity autobiographies: a deep sense of melancholy.

As I claimed in the introduction, the melancholic is only an "ideal type" — no blogger can be expected to feel or behave like Underground Man, and no resemblance between that literary figure and any real person can be assumed, especially since this study focuses on online representations of individuals, not on real persons. Moreover, it is hard to find similarities between Jason Kottke and Dostoevsky's narrator because the latter is not emancipated. Living on the margins, in the extremes, is liberating only in a very limited sense. Underground Man expresses himself freely, but lacks the balance necessary in a process of emancipation, between his self-assertion and the surrounding social structures and norms. The blogger, on the other hand, stands at the forefront of early twenty-first century society, a pioneer in blogosphere, which makes the signs of social marginalization and political passivity found in the blog rather interesting to watch. As we read the diaries posted over several years, melancholy becomes apparent in the form of withdrawal from reality to virtual reality, the formation of online relations that are more those of a cult than a civil community, and, most significantly, a tendency toward political passivity. Let me now show these variables as they emerge in "kottke.org."[1]

Preference for Virtual Reality

One of the main characteristics of "kottke.org" is the writer's location at the forefront of a brave new world inhabited by cyber-citizens whose lives are played out in virtual reality. In *This Virtual Life*, Andrew Evans defined virtual reality as the illusion of participation in a synthetic environment that either simulates the real world or creates realistic fantasy worlds.[2] The thousands of people following on a daily basis Jason Kottke's life-story are exposed, as in *The Matrix*, to a life that is mostly taking place in "cyberspace," defined as the arena, composed of computers and telecommunication, in which the above simulation is played out.

In his very first entries in 1998, this online diarist realizes, at some distance, the existence of a real world. According to one entry, he goes grocery shopping at the local superstore and notices a young couple in the parking lot hugging, kissing, and oblivious to the ten or so people watching them. "I was happy. Because I was witnessing True Love," Jason reports, "like in the movies" (20.3.98). Even in this early entry, the twenty-six-year-old Twin Cities boy, who admittedly never experienced true love before and whose life seems to him as "just sort of floating nonchalantly along" (18.8.98), associates love with the fantasy world of the movies.

Occasionally, the diary mentions sensations associated with real life, i.e., with life away from the computer. In September 1998, Jason posted an entry on shingling as "a welcome change from the computer. You're outside, getting a tan, wind in your hair, pounding nails, scraping up your knuckles on the shingles until they bleed, hoisting seventy-five pounds of shingles on your shoulders and climbing up a ladder. Ahhh...that's the stuff" (2.9.98). However, such entries become quite rare as the diarist gradually confines his life to the Web. Consider the entry of April 2000 titled "spring is in the air." The reader expecting a spring sensation is faced with the following statement: "Spring is in the air and that means leafy green Web sites are popping up all over the web" (26.4.00). Although this entry is ironic, in many others the abandonment of real-life experiences for simulated ones is stated in all seriousness. A "great day" for Jason is one in which his experience on the Web is fulfilling: "Today is one of those days. No, not one of those days, one of those good days for finding neat and interesting things on the Web. So much to link to and discuss" (5.4.02).

Cooking and exercising do not normally fit into his daily regimen and when he goes out to play basketball he admits: "I pretty much sucked because, well, all I've been doing for the last, oh, 6 months, is sitting around on my ass doing nothing" (13.9.00). And yet, doing nothing; that is, writing diary entries and answering hundreds of E-mail messages, is the essence of life in cyberspace in his perception, as illustrated in an entry written upon his return from an "Emerging Tech Conference" held in May 2002. He wrote that, just like in college, when new syllabi handed out on the first day of classes determined his life for the entire 14 weeks of the semester, he now felt "like this is my world, and not just for the next 14 weeks. I've been given a syllabus to follow; the future is uncertain but the path is clear" (17.5.02).

Sometimes, a conflict between the old reality and the new cyber-world can be identified. In one entry, Jason describes his difficulty to return to the Web after a vacation in the beautiful Alaskan wilderness. He assures himself, however, that this feeling will be over soon: "I'm sure I'll forget all about it in a few hours when the digital crack starts talking hold" (30.4.02). The purpose of this diary entry, he writes, is to remind him of that feeling once it is gone.

Life in cyberspace is an escape for many Internet users and this diarist is no exception. At one point he quotes from an article by another blogger, Jonathan Rauch, whose declared introversion resonates with how Jason feels as a person:

> The Internet has helped me a great deal in this regard. Email, IM, and my weblog allow me to communicate with people when I want and how I want, without worrying about all the things introverts worry about when interacting with people: small talk, first impressions, awkward silences, etc. With the web, I can carry on a conversation with a whole group of people and stare down at my shoes at the same time. That's an amazing and special thing for me.[3]

As a Web designer, Jason makes the most of the opportunities opened to him by his virtual presence. If in real life he looks at his shoes while engaged in conversation, in cyberspace he controls his presence to such a degree that he turns the introvert into an extrovert. What can be more fulfilling than placing a Webcam at his home for people to peep? "People seem to think the webcam is about me entertaining you," he writes in his diary. "That is incorrect. The cam is all about me establishing myself as a major Web microstar" (18.11.99).

Over the years, the Webcam is used to enhance his new—virtual—identity. At one point, he pulls a trick on the readers by replacing his own picture with that of an impostor. At another, he produces an image of himself for the readers to manipulate. The readers are invited to "play with Jason" (16.1.00). They can put sunglasses on his eyes and earphones on his ears, make a female figure kiss him or put a pre-programmed sentence into his mouth. Many people sent in the images they formed of their admired blogger but what is most interesting about the game is the sentence Jason chose to be placed in his mouth: "I am a big loser" (16.1.00).

This may seem strange in light of the celebrity status he acquired but it makes sense if we consider the sentence in light of the model of the melancholic. However cute the person behind the diary seems to his readers, and perhaps is in real life, as an actor in cyberspace (which is the only angle from which he is analyzed here) he shows defiance toward the real world. Jason does not live in a late nineteenth century mouse-hall but in some "reloaded" version of it; he is the resident of a new world in which many of the joys and sorrows of the old one are rejected. It is easy to imagine the following "kottke.org" entry as having been taken from Dostoevsky's *Notes*:

> I was helped by the singing cashier last evening at the local grocery store. He wasn't really singing...he was just very melodic. It sure cheered up the toddler with the couple in front of me in line, but it really didn't do much for me but annoy me. Bad singer and wasn't funny, even though he thought he was both" (15.1.99).

The singing cashier and the cheerful toddler, characters belonging to the *ancien régime*, are annoying to the resident of the new world, yet even when a daily experience is not annoying but sparks feelings of happiness, or a memory of such feelings, an effort is made to translate these feelings into cyber-language. For example, in June 2001, Jason, wandering in the park, saw two teams playing baseball. According to his diary, he found himself rooting for one of them that was not quite up to the task but nevertheless enjoyed playing baseball on a nice summer day. Three days later he felt uncomfortable about the story, which, he wrote, did not capture his feeling at the time. He never said what that feeling was but rather subjected the whole experience, which seemed so genuine when initially reported, to one of those exercises conducted on the Internet: "Instead of taking it down or just leaving it the way it is, I'm going to make a creative writing exercise out of it. Every week or so, I'll revisit the story and write a new version of it. The hope is that I will eventually arrive at a version of the story that gives you a sense of the feeling I had that day" (6.6.01).

One scene described in April 2001 is particularly striking in its resemblance to the *Notes*. Dostoevsky's narrator describes an encounter he had with an officer who pushed him without even noticing his presence, and expresses his frustration over his inability to take revenge for such rude behavior. Now here is the entry in "kottke.org":

> I was accosted by a Big Arm Swinger on the street today. You know the type, arms tracing full 180 degrees swathes in the air, taking up three times the space they should be on the sidewalk, making it nearly impossible for someone like myself to maneuver around them. A mobile windmill at maximum flow. Anyway, this particular BAS appeared in front of me without warning (I wasn't paying much attention) and caught me in the crotch with her backswing. Stumbling and wincing slightly, I sped around her rather than leaving myself open to further attack. Lost as she was in the freedom of her arm swinging, I don't think she even noticed hitting me. (3.4.01)

Dostoevsky constructed the character of the loser who fails to avenge the pushing and beating he suffers and subsequently places himself in a mouse hole. Jason Kottke, repeatedly referring to himself as a loser, constructed the figure residing in cyberspace. In doing so, both the nineteenth century writer and the twenty-first century blogger pose a challenge to the model of the citizen of the enlightenment who is not expected to escape reality but rather to make use of the new freedoms to hold a constructive public dialogue.

Formation of a Cult-like Community

Although the writing of online diaries is mostly an individual activity, the writers often form communities, in that they are aware of each other, post comments in or link to each other's sites, exchange information, and so forth. The community surrounding "kottke.org" can be characterized as a cult. Cults have been generally defined by three variables: an enchanting leader; a devoted group of followers; and a strong emotional bond between them. In blogosphere, Jason Kottke is as great a celebrity as those created by other media of popular culture, such as television or rock music. There is hardly an article on blogging that does not mention him or interview him. In one article he was labeled "über-blogger";[4] in another, "some sort of web god."[5] A special site titled "obscure logs" offers refuge to bloggers identified as beings *other than* Jason Kottke. His picture can be found in offline advertisements, and women often announce the crush they have on him: "If you haven't heard of Jason Kottke, you haven't surfed the web enough. [H]e is one of those brilliant designers whom everyone seems to know and adore. Cutting edge. Revolutionary. Sharp. I go to his weblog every single (week) day and pretty much take what he says as gospel."[6] There are profiles drawn of him in online and offline journals, notably a feature by Rebecca Mead in the *New Yorker* in November 2000 where his romance with another "über-blogger," Meg Hourihan, was presented in a fashion reserved for royal couples: "She is tall and athletic-looking, and has cropped spiky hair that last spring she bleached white-blond after polling the readers of her blog about her hairstyling options."[7]

There are various mechanisms that contribute to Jason Kottke's celebrity status—his frequent referral to himself in third person ("you can watch as Jason sneezes, scratches himself in inappropriate places, yawns, sits in the same place for very long time, and, most importantly, shudders uncontrollably as the 3 pm post-caffeine depression sets in and the subsequent dash for a Pepsi") (6.4.01); his mention of every piece written about him ("look Ma, I'm in a Book") (7.1.00); his hiding of self-indulgence behind a veil of irony ("kottke.org: Bigger Than Jesus") (14.4.02); his self-presentation as an ordinary guy facing big corporations ("The Internet today is increasingly in the hands of people concerned only with power and money. I'm going to do my small part to keep the spirit of the Internet founders alive") (14.4.99); and his capacity to activate his readers.

("Our household was all abuzz last night for the season premiere of The West Wing. At two hours the episode was a little long and not as neatly packaged as the show usually is. A bit disappointing but still the best thing on network TV. My questions to you are: 1) what do you think?; and 2) where's the best place online to discuss episodes after the fact?") (26.9.02)

It goes without saying that answers kept pouring in for 6 days and nights.

The readiness to respond to Jason's queries is amazing even in view of the familiar phenomena of call-in radio shows, talkbacks in media Websites or the March 2001 pilgrimage of thousands to a Web page on which the Virgin Mary was believed to appear. Jason Kottke's followers respond to any question, even if it sounds like a bored soldier's riddle on night guard, e.g., "You know when you wear an outfit with a black tie on a black shirt with a black coat? Or a white tie on a white shirt with a white coat? What's that called?"

The cult responds in mass when Jason asks them to vote for him in some Internet contest or when he asks for drafts of his victory speech should he win such a contest. He despises the "sheer stupidity of the masses" (5.9.00), but this does not discourage the masses from sending him greetings for his birthday, or for the anniversary of his blog. When he found one of his old pre-Internet diaries, other bloggers not only posted selected entries from that diary on their own sites (e.g., "life is the mayonnaise through which we squirt") (9.8.01) but sent in their own childhood diaries for him to post on his.

When Jason moved from San Francisco to New York, hundreds of people in cyberspace were holding their breath, reading all about the packing, the journey, the search for housing, the unpacking, the furnishing of the house, etc. In October 2002, no less than 126 comments were posted on "kottke.org" wishing him good luck, advising him where to find cheap housing, sharing with him various experiences about moving, showing sympathy over the difficulties that lay ahead, providing information about New York traffic rules, restaurants, street security, and what not. Although the community meets on the Web, bloggers from San Francisco expressed their regret that Jason is leaving town and New York bloggers rejoiced he is joining their city: "I am psyched to welcome you folks to my home city, even if I live in New Jersey now. You've got a friend in the Garden State (exit 165)" (20.10.02).

The cult-like behavior of the community seems to be enhanced by Jason's presentation of himself as an ordinary person. In one of the accounts of his past he writes: "I mainly recall coming home from school and watching Scooby Doo reruns whilst eating Nutty Bars. Come to think of it, that pretty much describes my current existence as well" (4.1.00). The worship of the ordinary has its foundations in all religions but its special cyberspace version deserves notice. Here, one has greater choice over the object of worship. Just as Jason allows his readers to manipulate his Webcam picture, so also they can decide who the person behind "kottke.org" is to them—the ordinary guy, the loser, the professional, or the celebrity. The appeal of this online diary may have something to do with its simplicity, which makes it easy for many to identify with Jason. As "Cam" expressed it in October 1999, "I think Jason and I are living parallel lives. My favorite book as a kid was also 'Cloudy with a Chance of Meatballs.' I also recently saw 'The Mummy' on DVD, and it did indeed suck."[8]

But the cult-like behavior may also be related to the nature of the new medium. David Weinberger presents the Web experience as a way for strangers to develop communal ties while remaining strangers:

> In our culture, we're suspicious of strangers. They're a threat. They lurk in shadows. On the Web, however, strangers are the source of everything worthwhile. Strangers and their utterances are the stuff of the Web. They are what give the Web its matter, its shape, its value. Rather than hiding in our tents and declaring our world to exist of the other tents near us—preferably with a nice wall around us—the Web explicitly is a world only because of the presence of so many strangers.[9]

Jason sometimes conveys a real-life loneliness as well as awareness of the community formed by all the lonely people who happen to link to each others' Web sites at the same time, thus forming what he calls "Linky love": "I bet if I link to a bunch of people here, that most of them will link back to me. They'll look at their logs and say: 'hmmm...this Jason guy linked to me' and then they'll write about it in their journal or weblog. Let's see what happens. And if I link to you and you're reading this, there's no harm in playing along, is there?" (14.8.99).

Whereas in traditional social contract theory such mechanistic connections between isolated units were seen as the foundation of a rational community, here rationality is replaced by what Ralf Dahrendorf called in a different context "a steam bath of popular feelings."[10] Strangers linking to each others' Websites develop emotional bonds, not because of any human contact between them but because of their very participation in the same endeavor at the same time. This is a new version of collectivism—a community feeling love while remaining estranged, as if a community of ants would begin to develop emotions by nature of their work on a common project.

It is interesting to follow Jason's description of the workings of blogosphere. He sees it as a complex system in which individual bloggers, acting in their own self-interest, post bits of information on their Weblogs. Then, a feedback loop starts; other bloggers take those initial bits of information, rework them, and feed them back into the system in the form of Weblog posts or comments. At the end of the line, a story may emerge that has been collectively edited by the system. Repeat this process millions of times a month with hundreds of thousands of participants, he writes, and you will get a few such stories a month. He rightly asks whether this means that the whole is smarter than its parts: "Is some higher level of structure or intelligence coming out of these 500,000 monkeys at their typewriters?" (25.2.02).

Whatever the answer, the perception of many individuals that they are part of a complex system generating a higher intelligence creates a new kind of bond. In contrast to the participants in an Aristotelian assembly of citizens, they do not have to develop their personalities, relate to each other's interests, negotiate, compromise, form coalitions, elect officials, fight wars, or make peace. They can, rather, hide behind nicknames; appear and disappear at their choosing, make far-fetched statements, and take no responsibility for the information they post. As suggested by the title of Jerzy Kosinski's well-known novel, all that is required of them is "being there," a precondition of the formation of cults and the worship of demigods.

Political Passivity

A common theme in "kottke.org" is the threat felt by the ordinary guy facing big business, big government, big Hollywood, and other giant forces. Here is an example: "business may be changing, but the power is still in the hands of the people who have been in control of things for quite some time. The more things change, the more they stay the same" (25.3.00). Another example can be found in an entry on the ubiquitous little cups for extra pennies placed by the register in gas stations. While this is hardly an earth shaking issue by any standard, it sounds like one:

> Let's stop to think about this for a minute. This means somewhere there is a machine (or possibly a whole factory of machines) punching out these custom penny cups. There are engineers designing bigger and better share-a-penny cups. Teams of marketing people are trying to build share-a-penny mindshare in the heads of gas station owners. Share-a-penny cup salespeople are out there going gas station door to door to gas station door selling their product. An army of delivery trucks are delivering these cups around the globe. Does this seem odd to anyone else? (17.2.99)

This esoteric entry espouses populism, i.e., the political ideology of the ordinary person threatened by exploitative economic and political forces. The blogger appears to be threatened by the phantom armies of delivery trucks he pictures roaming around the globe. There is however very little indication of public action (on any issue—large or small) in this blog throughout the seven years of its existence, as if the online recording of one's life becomes a substitute to changing it. Months may pass without any reference to elections, policy debates, leadership scandals, international crises, or any other political matter. Jason is uneasy, for example, about the marketing of certain products of popular culture to teenagers but his response, as always, remains passive: "I'm not exactly sure what I can do about the situation, but I do know that as time passes, I get more and more uneasy about mass media, advertising, and marketing in general" (6.3.01).

His uneasiness does not make him leave the computer in order to take political action in the real world. To the contrary, in one of the rare comments on political affairs, he reports a "burning rage" over Elizabeth Dole's drop out from the 2000 presidential race for lack of funds. To him, "it's all about money and winning, packaged in an eggshell-thin concern for the well-being of America and her constituents." His conclusion: "Politics makes me want to puke" (20.10.99).

Although many bloggers are politically alert and encourage political consciousness among their readers, it is hard not to feel that such expressions of disgust and apathy toward politics may be partly related to the nature of blogging as an activity demanding long hours at the computer, perhaps with the hope that the new medium of blogging would itself make a difference by its sheer mass. Jason, at any rate, conveys a clear sense of political passivity, which is nicely reflected in a mention of the old fable about the tortoise and the hare. While the fable's common moral is that a slow but steady tortoise wins a footrace against an overconfident hare, the diarist insists that "The race was not won by the tortoise; it was lost by the hare" (27.10.98). The tendency to wait for evil forces to disappear rather than search for the strategy needed to defeat them can be found in this blog again and again.

In light of this political passivity, it is interesting to observe the blogger's response to the attacks on the Twin Towers and the Pentagon on September 11, 2001. A report on "September 11 and the Internet" prepared by a study group a year later noted the function fulfilled by blogs on that day. With CNN alone receiving more than nine million requests for its main Web page every hour, the servers for major news outlets shut down. Blogs were subsequently reoriented and became alternate news sources. The report says that most bloggers were not particularly interested in becoming "real" news sources, but rather connected large audiences to sites they would not ordinarily visit.[11]

Jason referred his own readers to a large number of sites in which videos of the disaster and other updated information could be viewed. His interpretation of the events, however, was quite consistent with the apolitical nature of his blog: "All this talk of America vs. the world by our politicians is making me sick and uneasy," he wrote as early as September 11 at 10:17 a.m. "This is a human issue, not an American, democracy, or a freedom issue. Someone attacked us all, all if us on the Good Earth" (11.9.01).

Jason felt that being positioned at the computer at this critical hour was important: "Some people cope by hearing and distributing information in a crisis. I'm one of those people, I guess. Makes me feel like I'm doing something useful for those that can't do anything. Or something."

During the day, and the next few days, he distributed information and made statements such as one expressing fear that acts of revenge against Arabs may take place and calling to refrain from them. He published online sites through which donations could be made to the Red Cross or Salvation Army, called for blood donations, and demanded that the US not respond in haste. He mentioned the usefulness of blogging in providing eyewitness accounts and photos from people who were at the scene, thus lending "a more human take than all the analysis and politics on the television."

After the crisis, "kottke.org" became part of the process of return to a normal routine. While mainstream news media continued to stir the 9/11 tension by rerunning the images of the day and filling the airwaves with analysis, Jason spoke, for instance, about games he played in an arcade: "They even had a Bubble Bobble machine, one of my all-time favorites. Good, clean, dorky fun" (16.11.01). He explained the need to return to such themes by his restlessness vis à vis the mainstream media, assuring his readers he was not apathetic or desensitized to the situation. Whereas the initial media reports on the attacks had seemed to him honest and true, now he felt their spin:

> The PR machines of our government, large corporations, special interest groups, various agencies, and political parties have had time to mobilize. Everyone now has an 'angle' appropriate to their political/corporate/religious/cultural affiliation. It feels like I'm not hearing the truth from humans anymore, I'm hearing careful crafted and sanitized PR from government/company/agency/media spokespeople. (2.10.01)

He declared he would nevertheless continue to apply a critical mind to the information surrounding him, an act that he felt might help some of his fellow citizens out.

During the Iraq War of 2003, "kottke.org" also served as a source of information. It advertised the time and place of demonstrations and published the phone numbers of New York city officials who might be contacted in order to reverse a decision not to issue a permit for some demonstration or other. But political passivity continued to prevail. Even when Jason found himself in an anti-war demonstration in New York, he insisted he went there merely in order to observe rather than protest. He simply zipped along the outskirts of the crowd taking pictures. He noted that "The enthusiasm of the crowd was impressive; they really believe in what they were marching for" (23.3.03), but from his position in cyberspace, he did not share in that political enthusiasm. As he wrote on March 18: "If you're a regular reader of my site, you'll notice that I don't write about current events or world news much. And in spite of the impending U.S. war with Iraq, I'm going to continue to write about other things because war & politics are a means to an end and there's more than one way to get there" (18.3.03).

Getting There

To get where? Following "kottke.org" in subsequent years, one is struck by the political withdrawal of the blogger and his readers in the face of continued killings in Iraq, the massacre in Sudan, the tsunami and other natural disasters in Turkey, Pakistan, Guatemala, the U.S., and elsewhere. Occasionally, entries on these matters can be found, but the cult seems generally disinterested in anything happening in the world unless it is related to the cyber-world. A question posed, for instance, on what *The Matrix Reloaded* movie is all about, and what the next installment holds, received close to a thousand responses. The interest in the movie surprised even Jason himself:

> Back on May 15th, I wrote a 221-word entry on my first impression of The Matrix Reloaded. At last count (mid-afternoonish on June 17th), people have left 700 comments in the thread attached to that entry (7 of which are mine). Those

700 comments comprise a total of ~125,000 words (~180 per entry); that's about 3.3 150-page books... If you were to look at all the content of the site in the aggregate, you might come to the conclusion that kottke.org is a Matrix Reloaded-related site... (18.6.03)

At one point, Jason lists several topics he found under his name in Google. The list provides a pretty good picture of the concerns he and his readers seem to share: *Matrix Reloaded, Matrix Reloaded* discussion, addicting games, Christopher Guest, The Cognitive Style of Powerpoint, Gaetan Dugas, The Incredibles, September 11 photos, earthquake in Japan, Tom Hanks filmography, Calvin Klein dinnerware, NYC subway, Where is Raed, Daniel Pearl execution, Moby Eminem (1.8.03). This list includes a few matters of political concern, such as the Japan earthquake (to which three lines with links are devoted), and the execution of Daniel Pearl, the American journalist kidnapped and assassinated in Pakistan in 2002. The entry related to Pearl, however, is more in line with the blog's overall populist mood than a reflective piece on a disturbing political and security issue:

just watched the Daniel Pearl execution video. To say the least, it was disturbing. I'm not sure if I'm glad I watched it or not (if it helped my understanding of anything, etc.), but I am glad that I was able to make the decision without worrying about if my government or some network news department concerned with ratings wants me to or not. (24.5.02)

Living now in New York City, and enjoying its restaurants and cinemas, the blogger nevertheless continues to present himself as living on the edge of urban life. Consider this entry: "I work in midtown Manhattan and my walk takes me up 5th Avenue for a few blocks. I feel so out of place there. Everyone looks like they care so much about their appearance and I'm just wearing what they wear to fit in. I can almost feel it...deep down, they all know I shouldn't really be there" (9.5.03).

Or consider "Jason's rules for the NYC subway," resembling literary portrayals of the individual crushed by the urban masses:

1. Get the hell out of my way, I'm coming through. 2. Do not stop at the top of the stairs to put your MetroCard back into your purse/wallet. You are between me and my train. 3. Act more like a particle and less like a wave. When you're weaving all over the platform like a drunken sinusoidal, energetic particles like myself—who, in keeping with Newton's first law of motion, like to remain in a uniform state of motion until acted upon by an outside force—cannot easily get past you. (30. 5.03)

The perception of life on the edge makes political activity seem futile—something others are engaged in. It is hard not to sense that this perception, and its political conclusion, is not just related to this blogger but is part of a common trend in contemporary America. Here is Jason's description of his Independence Day activities, which are not unusual: "What Independence Day is all about:—

Watching a 145-pound Japanese man eat 44 1/2 hot dogs in 12 minutes in the Nathan's Famous Hot Dog Eating Contest" (7.7.03). This experience points at the degree to which entertainment and popular culture have replaced historical memory.

Even when an event of historical significance occurs, such as the capture of Saddam Hussein, the blogger is not particularly contemplative. He is mainly confused by the frenzy in the media and in blogosphere over the event: "Unsurprisingly, the small but particularly vocal segment of the blogos-whatever that can be identified by their non-ironic use of the word anti-idiotarian, is asserting that there is only one right reaction to Saddam's capture and any other possible opinion is incorrect. It's a toss-up these days as to whose coverage of current events is worse, cable news or that of weblogs. Fox News may have Bill O'Reilly, but reading the weblog coverage lately is like watching 1000 cable channels at once, each with their own O'Reilly arguing with all the other O'Reillys. Warblogs, you've jumped the shark. Next!" (14.12.03).

Jason himself is a major contributor to the frenzy in blogosphere. The most hilarious literary descriptions of futile human conversation cannot match the nature and magnitude of talk generated by the blogger in early March 2004, shortly after the suicide attacks in Karbala on Shiite Islam's most holy feast day when close to a hundred people were killed and several hundreds wounded, and a few days before the March 11 Madrid train bombings, asking his readers to "Plan Jason's lunch." Only a world devoid of historical and political consciousness, or seeking refuge from it, could be expected to generate responses for two whole days, until Jason himself is forced to close the thread down. For example,

> Is there an Indian or sushi joint nearby? Those are the two options that usually appeal to me when I don't feel like eating the same-old...pastrami reuben at a jewish deli...I hate that feeling, and I get it all the time. Not that I would recommend doing it, how about just eating half a (big) bag of your favorite chips or salted snack, then hope you feel like eating next time your appetite comes around?... how about a spiritual discipline for lunch: a one meal fast... i was just thinking what del was thinking: a one meal fast, plus drinking lots of water. but maybe take a midday stroll, buy a meal, to go, and offer it to someone less fortunate... (5.3.04)

What we have here is a large number of Internet surfers engaged in talk that has no apparent consequences for their own well-being or that of anybody else. Even the entertainment value of this activity is questionable, considering the seriousness with which some members of the cult are approaching the "subject." Quite striking is the self-righteousness involved, e.g., the proposal to hand a bag of food to the less fortunate, which has no practical meaning in the context in which it is made. Rather than serving some civil activity, this proposal becomes a substitute for it. Moreover, the more such meaningless chatter becomes a common mode in blogosphere, the more the chances that economic or political interests step in and manipulate the cult. When Jason returns from his lunch (which does not stop the flow of posts, as if they are now running an independent course), he promotes a New York restaurant, which opens the door to the use of blogs for advertisement by restaurant owners and others. Jason's suggestion to launch a "kottke.org book club" (2.8.04) also raises the prospect that books be promoted in blogs as they are on the Oprah show, which may turn a medium of emancipation into yet another commercial enterprise in contemporary society.

Jason is aware of this problem of commercialization. In September he posts an entry titled "The Revolution will be commercialized," in which he reports that out of Technocrati's top one hundred most-linked Weblogs, only sixteen do not feature advertising or are otherwise noncommercial. He laments the commercialization of Weblogs:

> the quick uptake of advertising on blogs, the increasingly false perception of blogs as inherently unbiased by commercial interests (and therefore preferable to "big media"), the continuing shift from blogging as a hobby to blogging for a variety of reasons, the number of weblogs launching lately that have ads from day one, the demographic difference between the typical circa-2002 blogger and the blogger of today, etc. (19.10.04)

Yet he himself turns his blog into a commercial enterprise.

> I'm asking the regular readers of kottke.org (that's you!) to become micropatrons of kottke.org by contributing a moderate sum of money to help enable me to edit/write/design/code the site for one year on a full-time basis. If you find kottke.org valuable in any way, please consider giving whatever you feel is appropriate. (22.2.05)

This shift, he writes, stems mainly from the difficulty to blog and, at the same time, engage in regular work. In turning himself into a full time blogger, Jason feels he is maintaining, through a modern day version of patronage, an enterprise that has been corrupted by commercialism:

> People leverage their blogs in order to write books, write for magazines or newspapers, pursue art or photography, go work for Gawker, Mediabistro, or Weblogs Inc., get jobs at startups, do freelance design (as I used to), start a software company, or as a vehicle to sell advertising. All worthy pursuits, but I'm interested in editing kottke.org as my primary interest; blogging for blogging's sake, I guess. (22.2.05)

He promises that this shift will not turn him into a journalist; the site will continue to be personal although he will now have time to do "the occasional bit of real journalism" (22.2.05). This raises an interesting question about the prospects of such journalism: can an alternate system of news reporting emerge from the personal Weblogs of individuals who are politically passive?

Some clue is provided in Jason's reporting during the Republican National Convention in New York City in August 2004. As it was held in his city of residence, the convention raised his political interest and several diary entries dealt with the convention and other matters related to the presidential elections. He turned into a journalist of sorts who, however, did not attend the convention but reported "on the effects of the convention on the city's population, if any" (23.8.04). This may be considered a form of journalistic reporting based on personal impressions but the problem lies in the lack of criteria about what is fit to print. Not that mainstream journalists do not often substitute impressions derived from New York taxi drivers for serious reporting, but here there is not even an attempt to exceed the narrow point of view from which one inexperienced individual observes the scene: "If this morning's commute is any indication, security is ratcheting up around Madison Square Garden. As I boarded the 1/9 at 14th Street around 8:45 am, a NYC police officer checked every single car of the uptown subway train before departure" (23.8.04). The next piece of reporting is based on the parties' Websites in which Jason finds too many personal attacks on the candidates. This, he writes, made him cynical: "A few Madison Avenue ad guys could run Jeffrey Dahmer for President and outwit these knuckleheads" (23.8.04).

When the campaign focuses on the false accusations that documents concerning George Bush's service in the Texas National Guard during the Vietnam War had been forged, Jason calls for a return to substance. He now engages in what he calls "collaborative journalism"—compiling resources for people who need to register to vote. This is where the blog becomes informative, focusing on deadlines and procedures for voter registration, information for people voting via absentee ballots, and the like. However, the information, compiled in a "Voters Information Guide for the 2004 US Election," is gathered from Websites or sent in by readers, which makes it hard to judge its accuracy and reliability. It is quite impressive though to observe a large group of Internet surfers attempting to sort out the incomprehensible information on voting. Jason also posts instructions on what to do on Election Day, how to avoid harassment in polling stations, and the like.

As long as the blog serves as a source of information-gathering and sharing it is an important tool of civil activity, but it loses its importance once it resorts to gimmicks. Jason can't help making a presidential endorsement: "Instead of endorsing a candidate for President (ok, short answer: voting strategically against Bush, not that my vote will make any difference in NY), I'd rather see who you guys are planning to vote for and make that the de facto kottke.org endorsement" (1.11.04). This endorsement may be partly a response by the "little guy" toward the media giants who are constantly engaged in such practices, and some bloggers' endorsements may actually have a political effect, but as it is presented here, it turns the enterprise once again into a cynical imitation of media practices by those perceiving themselves to be on the edges, rather than an effective tool of emancipation.

It is still early to assess the political effectiveness of practices such as Jason's calls upon his readers to send in their Election Day experiences, as a means to improve the voting process in the U.S. in the future. It remains to be seen whether blogging could lead to significant political reforms by gathering voluntary information on such questions as: "how did your voting experience go? Any problems? How did you find out where to go and when? Did you vote using a computer? Any better/worse than a paper ballot? Were election officials helpful?" (2.11.04). On the one hand, this may be the beginning of a civil effort aimed at bringing back into the political process disenchanted voters, including young ones, who have given up hope on the complex and incomprehensive electoral structures. On the other hand, considering the three variables discussed in this chapter—withdrawal into virtual reality, cult-like relations forming in blogosphere, and an overall political passivity, blogging may just add more noise to a political communication system that is already noisy, frenzied, dysfunctional and disenchanting enough.

Notes

1. <http://www.kottke.org/>
2. Andrew Evans, *The Virtual Life: Escapism and Simulation in Our Media World* (London: Fusion, 2001).
3. Jonathan Rauch, "Caring for Your Introvert," *The Atlantic Online* (March 2003) <http://www.theatlantic.com/issues/2003/03/rauch.htm>
4. Steven Johnson, "Use the Blog, Luke." *Salon.Com* (May 10, 2002) <http://www.salon.com/tech/feature/2002/05/10/blogbrain/index1.html>
5. "We've Got a Crush on You," (14 January 2000) <http://crush.pitas.com/kottke.html>
6. "We've Got a Crush on You."
7. Rebecca Mead, "You've Got Blog," *New Yorker* (13 November 2000) <http://www.rebeccamead.com/2000_11_13_art_blog.htm>
8. Camworld, 31.10.99 <http://www.camworld.com/archives/000254.html>
9. David Weinberger, "The Hyperlinked Metaphysics of the Web," (drafted December 3, 2000), quoted in Kottke.org, January 5, 2001.
10. Ralf Dahrendorf, *Reflections on the Revolution in Europe* (London: Chatto & Windus, 1990), 10.
11. "One Year Later: September 11 and the Internet", 2002. Pew Internet & American Life Project <http://www.pewinternet.org>

Chapter 3

Online Feminist

The new emancipation enabled by blogging is strongly related to the liberation of women. What can be more liberating than millions of women who formerly lacked a public voice, asserting new identities, blurring the private/public divide that kept women's issues away from the public sphere, and educating each other, and the world at large, of updated norms and values. Blogosphere has become a major arena in which feminist essays, novels, and other forms of expression are selected and brought to the attention of a wide audience.

"Megnut.com,"[1] a blog by a young woman called Meg Hourihan, is an intriguing diary to watch because it serves as a source of empowerment. The persona presented in this blog is that of an emancipated woman in the fullest sense of the term. Meg often calls upon women to assert their power in all spheres of activity, especially the technological sphere in which she excels. She co-founded Pyra, the company that developed blogging software, and Kinja, a Weblog media project based in New York City. She is a frequent speaker at technology conferences, mainly on Weblogs and other Web services, in which she expresses her concern over the lack of female speakers at such conferences. "Though I've been speaking at lots of conferences," she wrote, "there aren't many other women up there on the podiums with me. I know that conference organizers would like to have more women speakers, so we need more women to submit proposals" (7.4.03).

Meg also serves on the Advisory Board of a Vancouver-based gaming company and wrote a monthly column for the O'Reilly Network. In 2003, she was listed by MIT's *Technology Review* as one of the young innovators whose technologies are poised to make a dramatic impact on the world, and in 2004 was recognized by *PC Magazine* People of the Year. She participated in a panel of distinguished women engineers and human resources professionals to discuss ways in which companies can encourage and support women in technology roles, and attended "The Evolution of Women in the Workforce-Realizing Your Potential and Fulfilling Your Dreams" conference, which aimed "to highlight the achievements of phenomenal women who have forged their own paths, pursued their passions, and ultimately, fulfilled their dreams."[2]

"Megnut.com" fulfils many of the expectations feminist movements have of the World Wide Web. These expectations have been studied by GenderWatchers, a non-profit feminist research group specializing in women's equality and movements worldwide. In an article published in 2001, Christina Vogt and Peiying Chen reported the results of a survey of fifty women's Web based organizations in the US and Canada that use the Internet as their primary communication medium. According to the report, most of the respondents agreed that the Internet has affected the women's movement positively in allowing quick dissemination of information by feminist groups organizing insurgent actions, and in providing a fast and easy lobbying and recruitment device.

The authors of the study are aware that the Internet has not formed substantial new root coalitions, and has been strongly constrained by the digital divide, but they feel that it can nevertheless be a tool of empowerment. Vogt and Chen report that many women complain about information overload but argue that feminists have implemented hundreds of women's Websites, and channeled women into special interest niches. To Vogt and Chen, mass communication and protests are no longer the venues used to produce social change. Instead, they claim:

> today's postmodern women's movement is being waged on a more local front, around specific issues and goals. While this specialization may feel to some women as if the world of feminism is shrinking, it has allowed groups to provide richer and more comprehensive information resources and to make active involvement more relevant for the average person."[3]

The criteria used to measure the success of social movements, i.e., their ability to change policies or underlying cultural norms, cannot be met online due to the lack of interpersonal relationships; nevertheless, Vogt and Chen are confident about the Internet's capability to replace traditional forms of political organization. "To a certain extent, the Internet replicates the same characteristics in cyberspace that radical feminists sought to create in their own local organizations: non-bureaucratic and non-hierarchical structures that provide a context for meaningful interactions."[4]

"Megnut.com" sheds light on the nature of online feminism and sparks preliminary thoughts on the degree to which feminist messages may ultimately lead to "meaningful interactions." The lesson the blog conveys is that although this form of online feminism has a clear potential to empower, especially when the blogger deals with specific issues such as abortion, it also involves reductionism of feminist messages, by nature of their dissemination in cyberspace, to verbal statements that are quite meaningless from the perspective of political mobilization. Let us look at this dual nature of the blog.

Meg vs. Megnut

My name is Meg Hourihan and megnut is my personal site. I am originally from New England but lived in San Francisco from 1997-2002. I recently moved to New York City's West Village and am happy to be back on the east coast. I started megnut in May 1999, which is hard to believe since it doesn't seem like I've been doing it for that long.[5]

"Megnut.com" has become one of the best-known online diaries, partly because of the curiosity raised by Meg's developing friendship with Jason Kottke. Meg's life seems less confined than his to cyberspace, although she also spends many hours at the computer. On reading in 1999 that an average person uses the Web every thirteen days for an hour, she confessed that she uses the Web once a day, staying there about thirteen hours. She refers to herself as "very disconnected from reality" (15.10.99) and is concerned about a career that requires her to spend so much time at a computer screen.

When a weekend passes without posting and without work, she sees it as a treat, and when she begins to experience the public enthusiasm over blogging, she expresses skepticism about the phenomenon: "Argh, all this glorification of weblogs is beginning to irritate me! Big deal, a columnist got a weblog. Why is this surprising? He's is a WRITER! And acceptance? Acceptance by whom? Is that what we're all striving for?" (2.11.99).

Meg is ambivalent about recognition. Commenting on one of the early listings of popular blogs, she writes:

The more links one weblogger gets from another, the higher s/he moves up in the rankings. So if I were to post, say, something about how I love to read On-focus and Evhead [two popular Weblogs at the time] every day, and post that every day, they'd be more popular. Cool, and then maybe one of them could be like the homecoming king or captain of the football team, and then like, I could go on a date with one of them, if megnut becomes more popular, and we'd be like the coolest kids in school! (22.11.99)

These lines hint at the possibility that blogging may sometimes substitute for the recognition one has missed in real-life, or for the lack of real-life human relations in general. Consider the following entry: "I think I'm doing this great job of communicating when in reality I'm opening up to strangers, but am too afraid to open up to the people toward whom the sentiment is directed" (23.3.00). In another entry, she distinguishes between "Dot-com people" and "web people," the former working for start-ups but having no personal sites, while the latter "pour themselves into the web, with stories, with designs, with pictures" (14.4.00). To pour oneself into the Web is seen by Meg in 2000 as the natural thing to do, for despite her love of nature, she finds it uncomfortable to stay away too long from the computer. "I made the mistake of spending a big chunk of time away from my computer, and now I can't seem to get back in the saddle again. Nothing in my head seems like it belongs on the web these days," she complains (25.4.00).

On May 1 2000, Meg laments the lack of human dialogue in college:

> As an English major in college, I wrote lots of papers. I had lots of ideas and thoughts and theses I expounded which fell on very few ears, mainly my professor, and if it were a large class, a TA or two. That was it. Imagine how integrating the power of the web into the classroom: a simple app like Blogger to facilitate publishing, hand a discussion off it, require posting/commenting by students, and get people learning from each other, talking to each other."
> (1.5.00)

The blog contains many references to simple feelings: "yesterday it rained in San Francisco and for the first time in a very long time, I did nothing. I looked out the window and watched the clouds darken everything" (8.11.99). But in spite of the personal nature of the diary, the difficulty to establish human relations offline can be detected. Meg is very proud whenever a family member, including her grandparents on both sides, goes online or connects to E-mail. In August 2000, when she went to Hawaii for a week, she invited her Mom to substitute for her and post entries in her blog. Mom, incidentally, played the role beautifully, just like a mother who is forced into meeting for the first time her daughter's dates on the doorstep, and she later even began blogging herself. But such online experiments are not trivial in light of occasional references to real-world communication difficulties. For example:

> My Uncle Jay's gourmet pizzas are profiled in a Vermont magazine! As my mom writes, "Our family is just so 'in the news' these days." What's interesting about it is in reading this article, I learned more about my Uncle Jay than I ever knew before (he's my uncle by marriage, my mom's sister's husband). And I bet if he and my aunt Marcia read the article in the New Yorker, they learned a lot more about me than they knew before. Seems odd that one would have to learn the details of one's family members from the media, but I guess that's what happens when you live across the country from each other. (15.11.00)

Or elsewhere: I didn't know much about my grandfather's war experience—he never talks about it, not when I was little, not now. But in less than an hour poking around online, I was able to uncover more than I ever knew about where he'd been and the battles in which his ship had been involved (27.5.02).

The familiarity with people through online connections has its amusing moments. This is Meg describing a party she went to with her friend Sylvia:

> Some guy stops me and says, 'Don't I know you?'
> I look at Syl, who rolls her eyes.
> 'Um, I don't think so," I say (as if this wholly unoriginal pick-up line is actually going to work.)
> 'No really, I think I do. Your name is Meg.'

Odd. I don't recognize him at all. How could he know me?

'Huh, you don't look familiar to me,' I say.

Suddenly his eyebrows raise and he smiles.'Megway! You're the Megway!'"
(17.12.01)

Over the years, Meg can be seen as negotiating her Meg vs. Megnut identities, a process that is particularly interesting to consider in relation to the rise and fall of the Nasdaq. In October 1999, at the height of the Dot.com craze, the diarist, co-founder of the successful Internet company Pyra, would sometimes feel disconnected from reality, not even knowing what day of the week it was. In November 1999, during Thanksgiving, she gave thanks to the Web and to her online diary's readers; in January 2000 she indulged in her blog being fourteenth in some popularity rating ("I feel like a high school cheerleader who got an acne breakout the day before the prom!") (5.1.00); in May 2000, she jokingly reminded her readers that "I'm speaking to you as a dot com executive, ya know" (17.5.00); and in August 2000 she all but wrote a birthday poem to "blogger," the electronic portal developed by Pyra:

> Blogger application, Blogger application,
> Here's to you we sing!
> We all hope that years to come,
> May never sorrow bring…" (23.8.00).

However, subsequent years were miserable for Blogger and many other seemingly brilliant Internet enterprises, and we can follow through "megnut.com" the accelerating process that led to the dot.com burst:

> So boo.com went down the tubes…Boo hoo, who would have thought? But you know, this whole shakeup is a good thing. Perhaps people will start to realize that usability matters, that business models matter, that you can't just slap a www before a name and expect a company to materialize overnight like a fungus in a dark damp place. (19.5.00).

The writing is on the wall, but the diarist is still on top of the technological world, reporting in the same entry about her attempt to produce a "megnut t-shirt." August 22, 2000: "Last night Deapleap announced they were shutting down, and I feel like I've lost a member of the start-up family to which I belong" (22.8.00).

Although Meg is always in search of a balance between work and the rest of her life, and reports on various efforts to travel, climb mountains, and breath fresh air, it is not before the collapse of her own company that the diary begins to resemble that of a person rather than a cyber-hero. In the latter role, she refers to herself in the third person singular, consults with her readers what hair color to use, or activates them to check out the speed of some new technical device. In 2001, the year of the great collapse, the tone changes.

On January 16 Pyra's employees are laid off and Meg reports how she went into the office bathroom and burst into tears. Then she went home, got into bed, "and cried, and cried, and cried" (1.2.01). A few days later she resigned. At this point, to her rhetorical question of what is "the best part about watching your web company disintegrate?" she responds "Reading about it on the web" (1.2.01), but the search for a life behind dot.com begins. On February 5, Meg reports on a mini-rose and other plants that seemed to be dying. And while her devoted readers send her electronic signals of consolation, and even some real gifts, she looks for consolation offline:

> This was last Thursday, as everything around me seemed to be falling apart, as my world of the past two years just sort of crumbled down. Standing in front of the tree, in my bathrobe, staring at the budding little lemon, I realized my lemon tree wasn't dying—my lemon tree had entered a new cycle of its life. And with a smile on my face, I realized, so had I. (5.2.01)

Even to the point that Megnut-turned-Meg momentarily considers giving up the online experience:

> I'm really enjoying lazing around in my bathrobe, and you don't want to see that. Well, I don't want you to see that. On a less lazy note, I'm feeling unin-spired by the web these days, I think it's some sort of backlash thing. Anyway, I was contemplating taking this site down, but that seemed rash, and I realized that in a week or two, I'd probably be ready to come back to things. So what that means is: I may not be writing much (huh, I bet you didn't see that coming, didya?). (15.2.01).

At the end of the month she apologizes to her readers for spending little time online as she was painting the bedroom and was generally doing "non computer related stuff, like seeing friends and watching movies" (28.2.01).

This phase lasts about a month; in mid March she describes wildflowers in bloom and salty spray crashing against the rocky coastal cliffs she saw while on a hike, but at the end of the month she returns to the more familiar Megnut style: "I've reached that point, perhaps that age, where I'm ready for more commit-ment and more stability—I need a strongly types programming language" (29.3.01). A few days later, she describes a fantasy developed by a blogger friend about a best seller she would write about "Weblogging pirates" in the stormy sea of the new millennium, who use their Weblogs, updated from sea, to alert each other of potential targets. And in May, she goes on vacation, but not without leaving instructions behind: "I'll be back May 14th. In the meantime, there's two years of megnut content to your right. Feel free to read it, and by all means, real old content on other sites as well. Then let me know: does it stand the test of time?" (3.5.01).

From now on, the negotiation between real life and cyber-life will persist. Side by side with diary entries on afternoons spent cooking and drinking wine with friends, and picking fresh tomatoes from the garden, we find the familiar Web-exhilaration. "These past few days, I've been re-armoured with the Web through the simple act of doing research. I'd forgotten how amazing it is to have so much information at one's fingertips, and how powerful that can be. And it's got me all jazzed again about why the Web is so great" (30.8. 02).

Feminism and Politics

How effective is the Web as a means to disseminate Meg's feminist persona and ideas? This issue must be analyzed as part of her general attitude toward political issues. The blog is striking in its apoliticism: "Politics. I've been rather aloof to date with the presidential campaigns, and the candidates. Oh, I know who's announced their intents to seek nominations and all that, but platforms and beliefs-those are things I could only guess at until this morning" (22.11.99).

What had changed that morning; what suddenly caught the attention of the diarist about candidates' platforms, information that had been around for months? Two items were posted on a site on George W. Bush according to which the Republican presidential candidate declined to meet with a GOP gay group. These items are sufficient for the diarist to speak her mind in the most extreme fashion: "The two-faced hypocrisy of it all astounds me. Tell the fucking truth for crissakes—your 'inclusion' refers to people like you, George: white, Christian, heterosexual men and women" (22.11.99).

Such comments, based on esoteric news items dug up by bloggers, do not reflect political thought at its best. In fairness, Meg does not pretend to supply her readers with political thought. Occasionally there is reference to political events, for instance the 1999 anti-globalization protests in Seattle, but this usually consists of a few obscure news items accompanied by the expression of vague sentiments, e.g., "It's hard to believe this is America" (2.12.99).

Once vague sentiments replace political ideas, populism prevails. I refer to the tendency, analyzed in Chapter 2, to consider the polity as overwhelming the "little (wo)man" (13.6.01). Populism can be found in entries such as this:

> The thought of the federal government reviewing and inserting anti-drug messages into the scripts of some of America's most popular tv shows totally freaks me out. For the government to use television so subversively to spread messages to the public sets a dangerous precedent." What's to prevent a conservative White House in the future from spreading anti-choice or anti-gay messages through the same medium? Time for a new bumpersticker: US government out of my television! (14.1.00)

This is of course a legitimate political statement; what makes it odd, however, is the swift transformation from an Op/Ed-like paragraph to a bumper sticker. If the established media are often accused of superficiality, such a paragraph, even if accompanied by one or two newspaper items, becomes even more superficial. Consider the following discussion of international affairs that in no time turns into babble:

> This isn't funny (Puttin was elected by poll fraud, says report), it really isn't, and at some point perhaps I'll write about my concerns over what's happening in Russia (continued corruption, collapsing infrastructure, etc.) but the evil in me can't resist the snippet, 'a votes-for-Vodka scheme in Novosibirsk.' Hmmm, maybe if we tried something like that in America, people might actually 'participate' in the upcoming elections. (11.9.00)

In case this may seem like a call for political participation, Meg continuously assures her readers of her apolitical attitude: "Today I present megnut's thoughts on current events (feel free to stop reading right now, I won't be offended)." In that entry, she posts an item on the presidential elections accompanied by the following comment: "Ick. There's a reason I rarely write about politics. Bush scares me to death. Gore bores me to death." (17.8.00). No wonder that during the Bush-Gore standoff, Meg liked the idea of splitting the presidency between the two candidates. Although this was probably meant mainly as a joke, she did not express greater decisiveness when it came to a serious matter like going to war with Iraq: "I've been avoiding making a direct post about my opinion on the upcoming Iraq war because I've felt it's been so muddled and unclear" (18.3.03).

Feminism, however, is a political matter. To activate any liberation movement, one must be aware of the political environment and its delicacies, not just its bumper stickers. The apolitical nature of this blog therefore reduces the feminist discourse to a trivial set of comments such as this: "<u>One woman's</u> voice reminded me last night, reminded me of power? The power of art to change, of beliefs to inspire, of words to recreate this world" (10.7.99). The readers who clicked on the highlighted words "one woman's" found themselves in punk folk-singer Ani DiFranco's home page titled "Righteous Babe Records," in which the following statement is posted:

> i speak without reservation from what i know and who i am. i do so with the understanding that all people should have the right to offer their voice to the chorus whether the result is harmony or dissonance, the worldsong is a colorless dirge without the differences that distinguish us, and it is that difference which should be celebrated not condemned.[6]

The fascination with this statement is understandable as it sounds very much like a blogger's manifesto in its call for the right of all people to join some universal chorus. Yet, such slogans about a "worldsong," found on the verges of almost every ideology in modern history, may be inspiring in an emotional sense but not as motivation to act on actual causes. Blogging joins here the enthusiasm of DiFranco's fans in her concerts but it is hard to see its empowering role. Neither can any clear message be derived from an entry on the same day about the victory of the American team over the Chinese team in the Women's World Cup, if only because that victory had more to do with American patriotism than with women's liberation. Ignoring the fact that the Chinese team was also a women's team, the entry in "megnut.com" claimed that "<u>20 women</u> gave hope to an entire generation of American girls. *It's about time!*" (10.7.99). Time for what? For American women to become soccer fans in case they have missed the fun? To sit at their television sets and feel proud because the American team scored 5-4 against another team?

There is nothing wrong with such statements but their advancement of a feminist or any other cause is questionable. So are statements about the language used in various media, which this blog often exposes. Here is an example:

[E]ach day it seems I notice more and more 'Rambo' language in news articles to describe violent situations. No wonder we as a culture are desensitized to violence when this type of language is used to describe the murder of a young woman. Why do journalists employ the callous language of gangsters and action heroes? Have we no respect for the loss of life?" (27.9.99)

I could not pinpoint the news item this entry referred to but whatever the language used in the online journal that caught Meg's attention, it is hard not to wonder whether her emphasis on the way a horrible incident was described, with no further comment on the incident itself, stems from the fact that the entire communication we witness here—between the media, the blogger, and her audience—is dissociated from political commitment. The real is being reduced to the verbal.

Language is an important tool of social change, but the sole focus on language, stemming from the virtual environment in which the entire discourse is taking place, increases the probability that this change is not being accompanied by powerful action. Meg rightly complains about the exclusion of women from one of the sites listing, at the beginning of January 2000, the most influential high tech people of the preceding decade. The attention drawn to this exclusion, however, is not accompanied by an alternate list, but merely by the eruption: "How about including some WOMEN in your list, fuckheads? And two of the choices are Investment Bankers and Venture Capitalists, as if there aren't any women in those industries? Where do I vote for the Most Sexist Site of the Decade?" (5.1.00).

The relation between the apolitical nature of the blog and the apolitical treatment of feminist issues is demonstrated in the following entry:

So my plan has been, and will now continue to be, to leave the country if Bush is elected president. And I think my plan is also to leave California now that the absurd proposition 22 has been passed. Why is (are?) politics so frustrating? Why is the language on the ballot so convoluted? Why do we always seem to be choosing between two rich white males to run the show? And why do I always feel so demoralized after I vote? I get myself psyched up to make a difference, and then we always end up with the same old things: men who have no personality or charisma, who are as impassioned as planks when speaking, who seem to have sketchy morals, and who exist totally disconnected from the majority of Americans. ARGH." (8.3.00)

Many who share these feelings about American politics could find hope in female candidates such as Hillary Clinton, who in 2000 ran for the US senate. One could expect of a feminist blogger revolted by male domination of American politics, to relate to Clinton's political campaign by supporting or opposing it, but what we find in "megnut.com" is once again mere reference to language:

Hillary Clinton's site for her senate campaign contains only one instance of 'Clinton,' at the very bottom, in very small print. Every where else she's referred to simply as Hillary. You know, like Madonna. And now that I've looked over the site a bunch of times, the word Hillary is striking me as very funny and weird. Oh the hillarity! It's interesting how that happens to a word if you focus on it too much. (19.5.00)

The focus on words rather than on substance may stem from a degree of security. Had the blogger been really concerned over the state of the nation, she might have focused more on Hilary Clinton's politics than the sound of her name. The state of comfort can be found in entries such as: "I just realized I'm pretty contented, and there aren't a lot of things I'm craving" (14.6.00). We are definitely situated on the contented side of the world, where troubles such as those described in Chapter 4 do not necessarily require much change. Just like Jason in Chapter 2, who was preoccupied with the cups for extra pennies positioned by the cash registers in gas stations, Meg expresses concern over such matters as the treatment of customers in clothing store changing rooms.

That people are aroused about store policies that require customers to check their bags, or to take a number when entering a changing room to allow the attendant to check how many items are being taken in, is understandable. But placing such policies as issues of concern in the context of American constitutionalism, begs the question of whether blogging trivializes the constitutional discourse to the extent of turning it into empty words:

> I've been thinking lately about the assumption of trust in society, and how very little there seems to be of it. While innocent until proven guilty may be our constitutional right in the courtroom, the behavior outside of it seems to be more of the 'were going to assume everybody's going to attempt to do something bad' variety, especially when it comes to shopping. (17.7.00)

The trivialization of the discourse spills over to Meg's feminist messages, whose blogging version stands in contrast to what seems like her real-life status as an emancipated woman. Again and again, it is words rather than deeds that concern her, as when she complains that in *Fortune Magazine*'s list of the most powerful women, many hold the title "chairman" (2.10.00). Her feminist messages are often quite general and simplistic, as during the Bush–Gore standoff, when she heard that the head of Fox News's election night decision desk was George Bush's first cousin: "I know I usually don't post so many political links, but I just can't get over this. I think I was naïve, and this whole situation is opening my eyes. I guess I believed that the days of white male privilege and wealth were on the wane" (14.11.00).

The tone changes when Meg's attention is on matters such as the abortion issue. When the Bush administration came into office in January 2003 and she realized that appointees of the new administration, such as Attorney General John Ashcroft, were pro-life, she posted items on the subject and used the blog as a fund raiser for pro-choice groups: "I'd like to ask for your support," she writes. "If you've enjoyed reading megnut and are interested in giving something in return, I hope that you will contribute a small amount to one of the following organizations supporting women's right to choose" (22.1.01).

Meg's feminism is also less verbal and more practical when she is writing about women and the high-tech industry. She feels that better role models are needed to inspire the next generation of women to seek senior leadership positions. When invited to speak in conferences, she sees this as an empowerment tool:

> I realized I could whine and moan about the lack of female participation at these events, or I could do something about it, so I made a decision: I would try to speak at more conferences to rectify that imbalance. I'd demonstrate that there are women starting companies and building products and doing programming as well as men. Three conferences isn't much, but it's a start. As they say, a journey of a thousand miles begins with a single step. (25.8.01)

Such sentiments, however, are lost in the context in which they appear—a battle of words with another blogger who posted his thoughts on the evolutionary process, which he apparently felt made women inferior computer programmers. As might be expected, the heated debate over these thoughts, correctly referred to by Meg as "nice crock of shit about men being better suited to programming than women" (25.1.01), went on for days with lots of bystander involvement in the form of mounds of E-mails sent to the contestants. Had it not taken place shortly before the September 11 attacks, this debate, requiring so little political commitment, might have lasted forever. On August 31, Meg felt the debate called for real action, defined however merely as "a discussion/chat/coffee klatch about this whole women-in-technology thread" (31.8.01).

Only rarely does one find in this blog by an American feminist a political entry on the plight of women in other societies. The following is one of these instances "I keep thinking that one good thing that could potentially come out of this war on terrorism is the overthrow of the Taliban in Afghanistan and the restoration of basic human rights for Afghani women" (17.11.01). This entry is accompanied by a report by Physicians for Human Rights documenting the ways in which the Taliban regime has threatened the freedoms and health needs of Afghan women, a behavior unparalleled in recent history. Most of the time, however, the issues brought up are remote from these concerns, as when Meg preoccupies herself with some officer who assumed that the voice of battlefield assisting robots would be a female voice. It is hard not to tie this entry to the nature of blogging, which allows the posting of an occasional entry on women under the Taliban, and then returning to trivia.

In contrast to feminist fighters in oppressed regimes, this blogger hardly takes action to advance feminist causes, and even when she talks about taking action, it remains a hypothetical possibility. For example, after reading about the treatment of workers in the American food industry Meg wrote:

> If I could change the way people are treated at McDonald's, I would. If I could revolutionize the conditions in the meatpacking plants in Nebraska and Colorado, I would. Part of me wants to buy a franchise right now, and do it differently, or to fly to Columbus, Nebraska and slow down the line and yell at everyone, yell, 'What are you doing here? How can you treat the people who are

making you **your fucking money** like this?" (13.4.01)

Yet, this is only one part of her. The other part remains at the computer—blogging.

Meg is aware of the superficial nature of the blog as she writes at one point: "Oh God, I just realized that my posts have become the blogging equivalent of small-talk. All I'm doing is talking about the weather. I really need to get back to work again so I have more to talk about" (5.12.02). At the same time, pre-occupation with politics, without which the conditions of workers in Columbus, Nebraska, or anywhere else cannot be changed, depresses her: "All this writing about political stuff this week is making me very depressed" (24.1.03).

The tendency to engage in small talk may be related to Meg's increasing consciousness of her celebrity in cyberspace. In January 2003, she posts an entry by another blogger who played tabloid photographer and took a picture of her and her boyfriend in the park, which proved to him that the two are not "fake characters dreamed up by some evil marketing genius at Pyra to generate interest in the soap-opera potential of the weblog movement" (7.1.03).

As is common in contemporary media culture, the admired woman chased by amateur tabloid photographers begins to give other women advice. One of her entries is titled "Words of Wisdom," in which the memorable quotation appears: "Every woman needs the following: her 'fuck me' shoes and her 'don't fuck with me' shoes" (14.4.03). Another entry, explaining why Meg decided to go with her boyfriend to a movie she was not keen to see, is also phrased like a "know-how" column by a media personality: "People will tell you the key to any successful relationship is compromise. Without the ability to compromise, long-term love affairs don't make it beyond short-term trysts. Compromise done well is like any negotiation, the trick is to give so that in return you get something you want" (14.5.03).

One wonders about the nature of human freedom if an icon of the new emancipation like Meg Hourihan begins to sound like the established media that blogging was trying to change in the first place. Emancipation does not mean that those who have gained a voice on the Web must fit certain standards of po-litical sophistication. To the contrary, blogging is liberating exactly because such standards are absent. As already pointed out, blogosphere cannot be judged by the same standards set by high culture for literary works, and bloggers may be fulfilling an important task in exposing the exclusive nature of high culture and promoting an anti-authoritarian discourse.

The trivialization of politics, however, may produce the illusion of a politi-cal discourse when almost no political consciousness is involved. Consider the following office conversation recorded in the blog:

"Meg: 'Whoa. The Homeland Security Department's chosen Microsoft as its 'preferred supplier' for desktop and server software!'
Mark: 'That doesn't sound too good.'
Meg: (reading from article) 'Microsoft will provide the standard e-mail soft-ware for the entire department.'

Mark: 'So one I LOVE YOU virus and that's the end of Homeland Security'" (16.7.03).

This is illusory in that both participants in the dialogue remain on the periphery, taking refuge in jokes that point to political helplessness and alienation. They might, for instance, have demonstrated their disapproval of the action by joining a demonstration organized against a major government figure, John Aschroft, who spoke at New York's Federal Hall the following September. However, this is Meg's post about that demonstration: "there's a demonstration today...See you there?" (9.9.03).

Although the blog stresses the importance of the demonstration set to "demand the protection of our basic civil liberties, and counter Attorney General John Ashcroft, speaking in the latest installment of his stealth Patriot Act road show" (9.9.03), there is no further mention of the demonstration, or of her participation in it. The next entry, written on the same day, reads as follows: "If *Friends* final season begins September 25, and Ben and JLo are to be married September 14, and Joey Tribbiani's character will be spun off into a new show called *Joey* after *Friends* tenth and final season, which event will occur first: Ben and JLo divorce or *Joey* is cancelled?" (9.9.03). The entry after is about tomatoes.

The entries on food, sometimes accompanied by recipes, are of some practical use but the usefulness to anyone of the entries classified by the blogger as "political," is hard to determine. One such "political" entry refers to a Website attempting to challenge the way ideas are created and spread by creating and disseminating thoughtful, rational, and constructive manifestos on various topics of interest and importance. The hope of the Website's designers is that these manifestos will spread, "hand to hand, person to person, until these manifestos have reached a critical mass and actually changed the tone and substance of our debate" (17.8.04). The entry's title: "The return of the manifesto," raises hope for some new ideological era which ends abruptly when the readers are led through a lengthy discussion of the Website's format.

Back to "Real Life"

At a certain point, the blogger shows signs of fatigue. She writes she feels exhausted. "I had no perspective on anything, I was so deep into my world of weblogs and tech that I didn't have much sense of what was going on outside of my geek circles" (21.5.04). She even raises the possibility of not posting anymore, feeling the need to "just be" (21.5.04). What does just being consist of? Clamming, making a roaring fire with only one match, planting lots of alyssum and petunias, drinking many bowls of clam chowder, reading a murder mystery, etc.

It seems as if Meg has finally prevailed over Megnut. As she writes a few months later: "It's taken me several months of time away from computers and tech and geeks to accept the fact that computers and technology are not my passion" (14.9.04). She comes to the conclusion that her interest in the Web and in technology was always more about people. "With weblogs, it was making it possible for everyone to write online and share and communicate...But something was always missing, and I've realized that was true passion for what I was doing" (14.9.04). She now moves to something she feels passionate about—cooking.

Interestingly, the Web icon turned chef who now begins to report in her online diary about mundane activities in a New York restaurant, reports for the first time on feelings of happiness that have been almost completely absent in the earlier years of the daily entries in "megnut.com": "Yesterday at 3 PM I put on my black chef's clogs, my black pants and white t-shirt, pulled my Red Sox cap over my hair and got to work peeling and deveining shrimp. Seven hours later, sweatily scrubbing the kitchen floors, I was still smiling" (14.9.04).

Notes

1. <http://www.megnut.com/>
2. <http://pages.stern.nyu.edu/~swib/conference/index.html/>
3. Christina Vogt and Peiying Chen, "Feminism and the Internet," *Peace Review* 13 (2001): 373.
4. Vogt and Chen, "Feminism and the Internet," 373–4.
5. <www.megnut.com/about.asp/> (some of the content on this and other Web pages may have changed over time).
6. <http://www.columbia.edu/~marg/ani/>

Chapter 4

Iranian Girl

In early 1979, the Shah of Iran, Mohammad Reza Pahlavi, was overthrown by a popular movement inspired by Ayatollah Khomeini, a clergyman exiled to France in 1963. The return of Khomeini to Iran in February 1979 was followed by the application of theocratic Islamic-Shiite rule in the country, a trend strengthened in the 1980s as a result of a war with Iraq, a deteriorating economy, and ethnic strife. Despite hopes in the West that the new leaders who came to power after Khomeini's death in 1989, Ayatollah Seyed Ali Khamenei and President Hashemi Rafsanjani, would reopen the country to Western modernization, Iran continued to be a closed society ruled by clerics who used oppressive measures to impose fundamentalist laws and beliefs. The election of the more moderate Mohammed Khatami as president in 1997 has not weakened the rule of the Ayatollahs who managed to keep key positions of power in Tehran.

One of the strongest expressions of the fundamentalist revolution in Iran was the oppression of women. As Tayana Marshall observed after the public suicide of Iranian woman activist Dr. Homa Darabi in 1995, the revolution turned against the women who supported it. At the beginning, she explained, women took an active part in revolutionary activities, hoping the republic would bring gender equality to Iran, but this did not happen. In the early 1980s, laws were passed that forced the wearing of the hijab (Islamic modest dress) by women in public, and segregated the sexes in swimming pools, buses, and educational institutions. Women were banned from appearing on radio and television, purged from high-level government positions, and prevented from enrolling in fields like engineering, agriculture, or finance. Although they had the right to vote, they were denied the right to divorce and obtain custody of their children. The age of consent for marriage was lowered from fifteen to thirteen years. Contraception and abortion were banned.[1]

While occasionally troubled by news about the execution of women activists and the brutal clashes at student demonstrations, the West has not given the suppression of women in Iran due attention. There are several reasons for this: the Iranian government's success in concealing disturbing facts, the reluctance of Western governments with vested economic and political interests in Iran to uncover these facts, the general apathy of Western publics toward events occurring elsewhere, and relativistic norms discouraging debate over coercion in other cultures.

An important reminder of the oppression of women in Iran was Azar Nafisi's memoir *Reading Lolita in Tehran* in which she highlights the misery of Iranian female students, comparing their life under the veil to the ongoing rape of Nabokov's heroine. The book portrays women whose feelings, views, and ambitions divert a great deal from the West's model of the subdued Iranian woman, who is forced to dress and behave in ways that help the Iranian regime convey and reinforce that model. In an article in the *New Republic* in 2003, Nafisi noted that the crimes committed against women and other people in oppressive fundamentalist Moslem regimes are repeated three times: "once when they are forced into submission, once when they are represented through the very forces that oppress them, and once when the world talks about them in the same language and through the same images as their oppressors."[2]

In other words, not only are Iranian women suppressed, they are also presented as embodiments of the regime; the image of the submissive woman in traditional Islamic dress points to the Ayatollahs' success. As Nafisi expressed it in her memoir:

> we had become the figment of someone else's dreams. A stern Ayatollah, a self-proclaimed philosopher-king, had come to rule our land. He had come in the name of a past, a past that, he claimed, had been stolen from him. And he wanted to re-create us in the image of that illusory past. Was it any consolation, and did we even wish to remember, that what he did to us was what we allowed him to do?[3]

Many Iranian women thus feel the need to assert some form of free expression, which partly explains the influx of Iranian blogs, both in Farsi and in other languages. In an article in *The Guardian* of December 18, 2004, Nasrin Alavi noted that with an estimated 75,000 blogs, Farsi has become the fourth most popular language in blogosphere. Beginning with the first Farsi blog by Hossein Derakhshan in September 2001, many blogs have appeared signifying

> a new virtual space for free speech in a country dubbed the 'biggest prison for journalists in the Middle East,' by *Reporters sans Frontières* (RSF). Through the anonymity and freedom that weblogs can provide, those who once lacked voices are at last speaking up and discussing issues that have never been aired in any other media in the Islamic world.[4]

In a country in which self-expression is not allowed, dozens of media publications are closed by a hard-line judiciary, and bloggers get arrested (Iran became the first country to take action against Weblogs) the very mention of David Beckham, lipstick, or St. Valentine's Day in an online diary, writes Alavi, becomes a mark of freedom.

In 2005, Alavi published a book titled *We Are Iran*,[5] which includes English translations of Farsi blogs. This collection highlights the cat and mouse game played by the Iranian regime and the bloggers. It reveals, for instance, the announcement in 2004 of laws explicitly covering cyber-crimes: propagating against the regime, acting against national security, disturbing the public mind, and insulting religious sanctities through computer systems or telecommunications. Blogosphere is declared to be a network led by the CIA and bloggers are persecuted. Under these conditions, many members of this society 70 percent of whom are under the age of thirty take advantage of the relative anonymity provided by use of multiple servers, or foreign servers, to express themselves. Particularly interesting is the translation of a statement by Muhammad-Ali Abtani, the Iranian Parliamentary ex-Vice President, who called the Iranian virtual community too political, urging it to use Weblogs only for their intended use: as "clichéd daily diaries."[6]

What the Iranian leader overlooked is that such diaries can be no less subversive than explicit political statements. In a state in which morality squads in black cars patrol the streets to enforce dress codes and restrictions on contact between the sexes, the posting of clichés about the daily routines of one's dress, love, desire, and daily routine becomes a source of liberation. This is where the difference between this blog and the one discussed in Chapter 3 becomes striking. While in a liberal democracy a blogger's resort to trivia may divert attention from important political issues, in an authoritarian theocracy, similar trivia become a form of political protest. Moreover, while in the first case murmurings occur about oppressive political forces that are to a large extent imaginary, in the second case the reality of oppression makes the blog an exclusive means of emancipation.

The blog discussed in this chapter, "notes of an Iranian girl,"[7] is indeed a mark of emancipation. From October 30 2002, when a sixteen-year-old girl wrote her first "Hi," to December 23, 2003, when her last post appeared on the Web, a free voice is coming out of the totalitarian country. As one follows this blog, it is hard not to feel fear for the girl's life as well as admiration for her insistence not to give up, to keep sharing her thoughts with the world. It makes one realize how strong the urge for freedom is among those who are not blessed with it, as if the melancholy depicted in many other blogs is just the privilege of the free and prosperous. In what follows, I discuss "notes of Iranian Girl" as a limited and temporary yet meaningful celebration of freedom.

Teenager's Routine

"Hi...This is my first English weblog," writes the anonymous girl on October 30, 2002. Noting that there are many Iranian Weblogs in Farsi but not in English, she decided to "shout my words to the world from this little electronic page" (30.10.02). She apologizes for her poor English, which, she says, should not prevent her from trying to share her thoughts and feelings with the Western world: "It's my duty to tell others about Iran & the problems of a teen young girl. I hope that you (from everywhere of the world) come to my weblog & read the things you have never read. wish luck for me;)" (30.10.02).

At first sight, the blog is like those of other teenagers around the world. The blogger is frustrated when she does not find the time to post a daily entry and wonders, as bloggers do, whether anybody reads her diary. Most of the entries are written in moments of fatigue, or irritation over such mundane issues as homework. Many entries are written during hours of boredom and slight depression common to teenagers everywhere: "Friday afternoons always have the worst moments for me. It seems that they want to make me crazy by their boring hours that I really can't do anything on them. The best way for spending these minutes, is sitting behind the window & thinking & going through dream" (15.11.02).

However, what makes such a description of Friday boredom unique is the context; it is written during the student demonstrations of mid November 2002. These demonstrations erupted in Tehran and other cities following the death sentence given to Hashem Aghajari, a history professor and disabled veteran of the Iraq War with ties to President Khatami, who defied the Shiite clergy by suggesting in a speech that Muslims should be free to interpret their faith. In response to the harsh sentence, thousands of students held rallies, boycotted classes, marched in the streets, and shouted slogans. As the blogger puts it, "These days are really strange. Tehran is having special & important minutes. Streets are full of students, people, police cars & also full of blood" (14.11.02).

Iranian girl hopes that the lessons learnt from earlier demonstrations will protect the students from brutal treatment by the police. As a high school student she is not on the streets herself, but fears for those who are: "I feel a kind of fear. Actually I worry about the future. I see just a dark way in front & that makes me worry" (23.11.02). She is worried because she remembers how other demonstrations have ended: "I'm thinking of the students who are in prison, the ones who were died last year & who are going to die in the other demonstrations. I'm thinking of the people who in the whole history, never taste a real liberty; & I'm thinking of me, the 'me' who is a teen young girl that just can wait & see what will happen at last" (23.11.02).

During the turmoil, the teenager feels an obligation to tell the world what is happening. She is aware of the government's attempts to suppress free expression but assumes that blogs are harder to suppress than other media, which makes her critical of those who use their blogs to post nonsense or are only concerned with their own popularity. She considers blogging as a stage on the way to liberty and democracy: "Oh, so optimistic about the revolution...I am sure that it will happen. I don't know when but I know that one day that is not too far" (30.11.02). The revolution, however, will not take the form imagined in the West, she says. On November 29, she posts an article titled "Barbie in Iran" whose author, Shala Aziz, claims that while Barbie dolls are politically irrelevant in countries in which women are free to travel without their husbands' permission, in Iran, the doll provides a link to the free world. The very mention of such trivial matters as Barbie dolls in a blog thus becomes a revolutionary act.

Aware of the revolutionary potential involved in pursuing one's daily routines in a fundamentalist regime, the blogger writes regularly about her life as teenager. She tells, for instance, how she came home from school on a day in which she had to study for an exam but fell asleep for three hours, which subjected her to her mother's "nagging": "Oh, she nags, and nags & nags, it seems that there is no other thing she can do" (1.12.02). Despite the nagging, the girl keeps surfing the net where she finds a BBC news item on new Iranian divorce laws which allow women to file for divorce only with the permission of their husbands. According to the new laws, women seeking divorce have to prove that their husbands (whose permission they need) are incapable of providing for their family or that they are drug addicts, insane, impotent, or the like. She posts the news item in her blog, commenting that many Iranian girls are forced to marry men as old as their fathers, likening them to prisoners in cages.

In an entry on December 4, she mentions the destruction of a brothel district after the 1979 revolution, showing how the government manipulated portraits of the district's women to fit the moral lesson it tried to convey. She reveals that prostitution has not ceased as a result of the closure, only that the prostitutes' conditions have worsened. She blames the revolutionary authorities for imposing a ban on sex before marriage, thus leading to misinformation and to the spread of AIDS.

While she is writing this entry, uniformed and plain clothes police and members of the notorious Basij militia are beating up students on the streets, and the young woman is praying to God, emphasizing that the God she prays to is not the one in whose name prostitutes were burned alive in 1979: "I just wish that God takes a look at earth & see us & finally decides to do something for the people who are trying hard to have their country in the right way" (7.12.02).

The blog serves as a source of information for Iranian readers who can find in it foreign news items that are not available in the government-controlled media, e.g., a Yahoo News item of December 10 about an Iranian woman protester outside a Brussels building in which foreign ministers of the European Union were meeting. It also serves foreigners to get perspectives on Iran that the government prefers to suppress, e.g., about a fire in a prison in Northern Iran that killed twenty-seven people and injured fifty. While the official news agency promised that an investigation of the incident would be held, the blogger posted detailed information about the overcrowding in Iran's prisons.

Oppression

The blogger's own condition is often reminiscent of life in a cage. Alongside thoughts about the hardships of turning sixteen, the teenager goes through unimaginable experiences. For example, while writing an exam in her all-girls school she has to worry not about the right answers but about hiding her hands. She came to school with polish on her nails not knowing that the person sent to invigilate the exam was a "regulator," preparing lists of sinners. She realizes this may sound unbelievable to the readers in free countries:

> I want to say that girl high schools in Iran have some rules that may be unbelievable for others. removing hairs of face or eyebrow, having make up even a little, wearing anything except the Uniform, not covering all your hair behind

scarf & in some high schools not wearing chador (the black material that some
women wear) or not going to daily prays, are against the laws of schools &
would make troubles for students, Also having any CD, tape or other forbidden
things in their bags. (15.12.02)

This is written not by a subversive personality but by a young Iranian patriot. The blogger loves her country, is enchanted by the change of seasons, and
is often proud to tell about Persian traditions that preceded the fundamentalist
regime. On December 21, the longest night of the year, she writes:

tonight…yeah, it's Yalda night. Don't you know about Yalda night??? No matter, it's completely Iranian. perhaps the most Iranian night [of] the year…The
longest night of the year, The night for old & young persons of family to be together like before, the Night of water-melon, pomegranate & nuts, the night of
memories for grandparents & the night that is becoming just a name for young
people. I think recently I am getting more than ever sensitive about everything!!! Yes, Yalda night is the last night of autumn & is giving a nice Hi to
winter, & from long time ago Iranians used to celebrate it in their families.
(21.12.02)

This joyous description illustrates how devastating totalitarian rule is in its
attempt to break down family traditions:

Being up late & eat & laughing & tell stories & reading poems. And these days,
these nasty days that there is no time for being together I like this night a lot,
because that's still a reason to be with some relatives & have a happy night,
forgetting the problems, & for a lover of winter that I am it's an incredible
night. (21.12.02)

The blogger is saddened when her compatriots abroad are maltreated. During the roundup of Iranians in the US after 9/11 she writes: "I feel sorry about
my blood, Iranian blood" (19.12.02). She realizes the roundup is the result of the
fundamentalist regime's behavior. "look & see what has happened to this country with great [civilization] that one day was one of the best & richest countries
in the world & people had respect in everywhere, & today It is a poor country
that others look at the people as terrorists" (19.12.02).

At times she does not know whether to laugh or cry, as when the announcement is made that women can join the police force but will have to wear a
heavy black dress and the veil while on police duty. The blogger doubts whether
anybody in the West can grasp the absurdities women have to go through. She
occasionally translates items from Farsi Weblogs devoted to women's issues, as
when she brings the story of young students in a small town who were asked to
describe their dreams and responded by stating that all their dreams have been
lost. Having been deprived of the right to go to the cinema and the park, to hang
around on the street, or just to wear a regular dress, she writes, they no longer
have any dreams. Her conclusion:

Sometimes I get really angry with this bad situation that we have in Iran & I think about this chance that I was born here & I don't know why I should be here & [not live like?] a girl in my age, in US; but I when I read about these poor teens & their situation that is really worse than what we have in Tehran, I just don't know how can God be so cruel & share life like that. (7.1.03)

The Internet serves as a refuge. The Internet, she writes, fills her with a confidence that cannot be gained elsewhere. When she surfs the Web in search of posts for her blog, especially at night when everybody is asleep, she feels safe and peaceful, for the Internet is her window to liberty: "I just love to close my room's door, open my window & smell the whether that if I am lucky is rainy, & also break the silence of night with a favorite song, & through these electronic pages go to everywhere I want" (8.1.03).

No wonder the regime takes action. Shortly after a group of Farsi bloggers held a conference, sites were hacked and a site devoted to women's issues was covered by the electronic banner: "this whore-house is on sale" (28.12.02). Bloggers begin to be arrested. On January 13, 2003, Iranian girl reports that a student blogger known for his political activism has been arrested. She wonders whether he was arrested for his political activity or for his anti-government blogging. At this point, she is not worried about her own safety, probably because she realizes that the frustration she expresses about such matters as her confinement to the home only make the censors happy.

She tells how she and her cousin wanted to go out after an exam, as her brother did, but were told that two girls were not supposed to be seen alone in the street after dark. She also complains about being forced to learn Arabic, the language of the Koran: "OK; if you talk about Islam, I'm not a Moslem & have no religion & hate all your prophets, Koran, prays...& my also my God isn't the one that you created for us" (12.1.03).

Iran has a long tradition of scholarship and the girl is aware of the need to pursue her studies as no goals could be achieved without a good education. The goals she and her female friends can set for themselves, however, are very limited. Having to worry about such matters as the execution of women by stoning rather than about the pursuit of a career, they are often depressed: "I see many of my friends that are girls in my age crying & crying, I see many of them so furious, & getting upset by every little things. And also many times I find myself crying with no reason, getting furious & upset, thinking a lot & having a bad feeling too" (22.1.03).

She and her friends realize that the life they are forced to live has an alternative, that there are happy young girls out there in the world:

I see satellite channels, I see girls in my age in other countries, yeah, I see how they live, I see how happier than us they are & I see how we are breaking & [no] one hear us" (22.1.03). Following the American invasion of Afghanistan, she envies the women who were liberated there: "I don't have an exact view of Afghanistan but I think they are much happier than us & are free to breathe the air of their fatherland with liberty, not like us in prisons. (24.1.03)

The blog is ambivalent about the role the US should play in the liberation of Iran. On the one hand, it is concerned with the superficiality with which Iran is treated abroad. Iran and Iraq are bundled together and the US has no clear policy on how to handle either. Following a speech by President Bush in which he declared that Iranians have the right to choose their own government and determine their own destiny, Iranian girl wrote:

> I don't know, what I exactly think about Mr. Bush & his speech. I can't really get what he means by these few words about Iran & what will be the plan. It seems that after Iraq it's our turn, but what kind of strategy…will be required? How should these Iranian people choose their own government & determine their own destiny, by a new dependence? (31.1.03)

Although feeling that "thinking about such a big matter can't be done by a teen young girl" (31.1.03), the young teen exposes the shallow thinking of policy makers who are insensitive to differences between the states composing the "Axis of Evil."

On the other hand, as indicated in the entry about Barbie, the girl's visions of liberation are strongly associated with American culture. One of her greatest desires is to listen to American rock music and watch American movies, which are censored in Iran. She reports on a fourteen-year-old girl who threw herself off a bridge after being expelled from school for being caught with a CD, and of the arrest of a person who rented out DVDs. One of the ways to avoid censorship on movies is to watch them in film festivals:

> So the day before yesterday we decided to see 'the fifth reaction' film…so went to one of the best cinemas to get the ticket at 3 o clock, for the 7 performance. But we were just wasting time & it was impossible to get ticket, there were hundreds of people that had come since morning!!! The area in front of cinema had a situation like a war. (9.2.03).

When she managed to get into the movie theater, the girl was rather affected by the movie showing the anguish of female teachers in her country. "As a girl, I enjoyed the film a lot, but as I read in news, critics don't think very good about the film. I should say that most of critics are men & the film was [a]bout women's problems & some cruel things that some of men do to them" (9.2.03).

The government even cracks down on Valentine's Day celebrations after it finds out that young people have exchanged presents with members of the opposite sex. Reporting on the event, the blogger assumes that this crackdown will not be successful, for her generation will not give up on Valentine cards, chocolates, and dolls. She believes that the government's efforts to replace such old traditions by somber celebrations of the Islamic revolution will not succeed as long as there are intelligent youngsters like her around. During a week of celebrations in February commemorating the revolution, for instance, she realizes the spin involved and trusts the Iranian people are smart enough to realize it too and ignore the government's script. "Do you want to know what is going on now here?…many people tries to remind us that we must be happy about that big victory & again those old words about the Kin[g] who was...evil & Khomeini who came just as a angel & made that dirty & damaged land an Islamic, bright & great country" (10.2.03). When the government initiates an election to some powerless city board to try to camouflage its authoritarian rule, she assumes people will not go out and vote. They can't be fooled anymore by "every rubbish thing... that government does" (23.2.03).

On the other hand, she realizes that the damage caused by the revolution has been irreversible:

> Actually, Islamic revolution was a big & of course important act in Iran's history but a foolish & unforgivable mistake...a big mistake that can't be corrected anyway; who can rebuild all things they've damaged these days & destroy the rotten culture that they've made?!! Who can give back moments of our life's best years that could be so sweet but were spent in nasty confusions?!! (10.2.03)

This is the desperate cry of a young person deprived of her life by fundamentalist clerics, a cry oriented not only at "dirty mullahs" (10.2.03), it seems, but also at those in the West who are not sensitive enough to the quest for freedom expressed in this blog.

The Role of Blogging

Blogging has an important role in this regard; it makes it harder for Western observers to generalize about other societies without considering some of the nuances involved. It also raises forgotten dimensions, e.g., the stupidity associated with totalitarianism. The blog is often less concerned with compulsion than with silliness and irrationality. With every new occurrence in the Rushdie affair, for instance, the blogger is stunned. After years in which British writer Salman Rushdie was forced to hide due to a "fatwa" (call to take his life) issued by Iran's Revolutionary Guards, different ruling groups in Iran made conflicting announcements about the fatwa's validity and Iranian girl became furious: "It seems that there crazy men haven't decided to stop doing such foolish things & wanna make everybody hate them & their acts, I don't really understand what else do they want & why are they speeding up their crazy acts, instead of making things better" (16.2.03). On another occasion she reports on a government decision to sell nude paintings stored in the Tehran museum: "That sounds pretty foolish but the only thin[g] we can do is to feel sorry to lose these masterpieces" (26.2.03).

During the Iraq War, this blog, like others around the world, reported on events, worried about Salam Pax, the Iraqi blogger who disappeared from the Web for a few weeks, speculated about the fate awaiting Iran after the ousting of Saddam Hussein, etc. But while the discourse in other countries was more or less free, a crackdown on Iranian blogs took place during the war. In late April, Sina Motallebi, an Iranian journalist who published a popular blog, was arrested, as were other less famous bloggers. A few days later, Iranian journalists published a petition calling upon *Reporters Sans Frontièrs* and other human rights organizations to help free Motallebi. Iranian girl doubted whether the protest sparked by the arrests would be successful: "these years were enough for me to learn to think carefully & [be] doubtful about every thing…because behind every single event is a dirty trick" (22.4.03).

She became obviously concerned: "For some reasons, I won't be able to update my weblog regularly for a while…actually I'll write but I can't do as much as before; I'm really sorry about this but the present situation don't allow me to spend much time in the net, And also sorry that I can't reply [to] e-mails" (22.4.03). At the time this was written, additional oppressive measures were taken by the regime. A prominent actress was sentenced to seventy-four lashes for publicly kissing a male actor during an awards ceremony. On April 26, Hossein Derakhshan, an Iranian-born journalist living in Toronto who introduced blogging to Iran, reported on the fear felt by bloggers who supported Motallebi and called for his release.

On May 6 Iranian girl posted an article titled "Blogging for Revolution" by Pejman Yousefzadeh who expressed his hope that blogging might overcome the government's efforts to suppress free expression:

> The Blogosphere has already influenced politics, culture and society immeasurably. It was the first medium to pick up and understand the importance of Trent Lott's infelicitous comments at the 100th birthday of former Senator Strom Thurmond. It has won deserved acclaim in its coverage of Operation Iraqi Freedom and its discussion of the post-September 11th world in general. Let's hope the Blogosphere, and Iranian bloggers in particular, have the power to influence meaningful and effective change in Iranian culture and society. Keep tabs on Iranian bloggers and reformist Iranian websites. They could very well serve as the cyber-shock troops of a new Iranian revolution.[8]

On May 21, she posted an article by a former Iranian radio and television newscaster who cast doubt on the power of blogs:

> In the short period that I have been observing Iranian blogs, I have seen many pages that could very well have been authored by cyber-age toilet graffitists. The content on many of these blogs are, like the toilet graffiti I was familiar with, superficial, emotional, inflammatory, and of course, funny. Many bloggers are anonymous, as are the toilet graffitists. They receive inflammatory comments, are sometimes hacked by other bloggers, and - according to some reports … are at times shut down by the administrators for violating their terms-of-use agreement.[9]

On June 11, the BBC reported on clashes in Tehran between about 1000 students and police, the first major protest for more than six months. The BBC speculated it could be the beginning of a chain of demonstrations of the kind that shook Iran in July 1999. For more than four hours, it said, bursts of noise were heard at night when people set off firecrackers and sounded their car horns. The protesters, beaten by riot police, called for political prisoners to be freed and for President Mohammad Khatami to resign.[10]

The blogger was not there but felt something serious was happening. She cautioned about satellite reports from abroad exaggerating the event, reminding the readers that several protests in the past had led nowhere. She also disapproved of Iranian exiles sitting in their comfortable armchairs while encouraging the young people of Iran to give their lives for the cause they champion. Yet she believed the end of the regime might be close: "who knows; perhaps it ends up much sooner than we think" (11.6.03).

Two days later she and her father found themselves in the midst of the turmoil. The blog provides a rare firsthand account of the sounds and sights of civil protest in a totalitarian society:

[A]fter about half an hour walking we reached the main place that young boys had lighted fired & were chanting & also breaking coke glasses in the street...suddenly the whole alley became dark & some angry men with maces, chain & big knives started running to the alley from both sides. honestly, that was the most frightening scene that I had even seen in my whole life, but more than being scared of those men & also people who were throwing stones & glasses to them, I was worried for my father that he was really scared too & didn't know what to do, actually we didn't have any ways; you know, there was not a place for all people anymore, there were just some boys who were really so much brave that nothing even that big knives couldn't scare them. So we were afraid of the shouting & hitting & that fighting between people & Basijis...Finally we found a way a came out of those alleys & went to the street that car was parked, then tried to come there again, but in the car. This time things were much worse, you could only see fire & hear people chanting against government, Khameneiee, khatami & generally all kinds of Mullahs! They were shouting that they want mullahs dead; yes that is what everyone wants. And again Basij men with much more anger & violence came & started hitting people & arresting them, so some started escaping & we also came home....

Now I'm so much excited that I can't sleep & I'm just thinking about future that is not that much vague anymore, some bright points are seen. If things go on like this & these demonstrations continue just for one other week I bet that there'll be no need even to others' support... (14.6.03)

For the first time in many months, the blog is really hopeful: "I really have no doubt that the freedom is coming soon, so much sooner than even optimistic politicians expect" (13.6.03). The hope was however short-lived. Consistent with the politics of melancholy and isolationism, the Internet was filled with hope expressed by online protesters that success is close while forgetting the simple fact that they have not gained popular support. On June 16, Iranian girl reports of a boy who, in the taxi taking them both to school, spoke with enthusiasm about the recent demonstrations, claiming that once the uprising spreads to other parts of Tehran, the fundamentalist nightmare will be over. Yet no one else in the taxi seemed to listen to him or to care, she writes; the passengers were either pretending to be asleep or were too scared to respond. In school, the events caused great excitement—she even heard a rumor about girls who publicly took off their veils and started chanting in the streets, yet no popular uprising took place in Iran in 2003.

In late June and early July, two-hundred and fifty university lecturers and writers signed a petition calling for the abolition of Ayatollah Ali Khamenei's position as God's representative on earth. In the US, master blogger Andrew Sullivan made a plea to devote all the world's blogs to the struggle in Iran: "Many people have theorized about the power of the web to bring about change," he wrote, "and the young generation in Iran must know this as well as any group of people. So let's try and use it - if only to send a symbol of solidarity with those resisting the theo-fascists who have wrecked Iran for three generations...." Iranian girl was thrilled by the plea: "I'm sure that this work will be one of the most effective ones in this fighting for freedom, even more than street struggles & demonstrations" (18.6.03). Photos of Iranians committing suicide by setting themselves alight were posted on the World Wide Web.

As the 9th of July approached, she was sure the government ban on demonstrations would not be effective. "That seems foolish; no one was waiting for their permission & this fact that they would ban any demonstrations on July 9, will make no change to students' movement" (23.6.03). On July 8, the day before the planned demonstrations, the blog is fraught with tension and anticipation. Iranian girl is reassured by the fact that preparations for the demonstration had continued despite measures taken to stop them by breaking satellite dishes, issuing warnings, arresting people and closing Websites down. On the other hand, she is not sure whether the preparations were made with enough determination:

> You know, I have no idea what exactly will happen. Actually a while before this I used to think July 9 will be somehow the last day for this regime but now that it's less than 24 hours to this historic day I have a feeling that still the number of traitors is more than real Iranians who work for having freedom & a democratic regime. (8.7.03)

The End

The demonstrations planned for the 9th of July to commemorate the 1999 protest did not even match those that had taken place a few weeks earlier. The police were out in full force while the general public appeared indifferent. The blogger found it difficult to understand what went wrong. Something must be wrong with the Iranian people, she wrote, not realizing that the commotion leading to the protests on the World Wide Web was illusory. Or maybe she did realize it for the blog continued to appear on the Web for a few more months but lost its vigor. The dominant feeling became one of confusion and fatigue. "I can't stand this way anymore, I'm tired of everything and everyone" (29.7.03).

That summer, she wrote, was the worst in her life. It is supposed to be a summer of liberation yet the people are going about their usual summer routine. All hope for liberation has been lost: "You know, I really have no idea what is going on or what will happen, I'm just thinking of my optimistic wishes about this summer & now I see all were like sweet dreams & now there is no voice left to shout" (3.8.03). She realizes that the chance for improvement of women's conditions in Iran has been lost. She tries to develop a sense of internal freedom, "the feeling of being free just behind hundred doors & in a world that has become a prison" (10.8.03). Only a miracle can help her now, she writes in late August, and then comes the inevitable decision to stop blogging.

The girl who has provided us with rare insights into life under the veil forced on her understands the power of blogging, especially in light of the government's crackdowns. These simple Web pages, written by ordinary people, she believes, had gained much power and become a source of concern for government. She continues to mock the government's attempts to control blogging by organizing Weblog societies.

> Organizing weblogs!!! Oh, that's really funny, it seems like they know nothing about weblogs & the fact that they can never be organized by any societies. It's clear that their inability to control weblogs, still bothers them & they do anything to somehow find a way to avoid people write anything they want without even inspection. (5.12.03)

But she loses interest in the project and at the end of the year posts a farewell message:

> I can't believe how soon this fall came to an end! Calendar shows that the winter has come but as it's not snowing, I can't believe it! Final exams have also begun & this year I'm so happy! I really needed something to keep me busy... You know, It'd been a while that I was thinking of writing this post; a kind of ending post for a weblog that although never became exactly like what I wanted, but was like the only safe place for my mind... Anyway, it all was like a great experience, going through all personal, political & social events through this webpage with words & posts...and finding so many friends & realizing that there are others who think & care about you. Ok, that's all for now...although it's a bit hard to say; but...goodbye. (23.12.03)

Notes

1. Tayana Marshall, "Iranian Revolution Turned against Women who supported it," *The McGill Daily,* June 5, 1995, 5.
2. Azar Nafisi, "They the People." *New Republic* 228 (March 3, 2003).
3. Azar Nafisi, *Reading Lolita in Tehran* (New York: Random House, 2003), 28.
4. Nasrin Alavi, "Freedom in Farsi Blogs," *The Guardian*, December 18, 2004.
5. Nasrin Alavi, *We Are Iran*, (New York: Soft Sull Press, 2005).
6. Nasrin Alavi, *We Are Iran: The Persian Blogs* (Sample Chapter), <http://www.softskull.com/files/WeAreIran_SampleChapterLo.pdf>
7. <http://iraniangirl.blogspot.com/>

8.   Pejman Yousefzadeh, "Blogging for Revolution," *TCS (Tech Central Station)*, <http://www.techcentralstation.com>
9.   "Blogs and Toilet Graffiti," <http://www.persianblogger.com/english/archives/000018.html#more>
10. "Iranians Protest against Clerics," BBC News, 11.6.03. <http://news.bbc. co.uk/2/hi/middle_east/2980102.stm>
11. Quoted in "iranian girl," 18.6.03.

Chapter 5

Israeli Woman

From my own experience as an Israeli, I know it is not easy to live in Israel, a modern industrial state entangled in ancient religious rituals, a democracy engaged in occupation, a hedonistic culture whose citizens face the danger of being blown up by suicide bombers. The paradoxes of Israeli life are apparent on all fronts. Public opinion polls point to a desire for peace but hawkish candidates get elected to office, advanced health and welfare policies are applied but the economic divide is growing, a national pride prevails but masses of proud citizens are leaving the country, the lower classes support investments in the occupied territories against their own self-interest, thousands of orthodox youngsters are exempt from military duty in spite of severe security needs, etc.

Israelis often consider themselves as living in a madhouse. They are the focus of enormous international attention while being one of the tiniest nations in the world; they engage in endless debate over the direction the country should take while going nowhere; they love their land but systematically destroy its natural resources; they give to charity but kill each other in road accidents.

Living with paradoxes and contradictions requires mechanisms that will allow citizens to make sense of their surroundings. This is where the role of the intellectual as the interpreter of the human condition comes in. It is intellectuals who provide the members of every society with meanings and a sense of direction. There would be intellectuals in society even if there were no intellectuals by disposition, wrote Edward Shils.[1]

In different eras, different groups fulfilled the intellectual function. Generally it was the church that provided societies with meaning and guidance. In the modern era, as part of the eighteenth and nineteenth century enlightenment, writers, scholars, and artists took on this role. This changed the base from which intellectuals derived their right to be heard. While in the past, the source of their authority was transcendental, in the age of enlightenment it derived from civil society.

Civil society refers to the plurality of social groups operating in democratic states in relative separation from the state. These groups express concerns that are not necessarily given high preference by the political system: human rights, the environment, support of the arts, etc.[2] Intellectuals may be seen as the spokespersons for these groups. When the writer Emile Zola stood up during the Dreyfus Affair in late nineteenth century France and wrote "J'accuse" against the church, military, and political establishments, he did so in the name of norms of truth and justice sanctioned by civil society.[3]

The view of intellectuals as spokespersons for civil society raises the expectation that they get involved in issues of concern to civil groups, communicate with large strata of society, act toward the preservation of a pluralistic social structure, encourage civilized forms of public debate and take responsibility for occurrences in the world around them.[4]

In Israel, intellectuals have traditionally played an important role in developing the cultural capital that turned Israel into a democratic country. Writers provided the language and ideas that facilitated nation-building, scholars devised the constitutional and institutional infrastructure of the state, and artists participated in critical discourse over the direction it should take. Intellectuals stood at the important crossroads of a nation building process dominated by the state, helping to protect civil society from the socialist and nationalist forces that challenged it.[5]

However, in recent years, much of this has changed, partly because much public discourse is taking place in the mass media. Although intellectuals are still playing important roles in social causes, such as child protection or freedom of the press, their voice is mostly heard in relation to national political issues in Israel. They take partisan sides, join politically one-sided "think tanks," preach to the converted, and make little effort to reach out to wide strata of society. They often seem more concerned with promoting their own power and status than with the issues under consideration, and when appearing on television, their language does not differ much from that of Israeli politicians, who are not known for their civilized forms of expression. Rather than taking responsibility, they accuse anyone but themselves for the country's misfortunes. Generally speaking, a process can be identified (both in Israel and elsewhere)[6] in which intellectuals, or at least the salient elements among them, are being politicized to an extent that distances them from the concerns of civil society.

This distancing from civil society means that intellectuals no longer provide it with meaning and guidance. And if we accept Shils's functional assumption that every society needs a social stratum providing it with meaning and guidance, then we must look for it elsewhere. Many Israelis are definitely looking elsewhere, realizing that intellectuals may be "speaking truth to power" but are not speaking to them. In order to cope with the reality in which they live, citizens are taking advantage of the opportunities opened up by the Internet to shape new forms of individual and public discourse, especially in blogosphere.

Israeli blogs appear in portals such as "Israblog" and "Tapuz" which list tens of thousands of them, including many in English. As reported by Sarah Bronson, blogs by English speaking Israelis play a unique role in helping readers abroad to form opinions about Middle East politics. The immediacy and interactivity characterizing blogs is a great advantage in a country subjected to terrorist attacks. After a major event, bloggers all over the world turn to Israel's English blogs for immediate information. Moreover, as many English speakers in Israel are associated with right of center political positions, these blogs are often seen as an alternative voice to a world media known for its anti-Israeli stand.[7]

I would now like to follow the blog of a young Israeli woman who, failing to receive from traditional intellectual sources the insights necessary for survival, steps into the vacuum in search of meaning and guidance. The blog's name, "Not a Fish," hints at the blogger's urge to escape traditional modes of discourse for the sake of new ones. The title is taken from a Zen story which exposes the self-important nature of scholarly debates while providing a lively alternative consisting of simpler modes of expression. Here is the story:

> One day Chang Zzu and a friend were walking by a river. 'Look at the fish swimming about,' said Chuang Zzu, 'They are really enjoying themselves.'
> 'You are not a fish,' replied the friend, 'so you can't truly know that there are enjoying themselves.'
> 'You are not me,' said Chuang Zzu, 'so how do you know that I do not know that the fish are enjoying themselves?' (9.6.02)

Not only does the blogger mock such polemics, she presents a different mode of expression. Writing an online diary, she does not storm into the public debate once an issue emerges on the political arena but relates to social and political issues on a continual basis, communicates with a wider variety of social groups than many writers, scholars, or artists do, is far less concerned with her personal status, uses a rather moderate writing style, and depicts a deep sense of responsibility. Let me now follow this diary from its beginning in June 2002, observing its handling of civil concerns, analyzing its political contributions, and noting its advantages and disadvantages as a medium of public discourse.

Not a Fish

"Not a Fish"[8] is a blog written by "Imshin" who was described in an online profile in June 2004 as a thirty-nine-year old Israeli working mother. Born in Liverpool, she moved to Israel with her parents when she was nine and today lives in Tel-Aviv with her husband Bish, their two daughters aged nine and twelve and a half, and a tiny black kitten called Shoosha. Her work in an undemanding clerical job in the public service leaves her plenty of time to worry about current affairs.[9]

The blog stands out for its lack of pretense. Its logo describes it as "the meaningless chatter of your regular split personality Israeli mother trying to make sense of current insanity." As one follows the diary over two years, the insanity involved in life in the Middle East does not disappear but its interpretation from the perspective of one of its citizens rather than of politics, religion, history, or metaphysics, makes it easier to cope with. In a region of the world where political positions are expressed in messianic rage, it is refreshing to encounter an approach that combines straightforward observation with skepticism. Explaining the meaning of blogging for her, the diarist writes:

> I know the things I say are nothing special, probably not very different from the

thoughts and feelings of many ordinary Israelis. I'm no great scholar, no brilliant columnist. I'm not very right wing, or very left wing, by Israeli standards. I'm somewhere in the middle, a bit mixed up, swayed by emotions. I have no hidden agenda. I just say what enters my mind at a given moment. All I have to offer is my little angle of Israeli life. (3.12.03)

Imshin is aware, however, that her "little angle" may be useful in terms of the broader public discourse:

Could this not be useful for someone who wants to help peace along and needs to really know and understand both sides, and not just what he or she believes is right and just, based on previous life experiences from other parts of the world? Does compromise not take into account the dreams and fears of both sides in a conflict? Is my contribution so far less valuable than that of someone with fury in his or her eyes, standing on a street corner chanting mindless, inflammatory slogans that someone else thought up, and that mean very little, but serve to increase hatred between the sides? (3.12.03)

Imshin is neither a "peacenik" nor a warmonger. She is observing the violence in the Middle East with a sense of moderation that diverts from the rigid categories adopted by both right and left wingers to the situation. She calls neither for a hard hand nor for a soft hand by Israel toward the Palestinians but for a sober examination of the conflict and its solutions. The first entry in the blog followed a suicide attack in Jerusalem that killed nineteen people. In response, Imshin posted a letter written during the American Civil War describing Ulysses S. Grant's behavior after the first disastrous day of the battle of Shiloh in 1862. Grant refused to consider retreat, yet acted in sober serenity.

The technology allowing bloggers to link to a variety of materials, especially news items appearing in newspaper websites, and add their responses to them, makes them a kind of media watch group. On June 22, 2002, Imshin posts an article by Matthew Parris on suicide bombers, published in the *Times*. According to this, Parris assumes that both sides to the Israeli-Palestinian conflict would accept the notion that "encompassing your own death in the killing of other people may sometimes be justified, even noble. If you or I could have brought down the temple in which the Third Reich sat, killing ourselves too, that might (I presume we agree) have been a noble act" He is also quoted as writing that: "I do not think that in his heart an Israeli would deny that, if your enemy has taken land that is rightfully yours and occupied it, then not just your enemy's army but his wife and son and daughter and servants and all who, under his protection, come to live and make their living on the stolen land, are aggressors."

Imshin, who feels that the article simply justifies the killing of Israeli civilians, exposes the rhetorical technique by which this is allegedly done: justifying murder of a group by making assumptions about what that group seems to agree to. Responding to the above statement that no Israeli would deny the right to operate against the wives, children, and servants of perceived aggressors (which, incidentally, may be seen as hinting in anti-Semitic fashion at biblical justice), she excludes herself from the consensus imposed on her in that contention, which she can easily do because of the personal nature of the blog: "Wanna bet, Matty boy? This Israeli denies it. By this logic we should be shooting the children and younger siblings of suicide bombers." She also exposes the nuances used by the writer to squeeze in a vicious point: "Notice how he very subtly equates Israel with the Third Reich? You wouldn't even notice it!...I find this neat philosophical reasoning that makes such a compelling moral case for blowing up little babies extremely brilliant" (22.6.02). Two days later she exposes in similar fashion the homogeneous nature of the Argument page of the *Independent*: "I must say I haven't seen much argument on this page, at least about the Middle East. All columnists seem to agree that the Israelis are war criminals and Nazis and deserve to be blown up..." (24.6.02).

The problem is that blogging exposes violations of journalistic standards while it has no standards itself, and Imshin is aware of this. Having written analysis reports for a living, she doubts how long she will keep up with online writing. As a professional writer, she says, she used to work a few days or weeks on a piece, doing research and having plenty of time for thinking about phrasing before she even started writing. But blogging is different: "This is much more fun. I get to say whatever stupid idea pops into my head. And I don't have to submit everything I write to censorship by my boss, just because his name is also on it" (30.6.02).

The ability to voice whatever stupid idea pops into one's head is problematic in that it allows bloggers to spread unsubstantiated rumors and make irresponsible statements. Alan Wolfe has compared today's bloggers to the pamphleteers of the Colonial era in America. "Pamphleteering is what happens when no one—editorial writers, university professors, publishing executives—is doing much 'filtering.'"[10] The lack of filters does however have an advantage in that the blogger is not confined to any agenda but may comment on civil issues that are not solicited by any "boss." During a regular week in June, we thus follow Ishmin's feelings when she notes the last day of school for her two girls, the closing of a little zoological garden by request of the Society for the Protection of Nature in Israel, or her wonderings about changes in Ronaldo's hair. Save perhaps the latter, these issues, that are part of our daily life experiences, are not without larger public implications.

Take summer vacation for instance. While the readers of this blog are led through the familiar experience of the last day of classes, they are also exposed to an Israeli mother's concerns over the raising of kids in a region in which summer vacation may provide suicide bombers with greater opportunities to blow them up in public gatherings, such as ice cream parlors. Here is the entry:

> Summer vacation is an extra challenge for city dwellers with kids. Especially nowadays. If perverts and crazy drivers aren't enough, now I have to worry if it's safe for my elder daughter to have an ice cream at the ice cream parlor with her pals, or go to her favorite haunt—the local toyshop. Among some of the other mothers I'm regarded as very liberal, because I allow my daughter to ride the mini-bus to the swimming pool. What am I to do? Put her under house ar-

rest all summer? (2.7.02)

Such statements may sometimes appear in the established media. On the first day of summer vacation, a television crew would interview an occasional "man on the street," in an item appearing close to the weather report, which would turn the worries of civilians into a colorful episode. Here, however, the worries about one's daughters riding the mini-bus become an integral dimension of the Israeli condition, a dimension ignored by politicians and pundits (unless it temporarily serves a broader political agenda) but kept alive by bloggers. As we follow the fear of a citizen in an online diary, we get a more intimate understanding of it; when Imshin is awaiting a suicide attack, we are exposed to a lively picture of the symptoms accompanying the dread of impending disaster: "My throat feels constricted, my breathing is slightly labored and my heart beats way faster and harder than usual. Oh, and I feel nauseous. (No, I'm not pregnant)" (3.7.02).

She feels the traditional media cannot serve as her voice in such moments, not even a liberal newspaper like *Haaretz* priding itself for its appeal to the Israeli intelligentsia. Like many educated Israelis, Imshin has subscribed to *Haaretz* for many years, but came to realize it neglects her civil concerns. Commenting on an article by the newspaper's editor, she complains that although *Haaretz* still gives good coverage to events, the opinion columns, editorials, and in-depth stories have a common political agenda that does not account for the feelings of the great majority of Israelis. By this she refers not to the "silent majority" in the American sense, namely those who feel underrepresented by an allegedly liberal press, but to the civil society whose incumbents may share the columnists' political views but whose civil concerns are ignored. Imshin exposes a growing gap between journalists, who claim they provide objective coverage, and citizens who sense that the coverage of civil society is, at best, "patronizing and condescending" (4.7.02).

The alternative medium of blogging may be seen as a more authentic voice of civil society. It is not only the themes that are brought up in the online diary, compared to their omission in other media, but also the fact that we read them as part of an unfolding life story. One mother's worries during summer vacation are not framed in accordance with a political narrative, but we get to follow them as part of an overall summer experience, which includes, for instance, the presence of sandals in shop windows: "Time to go shopping. Now if I was still in my early twenties, I would a) worry that if I bought them now, they would be terribly out of fashion by next summer. B) not be able to afford them even at the cheaper prices" (9.10.02).

This allows a different reading of Israeli life than provided in the *Guardian* or *Haaretz*. It becomes a more complex experience in which the change of seasons, ignored by the media but not by the diarist, is accounted for without neglecting the larger political and security context. The presence of the larger context is demonstrated in the following description of Imshin's family outing in Northern Israel. The family swims in one of the sources of the Jordan River, sensing the refreshing effect of the ice-cold water and strong flow on a hot August day, but the blogger also recalls that this is the same river the Syrians tried to divert in the Sixties. Or consider this: "In the afternoon, after a rest, we took the kids to ride horses in nearby moshav [village] She'ar Yishuv, where seventy-three army officers and soldiers were killed, five years ago, when two air force helicopters collided in the worst military accident Israel has ever seen" (22.8.02).

This depiction of the little joys of life sought in a country living in the shadow of conflict may seem thrilling to some and disturbing to others, but the point is that a new medium is developing that allows such self-expression. Moreover, the new medium allows the blogger to negotiate her condition, to contemplate what her life is worth in view of her being destined to live it in turbulent times. Her conclusion is straightforward:

> Occasionally someone remarks how brave we Israeli bloggers are. Our life is so dangerous and still we laugh. What are they talking about? My life is wonderful. I am the luckiest of people (tfu tfu tfu. Sorry, it's a reflex). I have enough to eat and drink. I am healthy (tfu tfu tfu again). The sun shines every day and I am surrounded by love. What more could anyone possibly want? (a guarantee of immortality, you suggest? No, I pass.) If I get blown up tomorrow, don't re-read this post and shake your heads in sorrow. Be happy for me. I may be dead, but the day before I died was a great day. Who could ask for more? (21.6.03)

The Blogger's Politics

The civilian concerns identified in this blog do not imply a lack of interest in "larger" political issues. To the contrary, this blog takes on many burning political issues. The civilian filter through which the political issues are considered, however, leads the blogger to escape rigid political ideologies, a main component of political discourse in Israel. Imshin understands the need of many to cling to such ideologies; it helps them feel more certain about the future. If only their solution to the Middle East conflict would be accepted, the future would be secure. On the other hand, giving up rigidity for the sake of uncertainty is hard: "Uncertainty is a part of life there's no getting away from. But it's difficult to live with it staring you in the face all the time. The belief or hope that your children and grandchildren will have lives that are not living nightmares is helpful in keeping you from going mad" (7.7.02).

Yet, the blogger feels she has no choice but to live with uncertainty:

> Some here are stubbornly clutch on to the belief that an end to occupation will magically solve all. Some are just as adamant that we have a divine right to all of the historical land of Israel and that this right is holier than living peacefully with the people we share this land with. Most are somewhere in the middle, awoken from false hopes of easy solutions, but realistic enough to understand

the need for painful compromise to make the future possible here. (7.7.02)

She adds that the fear of what the future holds in store for her and for her descendants in this accursed part of the world is stronger and deeper than the everyday fear of terrorist attacks. Yet none of the firm solutions appeals to her: "Some have hardened their hearts and others have become remarkably compassionate for the other side. Compassionate to a degree that causes them to belittle and disregard the dangers we face" (7.7.02).

She thus continues to live with uncertainty and ambiguity. On the one hand she opposes those who have hardened their hearts, and searches for a solution to the Israeli–Palestinian conflict. On the other hand, the solution proposed by those who, out of compassion for the Palestinians would want the Jews to go back to where they came from, is unacceptable: "They don't seem to understand that we can't 'go back to where we came from'. We came from nowhere and we've nowhere to go" (7.7.02).

One way to overcome the difficulties of uncertainty and ambiguity is blogging. It is easy to identify the therapeutic nature of "Not a Fish" for the person writing it. "Do you know, writing this blog is like psychotherapy. I used to hate reading the Guardian. Everything I read used to infuriate me. Now it's one of my favorite reads because I know I can always make nasty remarks about it on the blog" (10.7.02).

The blog becomes the medium in which one expresses frustrations over political statements or events that seem wrong, or highlights those that seem right. Much attention is devoted to what Imshin perceives as anti-Semitic nuances in British public opinion. A typical example concerns her and many other bloggers' involvement in the scandal over the refusal of pathologist Andrew Wilkie of Oxford University to accept an Israeli doctoral student for having served in the Israeli army. Imshin posts Professor Wilkie's letter to the prospective student according to which he has "a huge problem with the way that the Israelis take the moral high ground from their appalling treatment in the Holocaust, and then inflict gross human rights abuses on the Palestinians." She responds to it by dwelling on her own autobiographical experience, describing the veiled anti-Semitic atmosphere in which her parents grew up in the North of England in the 1930s and 1940s where Jews were often blamed for the war. While some Jews tried to rationalize such behavior by relating it to the reality of a religiously diverse city in which everyone picked on everyone else, her parents, she tells, became active Zionists and left.

What has this undercurrent of anti-Semitism her parents experienced in Britain as children, during the war and after, got to do with present day discrimination in Britain against Israelis for political reasons, she asks. Her answer: Professor Wilkie of Oxford makes the equation between Israelis and Jews himself when he equates Israelis with Holocaust survivors although no Israel existed when the Holocaust took place.

Somehow I find myself terribly offended by the Holocaust sentence, rolled off so glibly and thoughtlessly. You get the feeling the good professor and his friends use this line freely in their stuffy cocktail party chitchat, without really thinking about it's meaning. (I am especially struck by the words *'appalling treatment'*. Appalling Treatment?! What a wonderfully British understatement)." (28.6.03)

This entry demonstrates the blogger's feeling that many British intellectuals are wrong in their treatment of the Middle East conflict. When she comes across the following piece from George Orwell's 1945 essay *Notes on Nationalism* she posts it without further comment:

It is, I think, true to say that the intelligentsia have been more wrong about the progress of the war than the common people, and that they were more swayed by partisan feelings. The average intellectual of the Left believed, for instance, that the war was lost in 1940, that the Germans were bound to overrun Egypt in 1942, that the Japanese would never be driven out of the lands they had conquered, and that the Anglo-American bombing offensive was making no impression on Germany. He could believe these things because his hatred for the British ruling class forbade him to admit that British plans could succeed. There is no limit to the follies that can be swallowed if one is under the influence of feelings of this kind. I have heard it confidently stated, for instance, that the American troops had been brought to Europe not to fight the Germans but to crush an English revolution. One has to belong to the intelligentsia to believe things like that: no ordinary man could be such a fool. (9.8.02)

The blogger makes every effort to deal with political affairs in a different way than do traditional intellectuals. When asked by another blogger what she thinks of Holocaust denial she writes that she is not very good at putting over a philosophical point at the best of times, especially while she is on a diet. She admits, as few pundits probably would, that the issue of Holocaust denial is simply too big and scary for her. While some like Professor Wilkie seem to see Israel's preoccupation with the Holocaust as some sort of manipulation, she is "still trying to come to terms, to grasp, to understand the meaning, or the lack of it, and to learn to live with the feeling of loss that somehow persists" (5.7.03).

The rejection of common intellectual modes of political debate and their replacement by personal reflections allows the blogger to make occasional arguments that are not fully thought through but do appeal to common sense, as when she deals with the controversial security fence built by Israel to separate the Jewish and Palestinian populations. Speaking of the Palestinians, she writes:

They want a state, right? The state will have an internationally recognized border, right? The state will also have internationally recognized passports, right? Palestinians wanting to work in a neighboring state will have to use those internationally recognized passports to cross that internationally recognized border in order to work in that neighboring state, right? So what's [their] problem with the security fence? Is it so important for them to be able to infiltrate the neighboring state, illegally? Why is that, exactly?" (20.7.02)

This outcry neglects important elements such as the Israeli government's policy of erecting the fence in accordance with the political interests of West Bank settlers rather than the economic needs of West Bank Palestinians. It does however expose the fact that the Palestinian opposition to the fence focuses less on concrete grievances than on an all-out objection to any conflict management measure: "They don't want to be fenced in, they say. Well, what the hell DO they want?" (20.7.02).

It is also interesting to follow the rejection of rigid ideological positions in the blogger's writings on internal politics in Israel. This may stem from a personal trait hinted at when Imshin mentions how the television set in her home serves as a place of refuge for some of her daughters' friends whose ideological parents ban television sets in their homes. A typical entry concerns the Eastern Democratic Spectrum, a radical political group pursuing the cause of "Sephardi" Jews (Jews from Arab countries). Imshin, whose husband is reportedly a Sephardi Jew himself, supports the group's lobbying for equality and impartiality in the distribution of state investments in education and housing, agrees that the rich history and culture of Sephardi Jews should be taught in schools, and praises the moderation she encountered in online communication she had with its leader. Analyzing the group's publications, however, she is unwilling to go along with the romantic yearnings she identifies in them for the past in Arab countries and the hatred conveyed in them toward towards Jews of European origin. "I agree there has been discrimination. I agree we must work to close social and economic gaps. I think investing in education in poor and peripheral areas is paramount. But seeing the discrimination as intentional and conspirational…is wrong and can be harmful" (28.7.02).

After being called a "leftie" by someone, she writes that she refuses to be identified as either "left" or "right." This refusal sums up the politics of the lengthy diary, whether it deals with religious fundamentalism, feminism, the right to die, the Palestinian leadership, the Iraq war, provincialism, globalization, and dozens of other issues. For example, she says she feels compassion for those who haven't been lucky, and donates generously to charity, but refuses to feel guilty about being relatively well off. She believes the state should supply all citizens with education and health care but also in strict law and order measures. She believes in taking care of the environment, but not at the expense of human lives. She thinks abortion is murder, but is nevertheless pro-choice. She even diverts from the trendy anti-globalization trend, seeing nothing wrong with Macdonald's, Coca Cola, and other multi-nationals:

> It is my responsibility, as a parent, to make sure my children get a balanced diet and I see no harm in these companies offering their wares, as long as they don't force me to consume them. Living as I do, in a little country, far from the affluent centers of "modern civilization", I am grateful for the considerable material (and even spiritual) improvement in my life that Globalization has brought about. Moreover, I fail to see how it is possible to globally solve global problems without Globalization. (12.10.02)

Meditation vs. Dialogue

This blog by a woman trying to survive the burdens of Israeli life sparks the idea that an alternative to traditional intellectual discourse may indeed be emerging in blogosphere. Imshin does not pretend to share the qualities attributed to academics, columnists, and other masters of public discourse; she does not present herself as cultured, highly educated, or endowed with charisma. Yet, judging by the responses she gets to her postings, her online diary probably appeals to more readers than many public speakers are able to reach out to. She has found a means of expression that allows her to make sense of her surroundings and make others think about them. This is particularly meaningful in a society in which individual concerns are not highly regarded.

At times, Imshin calls for dialogue with people of opposite views. She regrets the collapse of dialogue between Jews and Palestinians and expresses her unexplained urge to spend a Sabbath night with West Bank settlers in spite of her objection to them:

> I am strongly opposed to these people and their behavior. I think they should be evacuated, the sooner the better. They are serious obstacles to any possibility of peace in this region. So why am I fascinated with the idea of spending time there? Is it just an anthropological interest or is there something more?" (1.9.03)

But blogging, to her, is more a means of self-expression and self-exploration than of dialogue. For example, after an entry in which she took issue with an article about universal love and peace she got into an E-mail exchange with the writer of the article, and admits it was rather exhausting. "This blog is not a discussion," she writes. "You don't like what you read, you go read something else…I need to be around people who see things as I do" (27.2.02).

Meditation comes more naturally to her than communication. She has a great interest in Buddhism and her whole blogging experience may be seen as a meditation intended to maintain inner control when the outer world seems to go out of control. She is more an autobiographer than a journalist; her aim is not to make a point but to write a life in order to make sense of it. This is why she feels uncomfortable when she realizes that her diary sparks online debates: "I'm feeling a bit overwhelmed by all these lively discussions on my comments. I realize that I have certain responsibility for the content of the comments because it's my blog. So behave yourselves, you lot! Oh, and please don't use my comments for dealing in illegal substances or inciting to violence" (18.11.02).

While she sometimes acknowledges responses to her entries as eye opening, she admits she is detached from them:

> It's like: you kids feel free to chat among yourselves while I sit here quietly and stare out into oblivion. This will sometimes happen to me when I'm sitting with a group of 'real-life' friends. I lose track in the middle of a discussion and then I tend to either daydream; go check up on the bookshelves (if I'm in someone

else's home); wonder into the kitchen and end up helping the host/ess with the tasties; strike up a rival conversation or watch the smaller kids playing (usually most rewarding). (18.11.02)

This may be a source of concern for, as important as meditation is to the individual, society needs dialogue. It is hard to disagree with Karl Mannheim,[11] Karl Popper,[12] Martin Buber,[13] and others who placed dialogue at the center of both the advancement of knowledge and social civility. Bloggers are sometimes seen as engaged in dialogue. As Sorapure has suggested, the Web's interactivity and the immediacy of its publishing enhance that aspect of diary writing concerned not with solitary and private reflection, but with communication and community. To her, the online diary is anything but private, especially since many diarists use the medium to make connections with others.[14] Bloggers form discursive communities in that they are aware of each other, post selected media items for each other, exchange information, develop a degree of stratification, and even follow power and status hierarchies. As Cindy Curling puts it:

> People who write blogs tend to think of themselves as a community, and within that community there are neighborhoods of people with common interests. These neighbors keep in close touch, and spend time showing each other their best new information. If the neighborhood where you grew up was like mine, there were a few houses where all the kids gravitated because those folks had the swing set, the wading pool, the popcorn, and got the new Atari games first. Weblogs work in similar ways.[15]

However, it is hard to consider the exchange between bloggers as a public dialogue of the kind advocated by the above philosophers. For one, we know little about the online diarists besides their nicknames. We have just followed the diary of a woman nicknamed Imshin who may not even be a woman but the product of Web designers inventing her on the anonymous Internet. Or she may be a woman who decided to invent a false identity. And even if she presented to us what she considers to be her true identity, she is still not obliged to do so all the time or to provide us with more than passing thoughts that can alter from one day to the other. At one point she admits she is simply engaged in "chatter":

> The thing is we don't know what's right. Nobody knows. Is there any one answer to anything? Is there really any one path which, if taken will bring an end to all, or even most, ills? Can we ever say that about anything?...Let's take the middle way, said the Buddha, but where does that pass?...And we chatter on, because that's what we do. Round and round and round in circles. What's the point? Well, it passes the time, for one thing...So I'll keep on chattering on this blog. Just don't take me too seriously. Tomorrow I may very well be saying the exact opposite of what I was saying yesterday. (13.11.02)

This statement provides a rather realistic picture of the nature of blogging. Online life writing attracts us to texts without our having any way of knowing whether the identities presented in them are real or fake. This is acceptable in novels, plays, and movies that are situated between fiction and reality, but not in blogging, which involves the gradual formation of trust toward individuals who become selectors of media content for many people, substituting for a mass media that is widely mistrusted.

Thus, while emancipating us in one way, blogging subdues us to the well-known dangers of virtual reality.[16] Moreover, as we look at the new medium of blogging for meaning and guidance in a turbulent world, we face the danger of being guided or misguided by irresponsible elements. The Internet lacks responsibility. Nicknames come and go, statements can be written without their being given much thought, promises can be made that do not have to be kept, in short, the melancholic can easily take over the guiding function that the enlightenment attributed to the intellectual. However, as members of society we are in need of an enlightened dialogue in which ideas are exchanged, issues raised, interests articulated, and compromises made in an open, assertive, responsible way. Blogging provides an exciting new arena for public discussion, but it allows our Dostoevsky-like "ideal type" to flourish due to the anonymity of the Web. Like him, the Web lacks responsibility—the responsibility of human beings toward each other, and toward the maintenance of a dialogue conducted not in a mouse hole but in real life.

Notes

1. Edward Shils, "The Intellectuals and the Powers: Some Perspectives for Comparative Analysis," in *On Intellectuals*, ed. Philip Reif (Garden City, NY: Anchor Books 1970).
2. Dominique Colas, *Civil Society and Fanaticism: Conjoined Histories* (Stanford, CA: Stanford University Press 1997).
3. Enzo Traverso, "Intellectuals and Anti-Fascism: For a Critical Historization," *New Politics* 9 (Winter 2004): 91-101.
4. Jeffrey C. Goldfarb, *Civility and Subversion: The Intellectual in Democratic Society* (Cambridge: Cambridge University Press 1998).
5. Michael Keren, *The Pen and the Sword: Israeli Intellectuals and the Making of the Nation-State* (Boulder, CO: Westview 1989).
6. See Mark Lila, *The Reckless Mind: Intellectuals in Politics* (New York: NYRB 2001).
7. Sarah Bronson, "Web Diaries Become Hot Medium for Talk in Israel," Haaretz.com. 17.4.2004.
8. <http://imshin.blogspot.com/>
9. Normblog 2004, <http://normblog.typepad.com/normblog/2004/06/the_normblog_pr_1.html>
10. Alan Wolfe, "The New Pamphleteers," *New York Times*, July 11, 2004.
11. Karl Mannheim, *Ideology and Utopia* (New York: Harcourt 1936).
12. Karl Popper, *The Open Society and its Enemies* (London: Routledge 1945).
13. Martin Buber, *I and Thou* (New York: Free Press 1971).
14. Madeleine Sorapure, "Screening Moments, Scrolling Lives: Diary Writing on the Web," *Biography* 26 (Winter 2003): 1-23.
15. Cindy Curling, "A Closer Look at Weblogs," LLRX.Com (May 4, 2003): 5,

<http://www.llrx.com/columns/notes46.htm>
16. See Beth E. Kolko ed., *Virtual Publics: Politics and Community in an Electronic Age* (New York: Columbia University Press 2003).

Chapter 6

Canadian Baby Boomer

The increase in the birth rate in the US and other Western countries after World War II, accompanied by high growth rates in Western economies in the 1950s and 1960s, had a significant economic impact, especially because the post war generation became a major target for marketers. The emphasis on this slice of the market has also given rise to conceptions about the cultural uniqueness and impact of the "baby boomers," especially during the 1960s when many of them became university students.[1] Since the "roaring twenties," no decade has been mythologized like "the sixties," when a baby boomer revolution was allegedly taking place in the West. The mythology of that era is understandable in light of the fact that many writers, academics, and producers of popular culture whose university life was marked by a sense of protest, would look back to those years with nostalgia: "The sixties resound in our historical memory as do few other eras. It was a time when events went into overdrive, and the postwar social trajectory was deflected off line...Few who reached adulthood between 1961 and 1971 remained unmarked by the events of those years."[2]

This is only partly true. Many people who reached adulthood in those years remained relatively unmarked by the events led, as always, by an elite, which also dominated the historiography of the era, especially in the US. Even if they led a hippie lifestyle for a couple of years, participated in campus sit-ins and anti-Vietnam demonstrations, and cursed about LBJ and CIA, most baby boomers were no Abbie Hoffmans, Bob Dylans, or Jane Fondas. The "New Left," whose principles were extensively taught in American universities by its veterans, had little impact beyond campus walls, while the more significant social changes of the decade—the civil rights movement, the great society programs and feminism—were not necessarily the making of baby boomers. The great writings of the era, such as *One Dimensional Man* by Herbert Marcuse and *The Feminine Mystique* by Betty Friedan, were often written by incumbents of their grandparents' generation, and most baby boomers followed the psychedelic counterculture, the 1968 Chicago demonstrations, and probably also the "sexual revolution" mainly on television.

The gap between the myth of the sixties and reality was particularly wide in Canada which went through unique social and political processes while, as in other instances, adopting to a large extent the American myth of the era. The sixties were an important decade in modern Canadian history, marking a transition to modernization both in French and English Canada. This was the era of the rise of Quebec separatism, inspired by similar movements around the world, and the era of Pierre Elliot Trudeau under whose leadership policies were advanced that distinguished Canada from the US both as a welfare state and in pursuing an independent foreign policy. The Canadian transition in the sixties was no less profound than anything the counterculture in the US ever achieved. Moreover, Canada did not lack its own counterculture embodied, for one, in Trudeau's personality and behavior (e.g., his marriage to a twenty-two-year old carefree "flower child"), and coming to bear in the absorption of draft dodgers, the activities of the Canadian Union of Students, the siege at Sir George Williams University, the riots that broke out when the Toronto police tried to clear hippies off the streets of the Yorkville coffeehouse district, etc.

Yet, Canadians related the sixties mainly to processes and events occurring south of the border. For example, Tom Fennell, discussing the combination of "hippies, rock music and Trudeaumania,"[3] analyzed this experience mainly in relation to the American space program, the assassinations of John Kennedy and Martin Luther King, the American civil rights movement, the Vietnam war, and the Cuban missile crisis. And in her book *Long Way from Home: The Story of the Sixties Generation in Canada*, Myrna Kostash reported on three Canadian films made during the sixties, which, almost exclusively, however, portrayed images of non-Canadian figures, such as Alan Ginsberg, Jerry Rubin, Abbie Hoffman, The Beach Boys, Adlai Stevenson, Martin Luther King, etc. "My question was: what did Canada look and feel like in the Sixties?" she asks. Her answer: "It didn't look like anything. The Sixties took place in the United States of America."[4]

A general feeling prevailing among Canadian baby boomers is that the dream of the sixties, whether their own or imported from the US, has been shattered. As claimed in an *Alberta Report* piece titled "Perished is the Dream of the Sixties Set, Dissolved in the Harsh Light of Reality," the baby boomers' vision of a society animating a sense of community, national purpose, and moral obligation to others did not take hold. This, we are reminded, is not unique. The "Forties people," who won World War II and created a prosperous, church-going society, says the *Report*, have also seen their dream of Canada disintegrate.[5] It seems that every generation goes through a phase in which at least some of its self-conscious members realize their youth dreams have been illusory, which explains their disenchantment. "American boomers," wrote Barbara Wickens in 2003, "elected their first president, Bill Clinton, only in 1992. In Canada, we've yet to have a boomer prime minister-and likely never will."[6] Calling herself "just one more aging boomer," Wickens claimed that the nine million Canadians born between 1946 and 1965 were now somewhat risible. "Yoga, plastic surgery, Viagra? Pathetic attempts at trying to maintain our illusory youth."[7]

Whether pathetic or not, Canadian baby boomers, like their peers elsewhere, engage in negotiation of their identity, attempting to navigate between the myths of their youth and the reality of their lives. This negotiation process, begun when Leonard Cohen called upon them to "take Manhattan" while many of them were apparently more concerned with the success of Expo 67 in Montreal, can be observed in a variety of intellectual and artistic forums: coffee house conversations, book clubs, film festivals, and lately in blogs.

Let me now follow "Marn's Big Adventure"[8] which caught my attention because of its good writing style and its frequent reference to Canadian themes. As I began to read this "Life and times of a woman who makes Emily Dickinson look like a party animal,"[9] as one weblog directory describes it, I realized that this diary provides a rare glimpse into an instance in which Canadian identity is being negotiated.

The lengthy recording of a life in a Southern Quebec log cabin, whose most exciting feature is an occasional mouse hunted by Zubby the cat, may be read as a response to the disenchantment over "the sixties," and the reconstruction of a new/old Canadian identity that is more consistent with the tale of Anne of Green Gables than with the myths of Che Guevara, the Students for Democratic Society, or the Black Panthers. Although by no means representative of other baby boomers, as no life is representative of another, Marn's life writing reflects the thoughts of a woman who came of age in the sixties, and realizes forty years later that the past adventures attributed to her, largely by herself, were mostly invented on American television. Following one aging baby boomer's life story as it unfolds in hundreds of diary entries, then, may not satisfy the aspiration to learn about society through grand generalizations, but may be as inspiring to the student of Canadian society as it is to the hundreds of Internet surfers visiting this blog on a regular basis.

Cat Lady

The figure emerging in "Marn's Big Adventure" can be safely characterized as anything but an adventurer. According to the autobiographical note accompanying this blog, "Marn" was born in 1951 in Southern Ontario and has been married since 1974 to Paul because he also likes cats. The autobiographical note is dominated by descriptions of the family's cats because, as Marn claims, "Some of us include our kitties as family members."

This is an appropriate introduction to an online diary by a person who, while aware of the world around her and engaged in important philanthropic activity, seems to attribute no less importance to the well-being of her cats than to any other issue, be it political, economic, social, cultural, geophysical, metaphysical, theological, historical, anthropological, or mystical. It is not uncommon for a gifted writer to compose cat stories, even in diary form, but the emphasis found here on the pettiest elements of life becomes worth noting when written by a baby boomer in an era of great political turmoil. With every entry in the diary, Pete Seeger's question comes to mind: "where have all the flowers gone?"

Marn has apparently never been a "flower child" but she is very much a product of the baby boom generation. Born in 1951, she was no champion of the sexual revolution in her teens, but she belonged to the generation that announced it. "S-e-x was never talked about when I was growing up, never. As far as I can tell, my generation invented sex sometime in the 1960's" (3.4.00).

The expression "as far as I can tell" hints at some skepticism about the truism that the sixties were an era of large-scale sexual promiscuity. Before the 1960s, she writes, nobody knew anything about it. "They sure as heck didn't talk about it like we do, eh, so I have to assume **we** invented it. We sure talk about it enough" (3.4.00). Her wedding was "one of those hippie dippy, rollin' in granola kinds of weddings" (7.4.00). She made her own dress and wore Earth Shoes that made her stroll up the church aisle with a seductive, clod-hopping farmer walk that made brides at the time feel less stuffy. She followed other traditions of the era, such as living together with her future husband before the wedding, refraining from changing her last name to his, etc. And when describing an older friend, she considers him "a generation and a gender away from me, right wing, red white and blue, tough as nails and still has his military posture and hair cut to match," while she belongs to the baby boom generation: "I'm a flaming liberal, had a knee jerk antipathy to the U.S. military because of Vietnam, a feminista—I kept my maiden name when I married, which ain't unusual now but created a stink when I did it 25 years ago" (25.5.00).

Looking back, however, she realizes the gap between the images of the sixties and reality. Consider the tattoo culture adopted at the time by college students as part of their identification with cons, carnies, bikers, and other representatives of "low culture." Marn treats the possibility she could have ever been part of that trend, with irony:

> My tattoo dates back to my prison days. Me and my bitch we...Oh, **alright**, that's not completely true. Let me start again. I ran away and joined the circus when I was in my teens, my tattoo is a souvenir of...Stop it. Stop looking at me that way. Alright, alright, it was like this: I woke up after a three day crack and liquor soaked binge with 50 of my closest friends from the local Hell's Angels chapter. All I was wearing was my tattoo... OH, ALRIGHT. (10.4.00)

The bare truth is that Marn got her tattoo at a much older age with no romantic or revolutionary flavor accompanying the experience. In a confessional mood ("I'm now spilling my guts") she admits she could not even find the tattoo parlor in Montreal on her own for lack of a sense of direction, and that she took many precautions before allowing the tattoo artist to touch her, making sure the place was licensed by all the necessary health boards and professional organizations, that a new tattoo needle was used for each client, and that the building was immaculately clean. "Getting a tattoo wasn't a spontaneous thingie where free spirit Marn waltzes into any old place. Oh no, I'm too ummm Marn for that...As you can see, I am **not** a wild and crazy girl" (10.4.00).

What is she then? Marn is explicit: "I am one of those cat people. I adore cats and I'm a bit afraid that when I get even older and even more eccentric than I am now that I might end up one of those old ladies with, like, 89 cats or something" (30.3.00). Marn believes that "being one of those cat people" is not a matter of age, as she does not feel her life has changed much. Her identity as a cat lady is related to the revelation that the hopes and aspirations of earlier years have not given any other meaning to her life. This is what her frequent reference to her not having a life implies. The grand ideologies embraced by the sixties generation have not provided her with guidance on how to live her life. "Philosophers," she writes, "call it the leap of faith and truly that's what it is, a leap. It's not something you can will yourself to do, it's just something you do. Me, I lost my religion a long time ago. The closest I can come to believing is my daffodils" (1.5.00).

Not only does the diary express disbelief in the philosophies, ideologies, and religions of the age, but even when preoccupied with daffodils, Marn does not trust the pictures in garden supply stores, which are as deceiving as systems of ideas. She finds meaning in an activity no system of ideas prevailing in the sixties ever promoted:

> I take my new bulbs, a bag of powdered bonemeal and my trusty yellow handled shovel out to the meadows and start digging. My cat Zoe, who follows me everywhere with dog-like devotion, is particularly fascinated by this ritual. She loves the smell and taste of the flour like bone meal...I open a hole, toss in a couple of handfuls of the white powder and bat Zoe's black nose out of the hole so I can settle in some bulbs. Cover the bulbs with soil and repeat oh, about 35 times. She never gives up. (1.5.00)

As we follow the description of the annual bulb planting ritual by the lady and her cat, we are led through an all but religious ritual. "That moment when I nestle those ugly brown lumps into the ground, believing that they will survive the winter, that buried in their core is beauty, that we will meet in the spring...that moment is as close to faith as I come." (1.5.00). This scene includes mythological elements—burial, belief, survival, beauty, hope, meeting—that were incorporated in every modern ideology striving to replace religious mythology by a secular set of meanings. Marxism, in particular, mythologized the course of human life from birth to death, making it a redemptive journey. Marn, covering her daffodil bulbs with soil in rural Quebec of the early twenty-first century, finds an alternate meaning to her life.

Her writing, however, is not devoid of a subtle wish for redemption, or at least for the motive of commemoration after death sought by the ideologies and religions she has given up:

> Did you know that daffodils can easily last 50, even 75 years without care? Mine will keep our spring pact long after I break it, long after I am done composting in the cemetery across the valley from my home. I like the idea that someday someone will take a walk in the woods, stumble on my daffodil meadow, and perhaps wonder... (1.5.00)

It is not easy to derive such ideas from a blog written in light-hearted manner and including every cliché in the book. Underneath many meaningless phrases filling the diary ("A woman's gotta do what a woman's gotta do, eh") (7.4.00), a serious search for the meaning of life can however be found. "Some women, when they're blue" writes Marn,

> will buy themselves new cloths. Some will splurge on spiffy shoes, whilst others come home with new bits of make-up. Silly, deluded women. They've got it all wrong. The only place you can buy everlasting joy and happiness is a garden center. It is The One True Path. Can I hear you say, 'Amen?' Yes, brothers and sisters, emotional salvation can be yours if you visit a garden center. (12.8.00)

This church preacher's style is not incidental, for Marn attributes her pious gardening to a tradition of eight generations of Methodists in her family, which survived the modern revolutionary age. "I shed the faith but one of the hymns seems to have stuck...something about how one person's actions matter, something about 'you in your small corner and I in mine" (12.8.00).

The principle that one can find and sustain a meaningful life while hidden in a small corner is hard to adhere to in the early twenty-first century. Marn does not fail to realize that revolutionary events are occurring while she is in hiding. On September 11, 2001, for example, she knows she cannot simply continue to compose cat stories, although she hints she would have preferred to: "Oh, Lordy, there shouldn't be any New York voices in my head. I live in another country, in a tiny log cabin nestled in the woods. And yet...I hear New York voices" (11.9.01). When she hears of the attacks on the Twin Towers and the Pentagon, Marn recalls traumatic moments she did undergo in the past. She recalls, for instance, sitting at a small wooden desk at her public school on the day in which a tearful principal announced over the school intercom that John Kennedy had been shot, or being a student in Ottawa when the War Measures Act was announced. "Welcome to the new millennium, folks," she writes on September 11, "You might want to fasten your seatbelts, it looks to be a bumpy ride" (11.9.01).

Yet this is a rather exceptional entry, for mostly Marn remains aloof from the bumpy rides of the age, while being aware that the distance she takes may mean she is lacking a life at all. She often refers to the possibility that her readers would consider her life as one not lived, but her choice to maintain her seclusion from the world with the "spousal unit" and two cats, can be seen as stemming from the realization that the model of the world as spelled out for the baby boom generation by popular culture, one of "sex, drugs and rock and roll," was none but a set of fantasies.

In one entry, for instance, devoted to her cleaning the house with a "Mr. Clean" detergent, Marn revisits these fantasies: "For a while it was just me and the guy with the shaved head, earrings, and oh so muscular torso barely wrapped in that skin tight white tee shirt. Whooo yeah, I had that guy on the floor before he knew what hit him. Then Paul joined us and we were a threesome... Marn, Paul and...Mr. Clean" (16.7.00).

The rest of the text reflects on the demise of the wild illusions of the past:

> Oh yeah. Any time YOU'RE feeling depressed, feeling that YOU have no life, just mosey right over here. I guarantee that once you compare your life to mine you will feel much, much better. So while the rest of you spent Saturday wallowing in sex, drugs and rock and roll, the spousal unit and I just finished

lowing in sex, drugs and rock and roll, the spousal unit and I just finished Day One of our quest to create the illusion of order and cleanliness at our place. (16.7. 00)

It is easier for the diarist to reflect on the shuttering of the sixties' dreams when she talks about her husband:

Sometimes I regret paths not taken. I feel guilty about the domesticity, the harness of wife, child, home. I remember the beautiful long hands, the tapped fingers he had as a man-child, fingers always caressing a guitar, a paintbrush...Now those hands are calloused, some of the fingers scarred, the nails damaged by the work he does. I can't remember the last time he took his guitar out of its case...Husband, child, home have been a generous place for me, the microclimate I needed. I set aside some of my dreams for this but don't regret it. I hope he feels the same. (2.8.00)

It is hard to tell how happy the diarist is about her extreme domesticity. At times it seems that behind the irony with which she treats the "sex, drugs and rock and roll" illusions, she regrets they are gone. At one point, for example, she comes across a "Spark Slut Test" on the web and finds to her dismay that she is only 43 percent slutty, 2 percent below the norm. Her response:

It's not that I want to be in the top percentile or anything, but I WOULD like to be well, you know, as slutty as the girl next door. Is that too much to ask? Is it? Is it?...Or maybe...maybe I'm just going to have to accept who I am and deal with the fact that I've never been one to walk the well beaten path, even in matters of sex. Oh dear. (12.7.00)

The little glory accompanying her life seems to bother her more than her ironic style reveals. In a particularly sardonic entry she imagines a twelve men Greek chorus, resplendent in togas and laurel wreaths, accompanying her everywhere, but soon she realizes that the chorus would find itself in very unexciting locations like the village's bank machine. And even then, she would not be able to avoid such worries as how all twelve men could be put in the tiny bedrooms of the log cabin. "You can imagine my distress about this...I mean, one moment I thought I had come to a major life change, the next all my dreams are dashed on the rocks of practicality" (29.8.00).

Negotiating Canadian Identity

Whether or not "Marn's Big Adventure" represents the thoughts and feelings of others, I would like to suggest that what we are witnessing here is a negotiation process over Canadian identity, which can be closely observed because the blog tells the life story of a Canadian baby boomer whose construction of an identity is, for once, not done in response to social scientists' questionnaires. In what follows, I demonstrate this negotiation process in reference to the medium that facilitates it. My argument is that the redefinition of the Canadian baby boomer's identity is strongly related to the technical capability she acquired to speak to the world not as the spokesperson for a generation but as a common individual. As Marn's individual life story unfolds on the Web, many of the truisms attributed to baby boomers emerge, but so does the search for a safe corner in which life becomes a meaningful personal experience rather than a generational declaration.

Marn is aware of the liberating nature of her blog. She sees this new medium as a way to learn about one's own feelings by observing the feelings of others. "I like to mosey the diaries here, even though most folks are plenty young enough to be my kid. They talk about love, lust, loneliness. Fear of being dorky, all that staff...and I still feel those things" (5.4.00). This process of learning about oneself is facilitated by the Internet, for Marn admits that her capacity to express feelings offline is limited. Although having many acquaintances, the number of people outside her family she ever loved can be numbered on one hand, she writes. "Believe me, that statistics doesn't give me any happiness, it's something of a reminder that I have dried up raisin of a heart in many ways" (25.5.00).

Friendship is a form of story telling—friends tell each other about their hopes, fears and desires—but despite Marn's story telling skills and her professional experience as a writer, she always had difficulty to share stories: "it had been many years I'd made the effort to form a new friendship because I couldn't muster the courage or energy to share the stories you have to share to build a friendship. It all just seemed like too much of an effort." (25.5.00). She even found it hard to meditate in the "real world": "I can't imagine how someone can have the courage to look hard and deep inside themselves for a week. Me, I'm going to passing acquaintanceship route. What I don't know can't hurt me" (13.4.00).

Like many online diarists, Marn is ambivalent about the exposure of her personal life. On the one hand, she realizes that her grandparents, who did not have a similar opportunity to record their lives, have been forgotten, and nobody remembers anymore who the persons in the family's old picture albums are, while she found a medium of self-commemoration. On the other hand, the knowledge that some of her family members and friends may read the diary makes her uncomfortable; she prefers to expose her life to strangers, as in a conversation on a night bus:

> Have you ever been on a long bus trip at night, knowing that you're going to be hours on that bus, knowing that you won't sleep? I've done that, sat there in the dark beside a stranger, and begun a casual conversation to pass the time. Sometimes it evolves into something else and an incredibly personal story is told. The bus becomes a cocoon for a soft voice murmuring in the dark, features illuminated for a split second by an odd flash of light from passing traffic, a silver of a spirit in transit. When the trip is done you part ways, each to slip back into a life the other will never know, again a stranger without a name. That's how Diaryland feels to me. (15.5.00)

Blogs are indeed the appropriate medium for individuals who are restrained, shy, or otherwise incapable of communicating in the real world, and Marn, whose mother committed suicide when she was nine, and who consequently withdrew into herself, finds lots of satisfaction in the opportunity to record her present happiness in a humoristic manner. She realizes the revolutionary potential of the Internet in this regard.

> Isn't it interesting how many people we know are becoming so highly textual? Me, I'm betting that's what the web will be remembered for...not for the glitz, but for the fact that for the first time ever ordinary people had a simple, inexpensive way to get their words out. Welcome to the revolution, folks. Bet you didn't realize that when you were putting up a web page extolling the wonders of your cat, Fluffy, or your passion for the old tin façades they used to put on Victorian houses to make them seem posh...well, I'll bet you didn't realize that you were a revolutionary, eh. After all it's only words and maybe a few pictures, right? (19.5.00)

In the past, words have been controlled by money and power. "You won't see hieroglyphs telling the story of some guy who made pots for a living, and Homer wrote about gods and heroes, not about some guy who worked at a job he didn't like" (19.5.00). Even Gutenberg, she writes, did not set words free because a professional writing class had been established as part of the print culture, a whole business based on controlling tastes and selling words, that has to be mainstream. But blogs brought about a revolution in that words are no longer homogenized by mainstream forces, and ordinary folks can express themselves, as long as the expression remains online: "Here, in this little anarchist world of glowing dots on screens, as long as you can afford a computer and an internet connection, you can control words. You can publish yourself" (19.5.00). This is not only an emancipation of individuals formerly subdued to the tastes of publishers but a way for ordinary people to be remembered: "The lives, interests and best of all the words of all we ordinary folks are being preserved. Oh my" (19.5.00).

Marn makes the best of this revolution; once she has been given the opportunity to communicate with total strangers online, she not only meditates at great length about every intimate aspect of her life, but becomes the focal point of an online community of devoted readers who share in "Marn's Big adventure" in which Canadian identity is being redefined. The new Canadian, emerging from this blog, resembles the imaginary mansion owner familiar in the literature of the *ancien régime* preceding the bumpy rides of the twentieth century. Marn is explicit about the role of her blog in providing a redefinition of Canadian identity: "It strikes me that perhaps one or two non-Canadians stumble upon this diary, and so in the spirit of international understanding I will occasionally share little nuggets about what it means to be Canadian" (28.6.00).

It is not incidental that this declaration is made in an entry about laundry day in which the family's underwear-changing habits are shared in great detail with the world, as is the presence of plaid sheets in the family's laundry. Marn finds it appropriate to engage in such petty matters because she has given up on the glory and magic attributed to her generation: "Some diaries talk about seething sexual orgies, or unspeakably hot couplings featuring offbeat sexual paraphernalia. Me, I share the magic that is laundry day" (28.6.00).

The diarist apparently feels that the triviality of her present life applies to other Canadians, for how could one otherwise explain the rest of the entry:

> Our Canadian constitution promises peace, order, good government and plaid. Even the titans of multi-national big business have had to bow to the Canadian reality, and this is the typical dress code for men on casual Fridays in my country. (The fiddle is optional of course, but ALL the stylin' guys accessorize with a fiddle)…we are an unusual people, eh. (28.6.00)

National identity is defined in this blog less in terms of what is said about Canada than in terms of what is not said. Except for a few references to political matters, such as the claim by a nationalist French-speaking parent in a school meeting that the English language is given preferential status, Canada is portrayed as if it were a secluded log cabin in rural Quebec. Consider, for instance, the way in which international terrorism is treated; in this blog, Canada is immune from anything going on in the world. One morning, while having her breakfast toast and tea, Marn came across an article about travel safety in the New York Times magazine. The article included warnings by anti-terrorism experts on how to behave on a trip to Europe, suggesting, for example, not to wear khaki. Her conclusion was that she was safe for neither she nor the "spousal unit" had plans to go to Europe anyway, and none of them owned a khaki uniform. This conclusion was then applied to her compatriots: "Woo Hoo, we Are Canadian! We've been implementing anti-terrorist travel measures and didn't know it!" (9.11.00).

At a time when the world was concerned with the grave phenomenon of terrorism, and many people all over the globe were making desperate efforts to try and understand where human civilization was heading at the outset of the twenty-first century, one baby boomer in her log cabin in Canada felt perfectly safe and could apply her usual good humor to those who did not:

> And here I thought my tiny little life—the fact that I don't go anywhere, that I live in a country almost nobody knows about, and that I am almost terminally fashion-challenged—here I thought these things might all just be further confirmation of my general dorkiness. I didn't know I was simply practicing cunning anti-terrorist moves, eh. (9.11.00)

At one point, Marn makes an explicit reference to the *ancien régime* by comparing herself to Marie Antoinette, the guillotined French queen who shared her passion for roses. However funny the comparison, it is easy to picture Marn as an eighteenth century mansion owner looking at the flowers blooming in her garden. It is equally possible to imagine entries such as the following to have been taken from a diary of the romantic era:

The pond water is finally warming up; the waterlilies have awakened and are sending out their first leaves. Me, I can hardly wait until they start to flower, beautiful pale yellow blossoms with the most wonderful spicy perfume. My goldfish are also big waterly fans, just love hiding in them, but they also like to bask in the sun... (5.7.00)

This appreciation of nature becomes a major component of what it means to be Canadian. Based on "Marn's Big Adventure," Canadian identity is defined as if the turmoil of the last centuries: the world wars, the Communist revolution, the rise of fascism and totalitarianism, the Holocaust, the Atomic bomb, colonization and de-colonization, the Cold War or, for that matter, the sixties - left no marks on what the diarist calls "my little corner of the planet" (30.6.00). She is very concerned with genealogical research and tells fascinating and moving stories about her family members who were part of the great sacrifices Canadians made in recent history, but these tales often seem like old family portraits on the mansion's heavy walls. The important lessons that could be derived from Canada's participation in the world wars, for example, are lost in the pettiness of this online journal.

Let me illustrate this point by a diary entry written on Canada Day. Every year, Marn and Paul, accompanied by a group of friends (and of course by the devoted readers of "Marn's Big Adventure") join in a celebration of Canada's birthday in the mountains with a potluck, bonfire, and fireworks. Here is the description:

Oh Canada. Car windows down late in a summer afternoon, air around us full of the sweet smell of freshly mown hay, the soft spatter of gravel hitting the wheel wells, the grumbles of the engine as we climb some wicked hills. Oh July, a heady gift for a country that spends far too long under the icy boot of winter...Canada, a country with a constitution that promises peace, order and good government, a country that eased into independence. (2.7.00)

This pastoral description is of course contrasted right away with the United States, a country created through a revolution, but Marn has no objection to living in the shadow of the mighty neighbor to the south. "We Canadians live in the shadow of this world power, and often define ourselves by what makes us different from the 'Mericans, which amuses them no end, I'm sure" (2.7.00). The peaceful border between the two countries is assumed to remain peaceful forever, and no thought is given to such issues as the need to form an independent Canadian foreign policy, defense structure, or cultural identity. All these issues are treated with the same disinterest that Marie Antoinette afforded the problems facing eighteenth century France.

On Canada Day 2000, then, a group of Canadians are proud to celebrate the independence of a nation that lacks a political and cultural vision for the future. The model of the Canadian emerging in this blog is that of the rose that blossoms against all odds in Marn's garden. As she puts it in October, when the rosebush happily survives the first frost of winter, "I want to be like this plant, still trying, still creating, long after the calendar tells me I shouldn't be"

(17.10.00). It is this non-national, apolitical form of living that is celebrated by Marn and her friends on Canada Day: "When Richard lifted his flute to his lips and wove the notes to Oh Canada through a starry summer's night, joined by the voices of my almost invisible friends and neighbors, it was strangely haunting. Sometimes it's good to remember who we are" (2.7.00).

Community and Responsibility

On August 4, 2003, the American coalition was deeply involved in battles in Iraq, North Korea warned that discussion of its suspected nuclear weapons program at the United Nations would be a grave criminal act little short of a prelude to war, the Israeli-Palestinian conflict seemed as unresolvable as ever, the SARS epidemic was spreading in Asia and Canada, famine, AIDS and war were killing hundreds of thousands in Africa, and Marn's cat Zoe was put to sleep. By then, the cat was twenty years old, suffered from cataracts, deafness, and stiffening joints, was vomiting, and had blood in her stool.

Marn was understandably sad when the vet informed her there was no other choice but to terminate Zoe's life. She wrote that when her father was in palliative care, he felt that he did not have much to look forward to and chose to die, while Zoe, that tiny black creature, had trusted her for almost all her life and now her life was taken away from her. The trauma also brought up memories of the day in which nine year old Marn walked into the room when her mother was committing suicide.

Apparently nothing could have sparked more emotional reaction among Marn's readers than Zoe's death. Having followed the cat lady's tales for three years, many readers were now deeply touched. Each entry of the blog begins with the traditional "Dear diary" and ends with the diarist's signature "Marn." Then, under a label stating the essence of the blog ("Going nowhere and proud of it"), readers can post their comments. On that day, no less than seventy-nine comments were posted in what became a steam-bath of emotions. Here are some of them:

Oh, my poor Marn, I'm so so sorry. I wish I could offer you something to comfort you.
I'm so sorry. She was a beautiful cat, and you obviously meant a lot to each other. I wish there was more I could say.
Oh, Marn.
I'm so sorry, darlin'. Love to you.
Hugs to you from us and our four footed friends.
Oh Marn, I'm so sorry. I have so many hugs for you.
Oh goodness, I am so terribly sorry. No words can do this justice, but know all your readers love and support you ::big hugs::
Marn, No words to make it better. Thinking good thoughts for you, the spousal unit and Zubby..."
Rest in Peace sweet Zoe...Big Hugs Marn.

I'm so sorry for your loss. You did give Zoe a safe and warm and loving home, with all the petting and lovins a kitty could ever want. I'm sure she's watching over you right now – and purring...
"{{{Marn}}}"

Gestures like these are common and are not much different from sympathy cards found in drug stores. These expressions of sorrow are also probably mostly genuine. However, this outburst of emotion online is no trivial matter for it hints at the formation of an "imagined community." In the famous book carrying this title, Benedict Anderson discussed the formation of nations as a result of individuals imagining themselves to be part of a community by nature of their exposure to the same media, such as the novel and the newspapers.[10] Here, the national framework is missing but not the imagination. Dozens of people set in separate geographical locations, knowing each other mainly by nicknames, and having nothing in common besides their reading of "Marn's Big Adventure," engage in an emotional exchange that can hardly be witnessed in any real life situation.

This could be seen as a positive sign: individuals who are shying away from their next door neighbors or exchanging E-mails in the workplace in order to avoid face to face contact with their fellow workers are given an electronic tool to express deep emotions. The problem however lies in the illusion that a community is being formed.

The diarists who visit "Marn's Big Adventure," post this blog in their list of favorites, or read it on an ongoing basis do not satisfy one major criterion of "community": commitment. This criterion should not be forgotten as we follow the online exchange of emotional statements. The diarist who screams "{{{Marn}}}" following a description of a cat's death may feel strongly about the event at one moment and disappear into cyberspace at the next.

Online contacts may lead to satisfying offline relations but cannot replace them. Ad hoc meetings of nicknames in Marn's blog may make her feel, as she says she does, that she is surrounded by friendship and support but she is not. For friendship involves more than verbal expression; it is tested in hard and challenging real life situations. Online diarists are not there for each other; they are individuals who spell out real or fake portions of their lives, but this does not turn them into a civil group. The trust we may develop toward a blogger with whom we become familiar does not differ from what we often feel toward virtual figures like doctors or presidents played by actors on television.

Living in societies in which access to our own family doctor or parliamentary representative is becoming quite limited, it is not surprising that we are attracted to these actors. Similarly, living in societies in which we hardly know our next-door neighbors, it is not surprising we are fascinated by life writing on the Internet. Let us not forget, however, that another person's "big adventure" is not ours, unless we engage in communal interaction that not only stimulates our emotions but leads us to responsible civil action.

Notes

1. Stewart MacLeod, "The Curse of the Baby Boom Generation." Maclean's 24 (June 1996).
2. Irwin Unger and Debi Unger, eds. *The Times Were a Changin'* (New York: Three Rivers, 1998), 1.
3. Tom Fennell, "Mclean's and the 20th Century." Mclean's 108, (June 11, 1995).
4. Myrna Kostash, *Long Way from Home: The Story of the Sixties Generation in Canada* (Toronto: Lorimer, 1980), xi.
5. Ted Byfield, "Perished is the Dream of the Sixties Set, Dissolved in the Harsh Light of Reality." Alberta Report 21 (March 10, 1994).
6. Barbara Wickens, "Boomers Have It Tough, Too." Maclean's 27 (October 2003), 79.
7. Barbara Wickens (2003).
8. <http://marn.diaryland.com/>
9. Eatonweb Portal. <http://portal.eatonweb.com/weblog.php?weblog_id=6517>
10. Benedict Anderson, *Imagined Communities: Reflections on the Origin and Spread of Nationalism* (London: Verso, 1991).

Chapter 7

American Soldier

On December 9, 2002, a blogger nicknamed "The Indepundit," made the following announcement:

> MY EMPLOYER has offered me a once-in-a-lifetime opportunity to take on a leadership role in a major international venture. This project would bring a significant increase in pay and benefits, but would also involve incredibly long working hours and extensive travel; in other words, I would be "living out of my luggage" for the next several months.
>
> After consulting with my loved ones, I have come to the inescapable conclusion that this is an offer I simply cannot refuse. While my new work will undoubtedly bring untold stress, hardships and tribulations, the challenges are ones that I feel must be met, and the rewards will be legion. I have accepted the assignment. (9.12.02)

Most readers did not guess that the employer was the US Naval Reserve and that the diarist had been recruited to serve as an officer in the Iraq war. While serving in the Naval Coastal Warfare Group providing security to coalition ships unloading military cargo in the Kuwaiti Port of Shuaibaon, he continued to publish an online diary, but for security reasons did so under the assumed name, borrowed from a Simpsons episode, LT Smash.[1] With many soldiers on the battleships and on the ground having access to E-mail, the US military could not effectively ban blogging but the guidelines that were set for E-mail were applied, namely, soldiers enjoyed the openness of the medium while having to respect the rules of operational security, i.e., refraining from giving out locations, names of units or commanding officers, etc. This war blog became very popular, with over 1 million people estimated to have visited it during the eight months the diarist spent in service.

According to the blogger, the online diary served as a means of keeping his family and friends updated on his adventures, so much so that when he became too busy to post every day, he was reprimanded by his father in a stern email to the effect that he must post every day as mother worried about him. At the same time he realized that his family and friends were not the only ones who were interested; he was getting six thousand hits per day. This made him engage in an open chat with thousands of citizens at home who sent their questions, comments, greetings, and blessings. Here is a sample:

Q: You're such a brave man. Good men are hard to find. You military guys are into physical fitness, right? I like brave, strong men like you. I'll bet you're good looking, too.

A: Mrs. Smash sure seems to think so.

Q: Can I send you care packages?

A: No, thanks—Mrs. Smash, Mom, and Dad send me everything I need, and a PX trailer recently opened up at my camp. We get so many cookie crumbs through the mail now that I'm worried about gaining all the weight that I've lost, and the hand-written valentine cards from all of the elementary schools have really brightened up the tent.

Q: What about that guy in your unit who never gets mail—can I shower him with cookie love?

A: He's already taken care of. In fact, that guy now gets more care packages than most of the rest of us. We hate him now. But thanks for the gesture.

Q: Pay no attention to all those war protestors. Most of us are behind you 110 percent!

A: What war protestors? I have yet to see one out here. Not sure they actually exist" (13.3.03).

This exchange is amazing. For the first time in human history, a soldier in war is communicating in real time with the citizenry back home (one can only speculate about exchanges that might have occurred had the possibility existed during the Peloponnesian or Napoleonic wars). At every stage of the war, thousands of Web surfers were able to follow this soldier's thoughts and feelings about his comrades, his superiors, the food, the army routines, the weather, the enemy, the family back home, etc. Even the letters he received from his wife were posted on the Web, allowing blogosphere to learn, for example, that while the sink in the guest bath of the Smash family had to be replaced in April 2003, the hole patched in the wall required a new wall tile, and as a result a new shower door, a new shower faucet, a new medicine cabinet, new floor tiles, and new doorknobs and light fixtures.

The huge number of visitors to this blog cannot be explained only by public interest in these details but by the emancipating effect of their posting, as if the trauma of war were lessened somewhat by the combatant appearing not clad in body armor, helmet, and sword but as a human being. However functional it might have been in the past to separate soldiers from civilians by providing them with special uniforms, customs, and ethical codes, modern warfare, involving the public, the media, and the families back home, no longer tolerates such separation between the soldier and the citizen. With war no longer being fought in remote battlefields but affecting whole populations, huge attention is given to soldiers' letters, memoirs, novels, and other media describing their experiences as citizens turned combatants. Through blogging, these experiences are conveyed in real time.

Blogging thus marks a new phase in the relations between a soldier sent to war and the public. It provides the soldier with the opportunity to construct an independent narrative of the war set against the images of soldiers drawn by governments and military authorities, both during war and in its commemoration.

Let me explain this distinction between narrative and image. In chapter 23 of the *Poetics*, Aristotle deals with poetic art that is narrative in form. In this kind of art, the plot must be constructed, as in a tragedy, on dramatic principles. It should have for its subject "a single action, whole and complete, with a beginning, a middle, and an end. It will thus resemble a living organism in all its unity, and produce the pleasure proper to it."[2] Aristotle differentiates this form of art from historical compositions, "which of necessity present not a single action, but a single period, and all that happened within that period to one person or to many, little connected together as the events may be."[3]

Based on this distinction, we can differentiate between a war narrative whose beginning and end are rooted in a civilian context, and the freezing of the warrior's image in a way that ignores or even defies the civilian surroundings. Government and military authorities have often developed images of warriors who transcend their civilian surroundings as a way of glorifying war through the narratives of individual soldiers, which do not necessarily stress the glorious parts of the war experience. Blogging may thus be seen as a liberating force allowing the dissemination of individual narratives vis à vis imposed images. In what follows, I observe this process in the blog of LT Smash, showing both the emergence of an independent narrative and its partial yielding to images constructed by the authorities.

Citizen in a Republic

The departure note of December 2002 is accompanied by a quotation from Theodore Roosevelt's "Citizen in a Republic" address of 1910 in which the virtues of war are expressed in full glory:

> It is not the critic who counts; not the man who points out how the strong man stumbles, or where the doer of deeds could have done them better. The credit belongs to the man who is actually in the arena, whose face is marred by dust and sweat and blood; who strives valiantly; who errs, and comes short again and again, because there is no effort without error and shortcoming; but who does actually strive to do the deeds; who knows the great enthusiasms, the great devotions; who spends himself in a worthy cause; who at the best knows in the end the triumph of high achievement, and who at the worst, if he fails, at least fails while daring greatly, so that his place shall never be with those cold and timid souls who know neither victory nor defeat. (9.12.02)

LT Smash quickly gets into soldier mode, but his mood, and the style in which it is conveyed, differ greatly from the image conveyed by the quote above. For instance, when he finds out that his unit will not be home for Christmas, the blogger composes one of those soldiers' songs that is unlikely to be found in official speeches but, not surprisingly, becomes an instant hit:

Christmas here means nothing,
Another day will pass.
I won't be home for Christmas,
But Saddam can BITE MY ASS! (8.12.02)

Before the move overseas, LT Smash is preoccupied with taking care of last
minute civilian affairs, such as purchasing some more life insurance. This is an
obvious preoccupation for members of a reserve unit, which even when marred
"in dust and sweat and blood," is composed of mail carriers and small business
owners, laborers and engineers, cops, attorneys, and even a NASA employee.
The war rhetoric of presidents from Theodore Roosevelt to George W. Bush
ignores most of the issues discussed in this online diary, such as resisting the
temptation to scratch the itchy site of a smallpox vaccine, the difficult decision
to remain hungry or swallow the hot dog stew on rice, and the fascination of
meeting soldiers from different backgrounds: "About a week after arriving in
[the] country, I began to notice that there was a small group of people wearing a
slightly different uniform. From their funny accents, their use of the word
'leftenant,' and the rather silly habit of saluting with their palms out, I quickly
ascertained that they were British" (4.2.03).

In the televised meetings between President Bush and Prime Minister Tony
Blair, which conveyed an image of cooperation between the two countries that
will persist in public memory for years to come (just as the photographs of
Churchill and Roosevelt seated side by side at the Atlantic Conference play a
role in our public memory of World War II), the finer details of this cooperation
are glossed over by the two world leaders and their image makers. However, for
LT Smash they are all important. For instance:

If you have to interrupt someone with a foreign accent and ask them to repeat
themselves every now and again, that's not so bad. But when some lad from the
back streets of Newcastle is trying to send vital information over a radio circuit
that sounds like two tin cans and a length of string, that's a real challenge. I'm
sure they would say the same about a Texas twang or a New England drawl.
(9.2.03)

In other words, the war as experienced by the soldier is barely apparent in
the public image of war. Take love for instance. Families of fallen soldiers
sometimes publish love letters, and moviemakers often picture soldiers reading
love letters to the sound of a harmonica, but the ongoing pain of love and longings cannot be expressed in the moral scripts that make up the public image of
war. To illustrate this, the blog's entry on Valentine Day in February 2003 reads:

Happy Valentine Day! If you have a special someone in your life, do me a fa-
vor. Spend a little more quality time with that person today, just for me. I know
how it can be. When you have that person close at hand, there can be a tendency to take them for granted. Things are a little different, however, when
you're separated by over 7000 miles. I would give just about everything right
now just to hold her hand, or give her a big hug and tell her everything will be

alright. But I can't. (14.2.03)

The soldier's experience involves too many dimensions to be summarized in a set of images. An entry titled "Just another day" provides a fairly comprehensive narrative of a warrior's life involving nature, work, God, and power:

> The sunrise this morning was beautiful. There was dust in the air on the eastern horizon, magnifying the sun into the large, bright orange orb that seemed almost too big to fit off the ground. I was almost too busy to notice. Almost, but not quite. I paused for a few moments, to soak it all in. Then I got back to work. We're sharpening the sword...I pray that God will show mercy to anyone who stands in our way. Because we won't. (17.2.03)

Or consider this entry:

> After work today, a buddy and I grabbed a couple of cold beers, sat down on a park bench, and talked about football while watching the girls walk by.
> OK, the beers weren't cold. They were room temperature. And they were alcohol free. Oh, and the park bench was actually a concrete barrier. And there weren't many girls in the vicinity.
> But we did talk about football.
> It was a nice break, anyway. (6.3.03)

This is not to suggest that the image promoted in "Citizen in a Republic" of the brave warrior must be replaced by another image, say, of the American soldier in Iraq as an "anti-hero," or as a pawn in some chess game. Rather, I would argue that no image can capture the narrative that unfolds in this online diary. The diarist himself is often ambivalent about the image that might be drawn of him. "I'm not a hero," he writes at one point, "That is to say, I don't think of myself that way. I don't seek out danger. I'm not the type of guy who is always looking for the next adrenaline rush, or the latest thrill sport. I generally avoid dangerous activities" (22.2.03).

On the other hand, he is no coward either, he writes. What then is he? This is exactly what cannot be answered—no image can replace the life story unfolding here of an American Navy reservist, drafted shortly before Christmas of 2002 to serve in the Iraq war, definitely not one following a moral script. And the diarist is the first to realize this:

> There is no way to avoid this conclusion. I'm told to wear body armor and a helmet. I carry a weapon. We build fortifications. I lug a pack full of chemical protection gear everywhere I go. I've received so many shots, I feel like a pincushion. Sometimes, when I have a moment or two to think about it, I feel a bit scared. (22.2.03)

Yet generally he does not have time to think about the existential issues in the rhetoric of political leaders, retired generals, and—lately—talking heads on television, which become fused into public imagery. LT Smash is not unaware of his existential condition but his awareness develops as part of the story he takes part in day after day: "I'm here because I was called" (22.2.03), he rightly concludes.

When people at home were hearing the news about the army rolling through Baghdad, the diarist was engaged in "just another day of work. Like the day before" (6.4.03). And when embedded journalists transmitted images of the victorious men and women, the diarist fantasized, as soldiers have always done, about his first day off in four months: "I think I'll sleep in. Then maybe I'll read a book. Or play a game on my computer. Or watch a movie in the morale tent. Then sleep some more" (7.4.03). Interestingly, this very fundamental account of army life that appears on the World Wide Web day after day, is not easily absorbed by the thousands of readers following it, possibly because of their conditioning to be receptive to a more concise version of "army life" offered in such movies as "The Longest Day." As LT Smash writes, "Several people have written to ask me 'are you for real?' Yes" (15.4.03).

From Narrative to Image

As the fighting begins to wind down, the diarist is increasingly preoccupied with the discrepancy between his experience, and its representation in the various systems of communication and cultural production that are already operating at full tempo. On May 4, he reports on his walk to the library (a couple of shelves in the corner of a tent) where the cover photo on the April 7 edition of *Time* magazine showing two Marines in combat near Nasiriyah catches his eye. One marine is shown aiming his rifle at a distant target while the other has "got that classic thousand-yard stare of a man who has just suffered the terrible shock of violent combat" (4.5.03). The big headline asks: "What will it take to win?" The diarist is angry over the use made of the image of a soldier to serve the political agenda of a news magazine. He is also angry over "the flawed assumptions of the war strategists" (4.5.03), such as their praise of Arab news channels, while his own experience taught him that many Arabs treated these channels as providing comic relief.

Whatever the truth, the discrepancy between the soldier's impressions of the war, and the way it is being represented, frustrates him. This explains why despite the great sorrow he expresses over a comrade who lost his life, he refuses to participate in Memorial Day ceremonies at the end of May. The following excerpt illustrates the difficulty of making the leap from individual sorrow to public mourning:

> Yesterday was Memorial Day, and of course we had some observations here. There was a morning service that I couldn't attend because I was working. Probably wouldn't have attended anyway—I don't really have the emotional energy for memorials right now. I've already thought quite a bit about the young men and women who died in the conflict and reflected on the many who did so in previous wars. It's hard to forget about them here, where the machin-

ery of warfare is just part of the everyday background, and weapons are any-where. (27.5.03)

To him, the memory of fallen comrades is rooted in the everyday back-ground. It is part of a narrative that is largely overlooked during Memorial Day ceremonies. The public ceremonies do not capture his personal feelings on that day, for this is also his anniversary day, and he feels great longings:

> If I were at home, I would have something special planned. I usually buy her chocolates and a nice card, which I present to her in bed in the morning, before I leave for work. Once I had flowers delivered to her office...But I'm not at home this year. I'm over 6000 miles away living in a tent in the desert. (27.5.03)

The strongest expression of the void that exists between the soldier's narra-tive and the images constructed first by the military and political officials, then by popular culture, can be found in LT Smash's lengthy description of a tour of the battleground after the intense fighting is over. This is a fascinating account of soldiers loaded up with weapons, helmets, body armor, and cameras, being driven to the killing fields of Iraq to construct a shared memory that will exceed the personal narratives they have developed in their minds. As if foreseeing the commemoration efforts of the future, the diarist asks whether "a few years from now there will be any monuments or markers for the battle that was fought here, or memorials to the fallen soldiers" (16.5.03).

Overlooking an empty stretch of desert where major fighting took place, he understands that this may one day turn into one of those historic battlefield parks "where tour guides in period costumes explain the tactics of the opposing gener-als, and the hardships their brave soldiers faced" (16.5.03). This ironic entry is not too remote from reality for the guide relates the desert war to the image it is and will continue to be most associated with: that shown on television. He is quoted as saying: "If you stand right here, you can check out the same sight lines you might have seen during the battle on CNN" (16.5.03).

The process of forming the image of the Iraq war in accordance with the ab-stractions provided to the public on CNN and other media reached one of its peaks in President Bush's victory speech aboard the USS Abraham Lincoln on May 2, 2003, in which the swiftness of the victory was emphasized despite the continued killing of hundreds of coalition soldiers in the battlefields of Iraq. "In this battle," declared the president in presidential fashion,

> we have fought for the cause of liberty and for the peace of the world. Our na-tion and our coalition are proud of this accomplishment, yet it is you, the mem-bers of the United States military, who achieved it. Your courage, your willing-ness to face danger for your country and for each other made this day possible. Because of you our nation is more secure.[4]

Obviously, presidential addresses do not incorporate the narrative of any single soldier who participated in the war; it could not be expected that President

Bush would mention the new floor tile installed in the Smash home a month earlier. What is interesting, however, is the degree to which the images evoked in this presidential speech and other forms of public discourse began to overwhelm LT Smash's writings.

In early June, while still in the Port of Shuaibaon, someone discovered his writing skills and he was assigned the task of putting together the history of the deployment. He recognized that this would require a different form of writing than the online journal where the narrative of his war experience was presented. "yes, it's an important task, and one I take seriously," he wrote. "But it's not nearly as fun as keeping a journal. I have to stick to the bare facts—I can't really express myself" (3.6.03).

But what are the "bare facts"? Are they not embodied in the journal's narrative rather than in what the soldier would compose on the instruction of his superiors? It is interesting to observe how naturally the emancipated blogger accepts the subordination of his war experience to the historiography that is being composed with his assistance. As he puts it:

> Some future historian might one day crack open the history that I've been as-signed to write, and he or she might wonder how it FELT to be part of this op-eration. Unfortunately, there will be no cross-reference to be found in that his-tory to this one-or to the book that I'm compiling around these journal entries. (3.6.03)

He even raises the possibility that in the future he may be denied access to the records of his own memories: "A few weeks ago, I got an email from the Library of Congress requesting permission to archive this weblog for an histori-cal record of the war, which I of course granted. It would be interesting to visit the Library one day, just to see if I could get access to my own words" (3.6.03).

The question of whether in the future the soldier will have access to his own memories, in a real or metaphorical sense, is not an obvious one, for LT Smash is fast to adopt the public images of war being presented in the public sphere. Between June and late August 2003 (when he returned home and resumed his blogging as a civilian) the journal is filled with long entries that are more in line with the president's victory speech on the USS Abraham Lincoln than with the earlier narrative we followed over several months. These entries are marked by the wishful thinking that characterized the public discourse about the war during these months: "We launched a campaign to liberate Iraq, and thousands of Bin Laden disciples were urged to come to the defense of Baghdad. But terrorists armed with Kalishnikovs and RPGs were no match for laser-guided bombs and heavy armor. We slaughtered them by the thousands" (23.6.03).

At one point, the blogger writes an open letter to the president, which could have been composed by a presidential speech writer:

> Mr. President, I am writing to you, as a mobilized reservist, to express my ap-preciation for your courage and leadership as Commander-in-Chief. In the face of tremendous pressure and even outright opposition from both home and

abroad, you have maintained your resolve and kept your oath to defend America and all that she stands for. Along the way you must have endured many moments of loneliness and self-doubt, but in the end you did your duty. You did the right thing. Thank you. (2.6.03)

There is no reason why a soldier filled with patriotic feelings, should not post on his blog a note of thanks to his commander in chief. What is striking, however, is the rapid transition from a diary describing in detail the life story of a civilian turned soldier to a set of statements about the war consistent with the image constructed mainly by the White House. This transition can be seen in the soldier's refusal to take part in Memorial Day ceremonies in late May, when he needed no commemoration effort to remind him of the fallen comrades who were part of his life narrative, compared to his entry on the 4th of July, when he tied his own motivation to serve in the military to a slogan appearing on a national monument:

It's not the most visited monument in Washington, but it is easily one of the most impressive.
Built of marble and granite, and reflecting the architecture of his home in Monticello, the memorial to the author of the Declaration of Independence and our third President lies due south of the White House, across the tidal basin from the National Mall. As you climb the granite steps and pass underneath the marble dome, the statue of Thomas Jefferson stands tall before you. Surrounding the base of the dome, in deeply inscribed roman lettering, is the following declaration:

I HAVE SWORN UPON THE ALTAR OF GOD ETERNAL HOSTILITY AGAINST EVERY FORM OF TYRANNY OVER THE MIND OF MAN

This is a mission statement for all Americans, and every person in the world who loves Liberty.
This is why I serve. (4.7.03)

Thus, by the time we get to LT Smash's last entry on his war experience, we are already immersed in images, which, while still part of a personal blog, echo sentiments produced by others. Consider how strongly the personal emotions conveyed in the following paragraphs resemble images in war novels, staged photos, Hollywood films, and other media describing the return of soldiers to the arms of their loved ones:

We formed up in four rows at the foot of the staircase, while our loved ones watched from behind the security cordon, about 50 meters away. I searched the faces in the crowd, but I couldn't see her—had she not gotten the word about our early arrival?
We were called to attention, and the senior officers went through their routine, saluting and saying important sounding stuff.
Then the CO turned to address the troops.
Mission complete. Naval Coastal Warfare Group One, HOORAH!

HOORAH!
DISMISSED!
The formation dissolved. Families and sailors rushed forward, into a melee of hugs and tearful reunions.
Where was she? I felt a knot forming in my stomach, as I began to worry that she hadn't learned of our early arrival—Suddenly, off to my left, I heard a familiar voice: "SCOTT!"
Standing before me was The Most Beautiful Woman on Earth, surrounded by my family.
I dropped my bags, and closed the final yards in long, quick strides.
I was home at last. (26.8.03)

In *The Triumph of Narrative* Robert Fulford wrote:

Narrative is selective, and may be untrue, but it can produce the telling of events occurring in time; it seems to be rooted in reality. This is also the reason for the triumph of narrative, its penetration and in some ways its dominance of our collective imagination: with a combination of ancient devices and up-to-the-minute technology, it can appear to replicate life.[5]

In following the online war diary of one soldier active in the Iraq war we have been exposed to events occurring in real time and rooted in reality. The tale of LT Smash is spelt out in detail; never before have we been given such access to the ongoing thoughts, feelings, and deeds of a combatant. This blog, however, makes one wonder whether the narrative will be triumphant or will fall prey to the urge of individuals, who despite possessing the means to tell their own stories, participate in the dissemination of public images.

As we have seen, once the war begins to wind down, the soldier's narrative begins to give way to the public images. The distinction between "narrative" and "image" is of course not clear-cut—a war narrative may include images and an image of war may take the form of narrative. But the less he relates a story rooted in historical context and instead subscribes to the images created by political leaders and the mainstream media after the war, the more the blogger seems to give up an important element of his newly found emancipation, namely the narrated tale.

Notes

1. <http://www.lt-smash.us/>
2. Arisotle, *Poetics*. Translated by S. H. Butcher. The Internet Classics Archive. <http://classics.mit.edu//Aristotle/poetics.html>
3. Arisotle, *Poetics*.
4. CNN.Com/US, May 1, 2003. (http://www.cnn.com/2003/US/05/01/bush.transcript).
5. Robert Fulford, *The Triumph of Narrative: Storytelling in the Age of Mass Culture* (Toronto: Anansi, 1999), 15-16.

Chapter 8

Pop Culture Princess

On July 4, 2003, the monthly literary "webzine" known as "Bookslut" carried a lengthy interview with "Pop Culture Princess" Pamela Ribon, promoting her first novel *Why Girls are Weird*, her successful stage production of actress Anne Heche's memoirs *Call Me Crazy*, and her popular blog "pamie.com."[1] The interview was no different from thousands of similar interviews conducted with successful pop culture figures, with the obvious questions ("How is LA?" "Was it a career move?" "How did you get started?" "How many places are you going on your book tour?") and the obvious answers in which the princess tied herself to the kings and queens of contemporary pop culture: her book is no "chick lit," maybe a little more "Oprah book-y," she is "not pretending to be Carrie Bradshaw," and yes, she saw once Michael Moore in person.

What is fascinating about this interviewee, however, is the opportunity to follow her rise to relative stardom step by step, to observe the making of a princess in the world of pop culture. Being one of the first bloggers whose blog, named "squishy," appeared on the web from June 1998 to July 2001, and a year later was resumed under the title "pamie.com," Pamie is exposing us to the agonies, frustrations, humiliations, disappointments, hard work, expectations, moments of glory, moments of fear, and other dimensions of a free lance comedy writer who came to Los Angeles like so many other aspiring young men and women to get a share in the American dream. The young woman's journey described in her blog highlights the nature of contemporary popular culture, especially the blurring of private life and public performance prevalent both in Pamie's artistic work and in her blog. It also conveys a message about the relation between stardom and melancholy.

Life and Performance

Pamie is an engaging communicator. Upon her return to blogosphere in 2002, she is as personal as a kindergarten teacher returning to her kids after summer vacation. "I missed you too. I missed you very much, actually. I was lonely without you around" (27.6.02). Pamie admits that after she stopped blogging a year earlier she felt like a mom who has finally gotten her kids off to college and now finds herself in an empty house. And what does a blogger-on-leave do when

she finds herself in an empty house that is too quiet? Watch Oprah of course.
The obsession with "Oprah," mentioned several times in the first paragraphs of
the blog is not lost on the blogger who admits she cannot help it. She had lived
on unemployment for a time, wrote teleplays and screenplays that hadn't sold,
and had attended humiliating job interviews, but like so many Americans could
indulge in the perceived success of talk show hostess Oprah Winfrey. While the
miserable in past decades were able to find consolation in Jesus's love, today's
unemployed seem to indulge in affection for their own saints and redeemers: "I
love Oprah" (27.6.02).

She updates her readers that during the year of her absence from blogosphere her father died. In a manner reminiscent of Albert Camus's disinterested announcement of the death of his mother in the opening line of *The
Stranger*, Pamie gets the announcement over saying: "My father passed away in
February. Yeah, I'll just put that out there very quickly like I'm pulling off a
Band-Aid so I don't have to dwell on it and get all maudlin on you" (27.6.02). It
seems strange that she does not dwell more on his death, for while we are informed that she only rarely told her father about her deepest feelings, this generally does not apply to the readers of her blog. "My father didn't know all that
much about me," (30.7.02) she admits. She never told him, for instance, about
her writing—he just read her Web page. On the other hand, her relations with
her online readers were always close. When her father died and everything was
coming to an end, she writes, she really missed having the journal. "It's the hard
times that made this space feel very healthy. My thoughts and feelings were always validated" (27.6.02).

Judging by the number of responses she apparently gets to her postings (according to the biographical note in *Why Girls Are Weird*, "Squishy" was receiving close to one million hits a month) there are enough surfers in blogosphere to
validate any feelings. No wonder Pamie makes every effort to rebuild the community surrounding her blog after a one year pause: "So, here I am. I'll be here
if you need me. And please, please give me an email and tell me how you're
doing. We've got some catching up to do" (27.6.02).

The blogger is very preoccupied with the formation of a community around
her postings ("For those of you who have been staying up nights fretting over
the state of my laptop, it is now fixed" 17.7.02). She admits that writing a paper
journal bored her because of the absence of an audience. It is interesting to note
her irony toward paper journals, and her consciousness of their meaninglessness,
considering that the blog differs from them only in its public exposure. When
describing her work in the paper journal she is fully aware there are no real insights conveyed in day-to-day recordings of a life. Whenever she felt she had
something to write with any meaning, she says, she would work on a story,
novel, or screenplay. "I didn't want to 'waste' the words on just myself," writes
the blogger who sends thousands of words about herself into cyberspace. "What
a waste of paper. I've got like, five books filled with that drivel. Just me blab-
bing on like I'm stuck in homeroom, writing a note to some boy on a bus who
won't really read that note anyway" (4.7.02). This is the first hint at a life that is

considered worthy only when it is exposed to others, performed.

In *The Lonely Crowd*, David Riesman lamented the "other directed" vs. "self-directed" nature of American society.[2] Pamie is undoubtedly "other directed" in her endless search for readers' approval. Yet this blog also makes an important statement about self-directed existence. Various entries are produced in absurd theater style, exposing the meaninglessness of a life lived away from the limelight. These entries are interesting observations written by a talented playwright demonstrating what life looks like when it is just lived.

Consider the recording of a phone conversation, whether real, fictional, or a combination of both, between Pamie and her friend Anna Beth (AB) whose husband nicknamed Master V ran over their napping family cat a few months before and felt terrible about it. As the entry goes, Pamie and AB are engaged in a phone chat on work, gossip, and the like, when AB realizes the fish in her pond have died and are floating in the water. Pamie: "I'll tell you what you're going to do. You're going to take those fish and you're going to put them behind the tires of Master V's car and make him think he killed the fish by running over them" (9.7.02).

Although AB remarks that there is something wrong with a person who makes such sick proposals, she decides to try it because to her husband she is crazy anyway. The dead fish, worth 12 cents each (when alive) now become the center of the drama, being lifted from the pond with some chopsticks and a bowl. They are placed behind the car tires of Master V who is woken up from his afternoon nap and asked to get in his car in order to get some take-out dinner. When he runs over the dead fish he is stopped and the drama continues to unfold in the phone conversation we are believed to eavesdrop on. For example, when asked whether her husband laughed when he found out what happened, AB's answer is: "I'd say no. He just gave me that look. Pam, he thinks I'm a crazy drunk woman, that's what he thinks. Oh, man! These fish are so squished. You should see this. They were already small, but now they're just little fish puddles. Pam! That was so funny!" (9.7.02).

AB, the tiny woman who is dismissed by her husband as a crazy drunk but in a phone chat with a pal is deemed to be quite funny and daring is now being likened to pop queen Sinead O'Connor:

> At first glance you think you're dealing with a tiny woman who probably wouldn't cause any harm to anybody. Then she opens her mouth and you realize you've got a Banshee on your hands. She's tough, strong, opinionated, and you don't even remember you have to look down to see her. She's powerful and loud and yes, the perfect amount of crazy. (9.7.02)

There is an obvious duality in this diary entry; the story of two women deciding to commit a crazy act initially seems quite sad in light of the absurdity of the act and the apparent loneliness that leads to it, yet becomes a powerful tale about assertiveness and rebellion once framed by the familiar image of Sinead O'Connor. The tiny woman with the bombastic stage appearance becomes a frame of reference within which an absurd life gains meaning. In this blog, life gains meaning through stage performance.

The Wacked-out and Scary

Pamie's life is otherwise boring: "Nothing sounds interesting. I tried watching television. I tried reading my book. Short stories of Dorothy Parker just aren't grabbing my attention tonight. I worked out. I cooked dinner. I cleaned. I took out the trash" (18.7.02). This online diary is in many ways a stereotypical tale about alienated life in contemporary America. Pamie tells how in her family house in Houston the neighbors rarely come around. They are heard in spurts—when two people check the mail at the same time, or if two couples happen to be washing cars on the same weekend day, but neighbors never visit each other's homes for holidays or celebrations. "They are families that live near each other, and that's about it" (18.7.02). Moving to Los Angeles, she finds herself in a "real" neighborhood where kids are playing, dogs are barking, and the sound of fire engines is heard. But this is a source of confusion, as if Pamies' background in suburbia has weakened her skills as neighbor. She misses now her privacy as she can hear the neighbors talk, fight, clean, sing, and sneeze. She seems to regret that the fence around her house is only pretending to be a moat and a fortification. Her definition of a good neighbor is still a person who minds her own business. Hearing the noises around her in the neighborhood, she resembles herself to the hero of *Rear Window* and admits her restlessness about it: "I need to get out more. I shouldn't take entire days inside like this. It's not good for my head" (18.7.02).

Staying inside for whole days is partly a result of blogging. Pamie is aware she is spending too much time in front of a monitor: "Too much inside time. Not enough sunlight. Too much computers and cats. Cats and computers. My entire day is fixing the computer, fixing the cat. Saving the computer, cleaning the cat. Feeding the computer, feeding the cat." (3.8.02). When she manages to leave home for a few days, 726 E-mails are awaiting her upon her return.

This attention, however, is no substitute for a meaningful set of human relations; in spite of the community of readers forming around her, Pamie keeps writing about the insignificance of her life. "Lately I feel insignificant because I'm just a body that takes up space here until I'm gone" (30.7.02). She expresses a clear sense of a life being wasted:

> Maybe I'm not one of those people that make you sit back and go, 'what the fuck have I done with my life?' You know those people that just kick your ass with all they've done, and then you find out they're five years younger than you are? You get so mad at yourself for wasting time, for lollygagging around while that person was out kicking ass. That person didn't spend an entire day 'cleaning TiVo,' a process that involves burning the thirteen calories required to push your thumb on a button fifty times over five hours. (30.7.02)

It is interesting to detect a sense of insignificance in the writing of a blogger who apparently established a close relationship with hundreds of individuals. Pamie, however, is too intelligent not to realize that blogging places her in a separate world from the one where real people live and operate. She tells, for instance, about her difficulty to explain the nature of her online diary in the real world. Each and every time she tries to explain "Pamie.com" to a stranger, the meeting takes a strange turn as people generally fail to understand why anyone would be interested in stories about her cat or her coffee. "This place makes no sense out loud," she agrees. "It only works when it's one person in front of a computer. Whether that person is me or you. We're always alone when we're together, no matter how many people are reading" (22.7.02).

The above entry is followed by one on Angelina Jolie. This is typical of this blog in which the search for a meaningful life is conducted within the parameters of popular culture. In one entry Pamie expresses her need to apologize for not striving to be a scientist curing diseases, or a social worker helping orphaned children find families. She says she could have been a doctor or a lawyer if she wanted to; she has the discipline but she lacks the dream. Her dream is rather to live in Hollywood and write funny stories.

Nothing seems to get Pamie more excited than imagining herself on television:

> I feel really silly. This morning I got to drive through the Warner Brothers lot for a meeting, and I squealed like a child when I saw the E.R. set—the ambulance bay and Doc Magoo's. Then I bounced in the passenger seat when I realized we were next driving through Star Hollow, the fictional city where Gilmore Girls is set. I still get very star-struck and awe-struck at this town, this place that sometimes feels like I fell into my television. (30.7.02)

As the life story continues, we learn about how many of the actors we see on television "fell" into it. Before any television appearance is mentioned in the blog, we go through many uneventful days: "Started with Yoga. Then I wrote. I wrote some more. I emailed. Wrote. Lunch. Mail. Read. Wrote. Cleaned. Cooked dinner for friends. Watched *Driven*, which is the worst film of all times" (31.7.02). Then come the interviews in which the aspiring script writer goes through the humiliating ritual of meeting with those who have made it and are now in the business of blocking others from making it too:

> I go in and chat for an hour. Sometimes it's one person, sometimes it's a group of three or five. And I sit with a bottle of water or a cup of coffee and I tell my quick life story. I talk about what I'm working on now, what I'm working on next, what I worked on before, and what I'd like to work on if someone would just give me the money. (22.7.02)

This is what hundreds of aspiring actors, script writers and others are going through daily. The blog is quite insightful in showing the hardships of show business and illustrating that the choice of people to fill roles is mainly a matter of luck. As Pamie puts it: "As an actor you might be too tall, too fat, too skinny, too funny, not Hispanic enough. As a writer you might be too edgy, too political, too soft, too precious, or not manly enough. The truth is you just weren't the right piece for the right hole at the moment. It's nothing to do with you; it's just business" (13.9.02).

Pamie has aspirations; her ambition to make it in show business is partly reflected in the entries describing her unwillingness to have a baby. Although this makes her feel a little guilty in light of the warnings (mainly on television and in Internet forums) that the clock is ticking, she refuses to settle down, buy a house, stop renting, start planning for a future, get a savings account, or invest.

Giving up those routine practices does not, of course, assure Hollywood glory. To the contrary, the blog describes the seasonal depression during the Hollywood springtime when another season has passed and all the lonely people feel that nothing has happened in terms of getting auditions, contracts, or money. "What if this is another year where nothing happens? What if next August you're sitting in the same place with the same accomplishments with the same total in your bank account?" (13.9.02). So many Hollywood aspirants are out there, trying to get other people to like them, to pick them, to want them, a process similar to what they went through in their childhood when teams were picked for kickball. Pamie jokingly mentions that this condition could lead her to use drugs had she been able to afford them. "But right now we're a broke-ass talented family that should each have a sitcom or a three-picture deal. The coke comes later. Or so I've been told" (13.9.02).

The expectation that sitcoms or three-picture deals are awaiting the pilgrims arriving in Los Angeles is capitalized on by certain elements. In a series of entries, the blogger describes the messages Pamie gets as a result of a momentary mistake, stemming from loneliness, of posting some worthless lines masquerading as poetry on a site titled "poetry.com."

The detailed account of the messages, which seem like Spam of the kind we mostly discard, provides interesting insights into the style and practice of exploitation in today's society. While the correspondence quoted in the blog is quite vulgar, it is not hard to imagine more subtle yet no less frightening efforts to exploit the seekers of glory. The blog makes us follow in detail the sweet language in which "Dear Pamela" is approached. She is being told that her poem has been read and discussed "carefully," and that a "Selection Committee" has certified it as a semi finalist in an "International Open Contest." Pamie understands the psychology involved. The very attention given to a lonely person who sent a "poem" to a website, featuring (at the time I am writing this) over 5.1. million such poems, is, of course, flattering and may indeed spark the feeling expressed here ironically: "You see that? I'm a semi-finalist! I'm not one of those losers that just enter poems through the Internet and nothing happens" (8.8.02).

The happy semi-finalist is promised the chance of winning one of "104 cases or gift prizes" and of having the "poem" featured in a "Beautiful Coffee-table Edition!" which is even given the appropriate title "Letters from the Soul."

"Letters from the Soul" will be printed on fine milled paper specifically selected to last for generations with no obligation whatsoever to the poet who is only urged to proofread the work of art and add a biographical note (so the "media and public"—in that order—can have a greater awareness of her motivations, the meaning poetry has in her life, the story behind her poem, and her personal philosophical point of view).

As this goes on, and one shivers at the language of those marketing the American dream, it becomes more and more clear that the sweet-lipped offers made here before reaching into the aspiring poet's wallet are not only familiar from commercial fliers, posters, ads, telemarketing and the like but from much of the mundane communications in today's world, e.g., between untenured faculty and their senior colleagues, authors and publishers, job seekers and employers, etc., in which one's vulnerability—stemming from the need to fulfill dreams rather than live a life—is taken advantage of. The unfolding of the offers made to Pamie, line by line, makes this blog an important testimony to the way in which the language of dream vendors is blurring with the language of routine daily interactions. The offer includes, for instance, an ISBN number whose search on "Google" reveals that there were several people in the world who must have responded to the offer, as some poetry is posted on the Web accompanied by the statement that it has been published in "Letters from the Soul" or some other "anthology."

While Pamie uses her talent as a comedy writer to introduce us to this phenomenon, she is at the same time part of it. For instance, in an entry telling about another letter announcing her nomination as "Poet of the year 2002," and inviting her to read her poetry at "the single largest gathering of poets in history," in which she will be commemorated and receive an "International Poet of Merit Silver Award Bowl," she is also bragging about having been mistaken somewhere for film actress Naomi Watts. The composers of the letters are thus filling a genuine need hidden behind her ironic treatment of these letters—to experience just once what Naomi Watts and her like experience when receiving awards in front of an audience of millions of television viewers.

Again, while the letters posted in this blog resemble "queen for a day" contests in offering the prospective participants in the gathering of poets such attractions as strolling down the Hollywood Walk of Fame or taking a tour of movie stars' houses, they also reflect much of the communications we are subjected to in today's world. Many "calls for papers," for instance, attracting scientists to participate in conferences at certain locations, include similar language composed by public relations firms marketing the locations by appealing to contemporary dreams.

Moreover, while the letters in this blog seem particularly bold in the dropping of celebrity names who may join the single largest gathering of poets in history, as a means to make people pay the hundreds of dollars in registration fees (reduced somewhat for "poets"), organizers of the above mentioned scientific conferences, or other kinds of gatherings—professional, commercial, artistic, or whatever—often use false promises in their exploitation of other people's resources. Many in today's world can identify with the blogger's comment that while the letters she gets are addressed to "the world's most interesting and dynamic poets," they are actually addressed to the wacked-out and scary. Judging by her own repeated references to Naomi Watts and her pride at having been mistaken for her, Pamie rightly identifies at this point in time with the wacked-out. "So, it looks like I just won't be able to afford the Symposium this year. Maybe next year...Until then, I'll have to make my own bowl, sew my own medal" (7.9.02).

In the Limelight

On August 29, 2002 Pamie participated in a short segment on ABC television. She did not elaborate on the appearance besides mentioning she babbled about Gilmore Girls and John Ritter, but the entry provides us with preliminary insights about her "being there." She appeared together with another woman who was apparently the informed and pretty one and thus did most of the talking, while our blogger felt sweaty and exhausted.

Here is the description of the performer in the aftermath of the performance as she looks in the mirror and sees "Carrie Bradshaw" of course: "I just caught my face in the mirror, I'm still wearing makeup from the show. I never wear this much makeup. I'm writing a little column in my pj's with my aching feet, wearing too much makeup as I type on an Apple computer in New York. A little too much of a Carrie Bradshaw moment" (29.8.02). The next day she feels like Marge Simpson.

About a month later comes the real television story. Pamie is being called by a guy who invites her to be on *The Tonight Show* with Jay Leno. This might have been quite a breakthrough in the story of the aspiring comedy writer but is not. Mobilizing all her comic skills to describe the ordeal, Pamie gets us through an agonizing process. First she realizes she is being called because she is not unionized. "I'm not a 'real' actress yet, which means they can not pay me. Are you feeling the Hollywood dream yet?" (16.9.02).

The dream turns into a nightmare when she is asked whether she has an ample bosom. Since she does, she is designated to appear as a "Big Boob Girl" in some joke segment. Again, it is hard to tell whether the play that unfolds is real, fictional, or a combination of both, but it gets hilarious when "Mom" comes into the picture. For mom there seems to be nothing more "wonderful" and "terrific" than her daughter appearing at the Mecca of the American dream, *The Tonight Show*, even in the role assigned to her. Pamie, on the other hand, is aware of the humiliating process she goes through on her long road to success that may or may not come:

> See? I know you read this journal to get inside the mind of an aspiring writer/actress. And every single day when you see my one-step-forward-two-steps-back Cotton-Eyed Joe I keep dancing, does it make you want to cry? Or

does it make you look up with a tiny squint of proud passion and whisper into the air, 'Thatta girl, Pamie! Go, Big Boob Girl. Go! (16.9.02)

Going there means putting on one's "coolest" clothes and leaving home early enough to get to the studio on time. But it also means feeling terribly embarrassed about arriving much too early, trying to impress a staff that could not care less about the invitees, and learning that although the entire family (and all the family friends who have been alerted) is waiting for the appearance that night of the successful daughter, the segment may actually not go on air at all because "It's up to Jay" (18.9.02). Going there also means the filming of a parody of speed dating with Pamie's shirt taped to her bra so her breasts roll out the top, with her feet hurting, and with nobody offering her or her co-stars anything to drink. When the day comes to an end, the following entry can be found in the online diary: "Yep, just another fabulous night in the glamorous world of Hollywood Comedy. Time to update my resume" (18.9.02).

The résumé is enriched by other television appearances in some marginal game shows with Mom being disappointed they are not Jeopardy. The description of such experiences in the blog are as insightful as they are funny, as when we are told that "we had to bring something with our social security number on it, so I brought my final unemployment check, the one that said 'YOUR BENEFITS HAVE EXPIRED.' I found it only fitting" (17.10.02).

Following such experiences in an online diary allows us to glimpse the treatment meted out to aspiring Hollywood stars:

> They sent me home with a t-shirt, a new purse, sunglasses and a coupon for tennis shoes with roller skates built into them. I sent away for the skates in May. They still haven't arrived. The glasses, blue and square, made me look like an actual alien when I wore them. I do very much love the bag and use it all the time. (17.10.02)

This is all taking place within a cultural sphere in which the blogger cannot help showing her admiration for celebrities and her fascination with the fact she lives in a city where movie stars can occasionally be spotted. For example, one evening, leaving a concert hall to use the bathroom, she ran into Jake Gyllenhaal. Although she is conscious of the senselessness of her fascination with the event, she indulges in a series of fantasies, imagining, for instance, that the good looking young actor touched her or said a few words to her, while in reality he was probably just seen by her. The entry about this episode hints at the celebrity fan culture surrounding Pamie: "I walk back to my group and announce that Jake Gyllenhaal and me just had a tryst in the hallway. Everyone's impressed..." (30.9.02). As senseless as this fan culture may be even to her, it seems to play an important part in the construction of Pamie's identity, or at least her online identity. One wonders whether the episode described above is not one of the reasons for her labeling herself "Pop Culture Princess," which translated might mean "a comedy writer in Los Angeles who once saw Jake Gyllenhaal on the way to the bathroom."

But then comes success and Pamie herself becomes a celebrity. This does not come without hard work: "I'm trying to finish this screenplay and I'm at the part of the writing process where I hate it so much that I now have to just force myself to finish it. I hate every line, every character and every scene" (16.8.02). Beginning in December 2002, we read about the preparations for the theater show based on Anne Heche's memoirs, with the blog serving as a promotional device.

It is easy to see how people exposed to detailed descriptions of the pre-show excitement would be curious enough to want to come to see the show. "What started as a lark at a bar has turned into the real thing, and it's pretty exciting" (3.1.03), writes Pamie, engaging the readers who follow the process from the lark at the bar to the opening evening. Using the opening words of the show as a title for one of her entries, she conveys great enthusiasm: "i love it. i love it. i truly, truly love it" (7.1.03), as well as a sense of how complex the production is, involving producers, directors, music writers, musicians, lighting designers, etc.

The rhythm and hustle bustle of the preparations are conveyed very vividly so as to capture the readers:

> And the songs are running through my head, and I need to send an email to the cast to talk about ticket prices and I still have to get headshots from some of them and there's a rehearsal at my house in three hours and another one tomorrow afternoon and another one tomorrow night and then probably more on Thursday and then I'm at the theater all day on Friday until the show goes up that night. (7.1.03)

This is an interesting aspect of blogging—allowing thousands of readers to look behind the scenes of a production. The lines written after the preview performance, for instance, make the readers feel they are in the theater hall: "So, the show has opened. Cue the swelling orchestra music. Cue the spotlight. Cue the bow. Thank you. Thanks you. It was nothing. Thanks" (11.1.2003). The blog refers us to sites such as The Official Los Angeles Theatre Directory in which the show is announced and makes us participate in the diarist's anticipation and fear of the press. "Real press that come and see the show and write down notes while we act our hearts out and then maybe write nice things or back-handed compliments next to unflattering photographs of us. Can't wait" (11.1.03).

Pamie is clearly a performer: "It certainly gets an audience to make noise, and that's my favorite thing in the world" (11.1.03). When at the beginning the reviews are slow to appear, as are the audiences, she feels miserable. On one Friday night when there were only twenty people in the audience and Pamie felt sick, the scene of the sick artist is described in full vigor. Pamie is home alone and freezing in spite of wearing socks, shoes, jeans, a t-shirt, a heavy blue hoodie sweatshirt, and a scarf.

> I've become the whiny, pathetic, excuses-making, mopey, grumpy, blaming her period for her anger actress. And I'm the grumpy, unsatisfied, apathetic, weary, bratty director. I'm also the weepy, insecure, hunchy, bitchy, writer. I never

wanted to be any of those girls and tonight here i am, all three of those horrible women. (17.1.03)

As she goes on to describe her misery at having not eaten all day, at being cold, and, worst of all, at receiving no email, she is placing herself within the frame in which miserable artists are often described: "I am a pained artist!" she declares. And turning to more contemporary images she writes: "I am a Hollywood cliché!...I'm an unemployed web designer! Nobody will ever hire me again!...I'm a failed dot com" (17.1.03).

Interestingly, what Pamie herself calls "the constant whining, bitching and advertising about the show" (19.1.03) helps bring in the theater critics and the audiences. This is where blogging ties with advertisement. It is hard to imagine that readers who follow the whining on a daily basis would not have the urge to come to the blogger's rescue. As the theater fills up and the show receives good reviews in many forums, and later in the media in North America, South America, Europe and Asia, there is even more reason for the cheerful readers to jump on the wagon of success. The show, the celebrity culture, the book, and the blog all converge into one celebrity's success story, which is marketed to the masses.

The milestone in Pamie's life that occurred on January 29 is expected to become a milestone in the life of thousands of her readers. One can imagine them sitting at their computers, their blood pressure rising with the exciting news that Scott Thompson, from Kids in the Hall, is coming to see the show on Valentine's Day: "Scott Thomspon, whose sketches I would videotape and watch over and over. Scott Thomspon, who is so fucking funny I get sick and jealous at the same time. Scott Thompson, who's so cool I just spelled his name incorrectly twice because I'm so excited" (29.1.03).

From now on, events in the life of the blogger-turned-princess, such as the mention of her play in the tabloid press, is expected to (and probably does) become relevant to the lives of thousands. As in the case of rock stars, movie actors, and television personalities, the readers are becoming agents of Ms. Pamela Ribon's commercial success. Consider the following entry:

I'm wondering if you would want to help promote my book. It's gearing up for publicity time, so I need to send my editor and publicist people that are in the position to help promote the book. If you work for a bookstore, or know someone who does, if you're a reviewer, or know someone who works for a newspaper/magazine and would be interested in promoting a book like mine, or if you're working for some kind of talk show that interviews people like me, I'm looking for contacts. (3.2.03)

Success and Melancholy

Once success hits, ambivalence about her newly acquired status enters the frame, as if the shadow of melancholy is now cast over the whole endeavor. "I find celebrity to be a fascinating subject, and the lengths people will go to for attention astounds me" (8.2.03), writes the celebrity going to great lengths to capture the attention of all the anonymous people out there. Following a British documentary in which performer Michael Jackson discussed his relations with young children in front of fourteen million television viewers, she feels she needs to justify her own show's exposure of Anne Heche's life, and does so by noting that Ms. Heche herself decided to share her crazy and miserable moments in life with a large public.

Pamie seems to disapprove of such exposure: "And sure, you've done things you're not proud of, but when you really fucked up, did you issue a press release? Did you ask someone to make a documentary about your life? Did you read a book on tape? No. Because you didn't ask to be a public figure. You didn't ask for the ultimate attention" (8.2.03). Yet she does ask for the ultimate attention. At this point she seems to lose any awareness that she is playing the very role she is attributing to others: allowing the world to follow their life stories in detail and thus exposing themselves to mockery and criticism. As if she is not exposing herself just like Anne Heche, she writes that the show is not about the actress: "It's about what human beings will do to be seen, to be discussed, to be famous. It's about our drive to make ourselves bigger that we are. It's about how crazy we're willing to go, how crazy we can become if nobody is there to keep us in check" (8.2.03).

And nobody is there to keep her in check. Pamie sees Michael Jackson as lacking checks on his behavior because his closest associates have no interest in restraining him, but she also lacks checks, on her literary work for instance, due to a crowd of followers whose sheer numbers ensure that her books become bestsellers. It is hard not to feel that the wide attention given to *Why Girls are Weird*—a pretty good novel of its kind—stems to a large extent from the promotional power of blogging, and not necessarily from the literary taste of editors, critics, or even the general public.

The novel brings out the melancholic nature of blogging. It is the story of Anna Koval who posts an online entry on Barbie dolls under the name "Anna K," which instantly turns her from "a nothing-special-twenty-something, to Anna K: web celebrity."[3]

The author shows how blogging allows Anna to invent a personality. Just because Anna does not have a boyfriend, for instance, does not prevent her from creating one, especially since her fans prefer it this way. The readers of her blog identify with a life that is mostly invented and the easiness with which the deceit involved becomes a way of life is stressed: "It was so easy to write something and then post it online. The instant feedback was infectious. People loved Anna K. I was creating a celebrity."[4] The interactive nature of blogging complicates things because it makes the blogger herself identify with the persona she invented, as if Tolstoy would have received messages addressed to Pierre Bezukhov, or Orwell to Winston Smith, and the two had begun to live the lives of their heroes as interpreted by their readers.

Blogging usually serves as a means to negotiate one's life as a web designer, university professor, journalist, writer, etc., but here the novel serves the writer as a means to negotiate her blogging experience. The novel moves back and forth between what is described as the protagonist's real life and its online representation, incorporating whole pieces from her blog, after consulting with her online fans about which pieces they prefer. This literary experiment brings out the difficulty involved in living a life while representing it to others, mainly because of the discrepancies between the two Anna characters – the real and the imagined.

For instance, a relationship develops with a fan who applies to become Anna K's online stalker: "Think of it: You'll never be alone again! ... I'll be the person who makes you famous. I mean, you can't have fame without creepy fans."[5] As cute as this sounds, how desirable is it to have a stalker? How long can such a relationship develop without blowing up in one's face? When asked by another fan to meet her in reality, Anna is scared: "What if she saw right through me? What if I was disappointing in person? What if I found out that my biggest fan was someone I couldn't stand?"[6] Although this does not turn out to be the case, the real life meeting, like so many blind dates, is awkward because the only way to bridge the gap between the truth about real life and the invented lies on the blog is through more lies, such as spreading "guy things" in a single girl's apartment. The blurring of offline and online living reaches a peak with the fan spending a night in Anna's apartment and, during that night, reporting the experience on her own blog.

Melancholy sets in when in a later encounter with that fan Anna confesses her lies but this makes no difference because neither her real life nor her invented life is of any significance. "Who am I anyway?" the protagonist asks, "Am I my resume?"[7] The bare truth is that it does not seem to matter, even to her. The novel displays a strong sense of a loss of life Anna never had, which becomes only more apparent the more she babbles about her fake life in the blog.

This uncovers the twofold nature of melancholy as an unappeasable attachment to an ungrievable loss. Not only is the novel revealing a strong self-consciousness over an unfulfilled life, it also notes the small chance of fulfillment, due to the continuous representation of a fake life. In this novel the blogging experience is so overwhelming, that even when the various heroes meet in real life and try to tell some truths to each other, they are too entangled in the virtual images they have created of themselves and of those surrounding them to engage in candid interactions. "It seemed physically impossible to stop lying to her,"[8] says the protagonist after the confessional session with her fan. And when she is eager to meet her "stalker" in real life, he is reluctant to meet, realizing their relationship is only meaningful on the virtual level: "You wanted a friend and I've given you drama,"[9] he says in a voice message.

The novel conveys a clear sense of mourning over a life partly lived on the Internet: "'How did this become my life?' I wailed at the ceiling."[10] The author describes the futility of online relations that are not accompanied by real meeting of persons. When a nineteen-year-old reader of Anna's blog feels they have lots in common, while in fact they have nothing in common, she accuses the binary code of creating this confusion and heartbreak. "I was just some girl in Texas making up a few stories, wondering what would happen if I pretended to be someone better than I was,"[11] she complains. But nothing really happens. The protagonist tries to regain her life by deleting her online posts, but the pseudo-existentialist statements with which the book ends ("I'm going to be me for a change")[12] do not convince that a clear "me" can emerge from the ruins.

The novel is accompanied by an interview with the author who is asked how much of Anna's character is autobiographical, and there is no way to tell whether the answers are less spurious than the novel itself. Particularly interesting is the author's statement that her blogging stems from a life crisis in which she realized that her life did not resemble the life she always assumed she would have. This sounds like a return to the presumption made by her literary hero Anna Koval that her life could become meaningful if she invented a more attractive persona—one of the strongest manifestations of Riesman's other-orientation.

This orientation becomes dominant in the blog. Once the bloggers' celebrity is established, her online diary falls into a pattern similar to that of other pop culture princes and princesses. The young, talented, comedy writer turns into an icon of popular culture that provides others with advice about how to live their lives while feeling personally insecure, that professes to be involved in charity work while promoting its own projects, and invents a glorious life for the masses to identify with.

When the Iraq war breaks out, for instance, the blogger writes about her armpit problem: "I smell like a stinky guy, not a clean guy who just got out of the shower. I smell like the guy who ran all the way to the bus. And it just seeps into all of my clothes, and I sit around going, 'Who stinks?' And it's me. I stink" (23.3.03). It becomes clear that sharing this problem with the masses is related to Pamie's new celebrity; this is what pop culture princesses deal with at a time of war "Like when Martha Stewart just wanted to concentrate on her salad" (17.3.03). The blog's entries begin to be filled with stardust, as when Pamie tells of her being "Hollywood Cool" (26.5.03) because she was almost invited to some party given in Dustin Hoffman's house, or because Michael Moore has heard about a book drive she conducted on her Website and thought it was "inspirational" (1.6.03).

The more the waves of stardust spread over the blog, the more its melancholic nature surfaces. Alongside entries dropping the names of celebrities she met in Hollywood, providing "Dear Pamie" style advice over such matters as "Can girls tell when I'm checking out their breasts?" (5.9.03), or describing successful book tours, we find frequent complaints about neighborhood noise and lack of space when the blogger searches for some serenity on the beach or in a picnic area. The feeling conveyed is of a person suffering from an inescapable, noisy, urban environment and from a deep sense of loneliness.

The show business world, in which one is constantly waiting for something to happen, enhances that loneliness. As she puts it:

I've got to be honest here, part of me gets really bored with myself. It seems I'm always waiting on something and working on something else, and I imagine it's not even worth asking me what's going on anymore. If I have news, I share it. But if I haven't said anything it's because I'm working on one thing and waiting to hear on about three others. That's how it works. (6.10.03)

No wonder then that when the pop culture princess summarizes what her readers may envy as a successful year in the life of a shining celebrity, a deep void in that life surfaces: "Blah. Nothing. I've got nothing. I'm just babbling…I'm boring myself. Therefore I must be boring you" (30.12.03).

Notes

1. <http://www.pamie.com/>
2. David Riesman, *The Lonely Crowd: A Study of the Changing American Character* (New Haven, Conn.: Yale University Press, 1950).
3. Pamela Ribon, *Why Girls Are Weird*. (New York: Down Town Press, 2003), 4.
4. Pamela Ribon, 2003, 16.
5. Pamela Ribon, 2003, 79.
6. Pamela Ribon, 2003, 129.
7. Pamela Ribon, 2003, 199.
8. Pamela Ribon, 2003, 207.
9. Pamela Ribon, 2003, 208.
10. Pamela Ribon, 2003, 239.
11. Pamela Ribon, 2003, 290.
12. Pamela Ribon, 2003, 305.

Chapter 9

A Mother in India

One of the most important functions of blogging is the use of this new medium to construct narratives of illness. Sick persons, or their relatives, can share their feelings day-by-day, hour-by-hour, as the illness develops. In spite of some cases where online accounts of an illness have been faked, it can be expected that many people suffering from a physical or mental illness are comforted by the opportunity offered by blogs to post queries, gain and share information, give and get emotional support, and share their moments of agony, fear, joy, and happiness with others. There are thousands of blogs by persons afflicted with cancer, leukemia, depression, and other illnesses.

In this chapter, I follow a blog by an Indian woman whose daughter suffers from schizophrenia, one of the hardest illnesses for families to cope with. "A Mother in India"[1] stands out for its fluent writing-style, its interesting description of the illness, and its impact on the family. Also, the narrative is situated in a society in transition; modern India includes high achievers in the fields of computers, medicine, high tech, etc. while maintaining traditional cultural forms. This makes this blog extremely interesting, for both dimensions—social achievement, and tradition—are a nightmare for parents of schizophrenic children. It is also a good example of the use of blogging as a way to promote civic activity. Although the dualism of emancipation and melancholy, which in this study characterizes blogosphere, can also be found in this blog in that someone's misery is presented in full force but not solved, this blogger combines her online diary with civic efforts, thus making this blog into a good example of the use of blogging as a means of communication within the boundaries of civil society.

Schizophrenia and Life Writing

Schizophrenia has been described as a contentious construct used to describe a wide range of cognitive and emotional dysfunctions.[2] These include "withdrawal from reality, illogical patterns of thinking, delusions, and hallucinations, and...other emotional, behavioral, or intellectual disturbances."[3]

The disturbances associated with schizophrenia are inconsistent with norms of achievement in society. As Catherine Chesla argues, "Schizophrenics fit poorly into a society that values achievement because the illness drains the individual of motivation to accomplish valued goals."[4] The negative symptoms of the illness, she writes, "read like a list of vices in our culture: apathy, social withdrawal, anhedonia, amotivation. Matters are worsened by the fact that these symptoms are present in physically healthy adults, who appear to be able to work."[5] But long before achievement has become a central norm in modern societies, families with members suffering from mental illness have been subjected to social stigma.

Many have exposed the stigma attributed to the mentally ill and their families to be mainly the result of fear and superstition,[6] but only recently have researchers begun to sort out its many manifestations. In studying the effects of caring for a child with schizophrenia on maternal health, Greenberg and others have described some of the effects of perceptions of this stigma. Parents may be reluctant to invite friends and neighbors to their homes or may restrict public activities to avoid encounters in which their son or daughter may feel stigmatized by the illness.[7] Experience has shown however that the way to cope with stigma is not to hide but rather to share the child's condition with the world, bring the facts haunting the family out into the open and thus reduce the fear and superstition that produces the stigma.[8]

This is what many families are now doing. There are several projects that encourage members of families of schizophrenics to speak out. One project, initiated by the *Schizophrenia Bulletin*, publishes a "First Person Account Series" intended to provide mental health care professionals with the opportunity to learn first hand about the issues and difficulties faced by families. The series gave rise to important insights such as Sarah Ben-Dor's account of the events leading to her schizophrenic son's suicide, which demonstrates the misunderstanding that exists between the family and the outside world. While for the family the child was sick, for the rest of the world he was simply crazy. Ben-Dor demonstrates the importance of support groups in which parents share their grief, anger, and feelings of helplessness and fear. She describes, for instance, how both the sick persons and their family members feel warmth and encouragement when accompanying other families on, say, picnics—occasions when the stigmas, for once, do not exist.[9]

Such autobiographical writings enable both professionals and the general public to appreciate the hardships involved in caring for a sick child, and researchers are paying increasing attention to the narratives of patients and their families. The problem lies in the limited access to such narratives; the narratives collected in the "First Person Account Series," for example, mostly unfold in a controlled environment.

This is where blogs are invaluable. Blogging software provides the mentally sick and their family members with a means to spell out directly and with immediacy their personal narratives and to describe the development of the illness. Although the person described in this blog became ill before blogging was available and the first of the mother's entries are in the past tense, the continuous structure and personal nature of the blog allows us to follow step by step the heartbreaking events in the life of one family coping with schizophrenia.

A Tale of Helplessness and Fear

The first entry in the blog appeared on February 22, 2004: "February is one of the pleasant months of the year in Delhi. February is also when I relieve the pain, turmoil and helplessness I had to go through eight years ago. My daughter was going through hell too, far worse than mine—her mind wracked by the demons of the past" (22.2. 04).

It all began when the mother asked her daughter why she was looking so sad. "'Mamma I am losing control of my mind,' she said in a calm voice. I could not understand" (22.2.04). This lack of understanding is the story's motif. The expression "demons of the past" is indicative of the mythological interpretation given to an unfamiliar illness.

At first, the family treated the matter using traditional means, hoping that a lot of rest would make the girl better. She enrolled in yoga classes, which were of no help as the sick girl could not even do a simple exercise such as lifting her feet. Although the family tries to be understanding and supportive, this does not have much impact on the daughter's condition. Most nights she lies awake, and talks about incidents from her past that deeply hurt her. She can lapse into silence, not listen, and takes no care of her appearance.

The mother provides a detailed and complex picture of the girl's condition which medical anamnesis can hardly match. "Her movements seemed to be regressing—the way she walked, not swinging her arms but handing lifelessly by her side. When she ate her meals, crumbs fell on her dress and she was unaware of it" (22.2.04). The girl develops a different sense of time: "Sometimes I felt she was in a desperate hurry to do what she liked to do before something catastrophic happened" (22.2.04).

The diary entries, often posted late at night, allow the readers to share in the mother's helplessness and fear. The girl is given cloth and embroidery threads so she can embroider and sew, as a cure for her schizophrenia. The family is not familiar with medication for the treatment of mental illness. Initially, the girl is not taken to see a psychiatrist for fear of the stigma that will be attached to such a visit. "Who would marry her, I thought then. Desperately I read books on Naturopathy which said a diet rich in almonds, saffron and cardamoms were good for the brain. I gave her large amounts with milk. She got worse" (22.2.04).

When the girl finally gets to see a psychiatrist, he happens to be a private practitioner in his seventies who tells the parents that she is a deep introvert undergoing a nervous breakdown. He prescribes medication but offers no explanations, and the parents are too terrified to ask questions. On discovering that the medication prescribed is intended for the treatment of schizophrenia, the family lacks the means to evaluate this detail. "I walked, I don't remember where but thinking with terror that my daughter was turning into a split personality" (22.2.04).

The family begins a desperate search for information. Told from the perspective of one mother, we can see the resources families have to mobilize to find their way in the unfamiliar world of medical terms and practices. The

mother looks up the meaning of "schizophrenia" in a dictionary, where it is described as a person's split from reality. The lack of reliable information is striking: "The next day I called the p-doc and asked him whether I should buy a dog
because my daughter wanted us to buy one. He told me not to as she could be
manic" (22.2.04).

The mother calls up a distant cousin who practices medicine in a government hospital and asks her to check with a psychiatrist about the medication that
has been prescribed. She discovers that it is very strong and may have lasting
side effects. This increases the family's feelings of helplessness and fear: "Terror ruled our lives because we felt so helpless. Sometimes we wish that we
hadn't stopped the medication then. But then we console ourselves that what we
did was because of our ignorance" (22.2.04).

Ignorance about schizophrenia also prevails among the medical professionals. A psychiatrist the daughter sees in the government hospital says the girl will
be fine after taking some tonic for her nerves. "As you can see," he says, "she is
in a state of conflict. She either wants to be married which her grandmother
wishes or take up a career her mother wishes. There is a big fight between the
two personalities and one will emerge" (23.2.04).

The next encounter is with a neurologist who screams at the parents demanding how they dare bringing a psychiatric case to him. So the intimidated
family returns to the former "p-doc". The mother expresses her feelings of guilt
about her failure to be more assertive in the face of intimidation. "Why was I
frightened then to ask the p-doc questions about my daughter's welfare? Why
didn't I confront him then about his earlier statement that my daughter would be
well? Why didn't I ask him about the medication and its side effects?" (23.2.04).
She realizes that her lack of assertiveness stems from the conditioning imposed
by society against questioning something shrouded in ignominy, but this does
not relieve her guilt.

The girl's father is in the air force and the girl therefore is eligible for treatment in a military hospital where she sees a psychiatrist who is responsive and
establishes a rapport with her. The medication he prescribes eventually produces
a smile. Unfortunately, he is moved and the meetings with the new psychiatrist
soon lead to a return of the sense of helplessness and fear. "Most of his patients
were men from the armed forces who had served in the high altitudes of the Himalayas. They were simple men from the far flung villages who looked even
more befuddled when they came out of his room. Sometimes we could hear him
shouting at his patients" (26.2.04). The family is then transferred to another town
and thus relieved of having to visit this doctor, but faced with the unlikelihood
of finding another receptive doctor in a society of a billion people served only by
four thousand psychiatrists.

Over time, the parents' ability to gather information and relate to the daughter's condition improves: "The thick veil of ignorance about mental illnesses
which clouded our lives in the earlier years have torn with the knowledge we
have gleaned. Knowing about the illness and its symptoms makes it so much
easier to communicate with the p-doc" (27.3.04). What is not changing over time

is the stigma; relatives, even those who have themselves experienced mental sickness, keep agonizing the mother who wonders: "Is the only way to feel empathy towards someone afflicted with Schizophrenia...living with that person?" (30.3.04). She refers to those who live with schizophrenia as "the chosen ones who not only have to help our loved ones battle this illness but also undergo torment when someone derides them" (30.3.04).

The extended family proposes traditional healing practices. In a distant town, the girl's grandparents match horoscopes with eligible men, find a man who is suitable and arrange an engagement ceremony, assuring the mother that once the girl (who by now can barely walk) becomes engaged, she will be fine. The extended family refuses to read material about schizophrenia. Its main concern is to prevent people from finding out there is mental illness in the family (it has apparently existed in the family for generations). Most of the time, the topic is discreetly avoided. The mother wants to scream but the years of conditioning, she writes, "froze the words on her lips." She breaks ties with family members who engage in malicious gossip about the case. "My husband and I have tried so hard to make my parents and his family understand this illness so it be treated like another illness. It is like hitting your head on a wall crying to be heard while people walk past not seeing you" (6.3.04).

All this is written amidst unbearable daily routines which are described in detail: "I used to take turns with my husband sitting next to her waiting for her to fall asleep or just sit near her when she wanted us to" (6.4.04). The mother shares with us the thoughts that go through her mind when she is sitting at her daughter's bedside, which always involve guilt:

> I thought about the way I would live life if given another chance. Perhaps I would have been more firm? And made a home with more stability and reduced the accompanying strife? It went on and on. I had to constantly reassure myself that I had done my best and shake off the mantle of guilt that constantly threatened to put me in a state of gloom. (6.4.04)

She also feels guilty about her lack of sensitivity in the past toward people who probably had schizophrenia. She remembers a relative who was not working and stayed at home with his parents, realizing only now that he may have had the illness. She also mentions a cousin who on the way to college often became confused and disoriented and regrets not having been more sympathetic: "My aunt passed away eight years ago. I wished that she was alive so I could tell her that I understood her pain" (6.4.04). But there is nothing she can do about it besides noting it in her blog.

The Blog's Contribution

Let us now analyze the blog's contribution both to the readers and to the blogger. First, it allows the readers to glimpse some of the unique features of traditional India, which are important to absorb not for the exotica involved but for their inspiring lessons conveyed on life and on life's tragedies and joys. In July 2004, the mother leaves for a two-week spiritual sojourn in the Himalayas, by the holy river Ganges.

> I sat for long periods on the banks of the Ganges, contemplating, meditating and sometimes just drinking in the beauty of the river and the mountains. I bathed in the cold water of the river…I also spoke to learned men in ochre robes who had studied the age old scriptures. They seemed timeless, so thin but their faces glowed though they may have been in their seventies. I asked them so many questions which no elders in our families could answer…They all did talk about the power of love, compassion and prayer so I prayed by the banks of the river. (9.7.04)

The modern Indian woman is aware that such a spiritual sojourn has limited effects. When she returns to her routine, she expresses the difficulty to maintain a balance between the quiet meditation that she experienced on the banks of the Ganges, and the need to talk, if only as part of the managing of the mundane routines of a house with a sick child. "So many mundane things one has to talk to maintain peace in the home. And the irony—when one doesn't talk much, there is so much of peace within oneself. I hope God gives me the strength to strike this balance" (17.7.04).

But the balance is there. This mother displays a rare capacity to handle the mundane tasks of life, yet to reflect on them in ways that endow them with a sense of serenity and spirituality. Take the routine description of when the daughter asks for an old quick-stitch kit nestling amongst knitting needles, embroidery threads, and sewing paraphernalia: "I feel a sense of gratitude to God when I see her beautiful face lit by the glow of the lamp as she bends over to sew the stitches which make a pattern" (23.7.04).

Or consider the following description:

> Last week we went to the psychiatrist. It [is] a monthly visit-these days. After coming out of the clinic, we saw a man sitting on the kerb, with a basket on his lap. He stood out because of the way he dressed. He was from the countryside. Looking at him, I was so sure that the basket with the lid would have a snake. It did. When I asked him he opened it and predictably a huge, spectacled, black cobra uncoiled itself, spread its hood and hissed threateningly. I felt suddenly happy for watching the man and his snake, brought back pleasant childhood memories when life moved at a slower pace and snake charmers were a common sight. As the man explained how he made a living with the snake, occasional[l]y selling its venom, he struck such a contrast to the chaotic traffic behind him. (27.8.04)

The serenity of the situation is not lost on the daughter who remarks that the man seems very content despite not knowing where his next meal will come from. The mother then shares with us her thoughts:

> As I thought over her words I wondered if that man had achieved or was

blessed with that rare quality of equanimity, where he could exist in peace amidst the chaos. The wise ascetics and the ancient scriptures urge us to stay calm in this eternally changing world. With schizophrenia in our lives the magnitude of turbulence in our lives, at times, is at unimaginable levels. It is so difficult to always stay calm, it is so difficult to love and yet stay detached, so difficult to give while overcoming the desire for a return...the list is endless. Perhaps some are blessed and for some, well—they have to take different paths to achieve that state. (27.8.04)

Our exposure to the online diary of a mother caring for a schizophrenic child makes us realize how little concern there is in society about this illness and other conditions, and how little we as individuals are concerned with such things unless they affect us personally. At the same time, the unfolding of the story of the sickness in the first person singular reduces this distance. It allows us to reconsider a variety of truisms and stereotypes, such as the assumption that suffering in the family is a uniting force. The blog reveals the chasm that develops between the daughter's parents and grandparents who will not abandon the idea that their granddaughter's lack of marital bliss is the cause of the illness. "Angry and bitter words were spoken. Exhausted I used to weep in the bathroom. I had to decide as to who needed me more. I had to take care of my daughter, so I stopped speaking to my parents" (26.2.04).

One stereotype that is shattered is that of the suffering masses in traditional societies being apathetic and helpless. In this blog we hear of poor peasants with dust-encrusted feet, nut brown faces etched with lines of toil, and crumpled clothes arriving at the hospital after long journeys. While they may come from far-flung villages where superstition about mental illness is rife, they show strength and determination: "Talking to some of them, I was amazed by their attitude. They said that they were not well, so they couldn't work, hence they had come for treatment to get well to earn something or look after their families. No formal education but so much of awareness!" (10.2.04). The blog also reveals how kind people can sometimes be. An enlightened family friend risked a fifty-year friendship with her own father and stood by the secluded and isolated family.

The continuous nature of the blog allows us to share in occasional moments of joy amidst the suffering: "today has been a perfect day spent with an affectionate nice and an old loving friend and her family who try to understand this illness when I tell them about it. A day that will be imprinted in my mind to recall and relive. I feel a sense of gratitude when I am blessed with such moments" (27.3.04). The blogger looks back to the day eight years earlier, when it all began and feels a degree of hope: "I feel hope this year because my daughter is able to take care of herself, our two cats and also cook while I am away. These may be normal activities for the normal people. But for her I know now they require a great deal of effort" (27.3.04).

As to the function of the blog for the blogger herself, she seems to gain strength from writing and from the comments she receives. The comments are mostly from people expressing familiarity with the situation. The exchange with commentators sometimes reveals a tendency identified in other chapters of the engaging personal narrative being reduced to a set of clichés, "know-how" tips and shallow emotional expressions such as the following: "Pain and sorrow or happiness, these are just two faces of the same coin which the controller of our destinies keeps tossing into the air and whichever face that falls on the road which we travel on, decides the moment" (26.2.04).

It is hard to assess the long-term contribution to a person suffering great agony over a sick child of comments like "hugs to you," accompanied by icons symbolizing hugs. Some comments however do seem genuinely comforting, for instance, that of another mother of a schizophrenic child who advises the blogger not to neglect herself while she is taking care of her daughter. An American woman living thousands of kilometers distant provides insights about how her own daughter's illness has taught her humility:

> Life can be so sweet and grand and suddenly one can be struck down with such sadness and sorrow. It makes me appreciate all the good things even more. I want to believe there is a reason for everything that happens to us in this world...I don't know for sure what it is...but I'm sure the creator knows the answer even if we don't. Take care and be good to yourself. There are many people reading your journal and praying and thinking of your family. (3.3.04)

When the blogger is involved in a road accident, neighbors rush to help, cooking meals for the family and attending to the daughter's needs. Two women visit the mother in hospital, one sings songs in her native language, and the other translates them. Such neighborly gestures seem much more effective than online hugs, but the blogger finds comfort in the exchanges with others and a support group begins to form, first online, then offline. Once she has access to the Internet, the mother finds the Website "schizophrenia.com" comforting because it exposes her to others who are suffering similarly. "There was no place we could air our grievances because psychiatric patients and their relatives were not taken seriously. A patronizing tone was used with the patients" (10.3.04). The therapeutic function of the blog becomes clear when the mother spends a couple of weeks in another town where she does not have access to the Internet. She misses the putting of suppressed feelings into words. To her, writing is "like letting free a bird which was trapped in a cage" (27.3.04).

In April, the blog begins to record offline meetings between individuals who share the mother's situation.

> Last Sunday probably was like any for most people. A hot summer day in a city that seemed bleached and exhausted as a blazing sun shone relentlessly from a clear blue sky. For me it was a special day. I met two people. One, a petite, beautiful mother whose son was struggling with this illness and the other a young soft-spoken man who was courageously coping with the illness that has touched him. (22.4.04)

The description of the meeting reveals the unique nature of meetings between people who share a condition that is not understood by the outside world.

"Whatever was spoken was understood" (22.4.04). The blogger invites the young man to her home, where her daughter for the first time in her life meets another person battling the same illness. The bond formed that afternoon between strangers, the mother concludes, would not have occurred were it not for her Website.

In the weeks to come, she becomes socially active. In late May, "Schizophrenia Awareness Day" occurs and she rings up a leading Indian newspaper. It is generally difficult to get the media pay attention to schizophrenia but the suicide of a young girl who suffered from the illness provides the mother with an opportunity to get the attention of a reporter. She tries to raise awareness about the illness and the need for measures to be taken to avoid suicides. She tells the reporter about the support group forming through her blog and recommends that the mainstream media take similar action to provide patients and their families with ways to get together. The reporter, writing a column on "ordinary people who do extraordinary things" is sympathetic. On June 4, in the Sunday edition of the *Indian Express*, an article appears in which the daughter's story is related under the offensive title "Little Jekyll, scared Hyde" (17.7.04).

Beginning in February 2005, the blog deals with the government decision to reduce accessibility to drugs, including those helping schizophrenia patients, thus threatening to bring back "the Dark Ages of Institutionalization coexisting with the Silicon cities of India" (8.2.05). What the blogger refers to is the patenting of drugs in accordance with the World Trade Organization. Since drugs in India were cheaper than elsewhere (because Indian drug companies have produced generic versions at low prices), the Indian government was asked to abide by international trade covenants as part of its role in "globalization." The blog exposes this dimension of globalization from the perspective of one family:

> In a country like India, there are over twenty million people with major mental illnesses and more than 70% of them live with their families. The family is the backbone of support and care. Any policy affecting the treatment and healthcare of those with mental illness will also affect the quality of care provided by the families to their loved ones. India is a poor country and people with major mental illnesses in India, have no Disability Insurance or Benefits, no Medical Insurance cover-unlike cancer, no Government programs like Social Security Disability / Employment/Insurance, no Sheltered, Transitional or Supported employment, No Clubhouses for Social Rehabilitation/not enough Mental Health Facilities for hospitalization, few crisis intervention centres and now - no choice for a drug that is crucial to control their illness because they will no longer be affordable. (8.2.05)

The mother decides to take action and records her Kafka-like endeavors. She contacts the Ministry of Commerce to check if the new patent ordinance applies to the drugs her daughter is taking. She is told to contact the Ministry of Industrial Promotion & Policy, which refers her to the Ministry of Patents. The undersecretary at the Ministry of Patents speaks enthusiastically about patented software and when asked about the impact of the patent on the price of drugs responds in political rhetoric designed to humiliate the person posing the question. The blog leads us through the "dusty and daunting" (8.2.05) corridors of government offices where bureaucrats are sometimes nice but not very helpful.

As I conclude this chapter, a forty-nine-year old mother in India caring for her schizophrenic daughter is still walking between government offices in Delhi, remaining polite while sharing with us her urge to cry aloud: "Where should I go next? Please help me. Is there no one who cares for these people who suffer so much?" (19.4.05).

Notes

1. <http://www.schizophrenia.com/indiam/>
2. Sarah Baker et al., "Client and Family Narratives on Schizophrenia." *Journal of Mental Health* 10 (2001): 199-212.
3. *The American Heritage Dictionary*, 4th Edition (2000).
4. Catherine A. Chesla, "Parents' Caring Practices with Schizophrenic Offspring." In *Interpretive Phenomenology: Embodiment, Caring, and Ethics in Health and Illness*, Patricia Benner ed. (Thousand Oaks: Sage, 1994), 168.
5. Patricia Benner, 168.
6. See Michel Foucault, *Madness and Civilization: A History of Insanity in the Age of Reason* (New York: Vintage, 1965).
7. Jan Steven Greenberg et. al., "Mothers Caring for an Adult Child with Schizophrenia: The Effects of Subjective Burden on Maternal Health." *Family Relations* 42 (April 1993): 205-211.
8. See Louise Wilson, *This Stranger, My Son: A Mother's Story* (New York: Putnam's Sons, 1968).
9. Sarah Ben-Dor, "Personal Account." *Schizophrenia Bulletin* 27 (2001): 329-332.

Chapter 10

African Exile

"Hello World. This is my first post. Many more will follow" (5.6.03). The beginning of the blog called "On Lesotho,"[1] seems like that of many others. The blogger is enjoying the new software he has acquired and in the coming days fills the Web with what seems like linguistic nonsense:

Friday, June 6: "My friend, Rachel, says, 'In American English, quite means 'very' or 'really', (as in, *Your site is quite good! I really like it!*) In British English, however, it means 'not that much' or 'a little', or even 'not good at all', (as in, *Yes, the weather's quite alright—it's not flooding yet*)" (6.6.03).

Saturday, June 7: "Take the question of prepositions... We're supposed not to put them at the end of a sentence. But that often leads to stilted, non natural-sounding speech. As Sir Winston Churchill supposedly said, *that is nonsense up with which we should not put*" (7.6.03).

Monday, June 9: "I've heard some native speakers make their share of mistakes on *who's* and *whose*. I've heard, for example, *Who's car is that?* But you know better, don't you? You would not say *Whose making that awful noise*, would you? I didn't think so" (9.6.03).

Then the focus changes; the linguistic comments begin to relate to the African state of Lesotho:

June 17: "Yes. Lesotho is too often called THE SWITZERLAND OF AFRICA. What do the two countries have in common? Quite a lot, actually, if you disregard the dosh: Mountains, Surface area, Being chums with everyone. But why the dickens is Switzerland never called THE LESOTHO OF EUROPE? Huh? Know what I mean?" (17.6.03).

Not quite. We still do not know what the blogger means, until the blog, written by an African in exile in France, begins to remind us of a familiar theme advanced by another famous exile in France, Franz Fanon, who stressed the role of language in colonial oppression and in the liberation from colonialism. Fanon, a black psychiatrist from Martinique, inspired the Algerian struggle for independence. His books *Wretched of the Earth* and *Black Skin White Masks* were among the most influential writings of the anti-colonial movements of the mid twentieth century. Colonized people, he claims, have an inferiority complex planted in their soul by the death and burial of their local cultural originality. When they find themselves face to face with the language of the civilizing nation, they try to adjust to it in pathetic ways. The educated among them distance themselves from their black brothers and sisters and speak like the colonizers, which only accentuates their otherness.[2]

Fanon ventured to liberate black people from that inferiority complex, concluding that since it has deep psychopathological causes, violence is the only effective means of liberation. "At the level of individuals," he wrote, "violence is a cleansing force. It frees the native from his inferiority complex and from his despair and inaction; it makes him fearless and restores his self-respect."[3] In Fanon's work and legacy, violence is not only a tool in the colonized people's struggle for independence but the cornerstone of a new civilization free from racial oppression.

The blogger, Rethabile Masilo, differs from Fanon in his moderate style and non violent approach. Yet, like Fanon, he has a profound understanding of language and its role in oppression and liberation, which makes this blog interesting to follow. Here is a blogger who does not replace the emancipating power of blogging with the fetishism of words we associated with melancholy but makes an effort to utilize the power of words as a means to advance a political cause: the cause of the dying continent of Africa. As in Chapter 9, this blog allows us a view of online life writing not as an end in itself but as a means to make changes in the real world.

In light of the enormous difficulties facing Africa today, and the little aid given the people there despite worldwide awareness of the gravity of their situation, it can be argued that one more expression of frustration does not promise change, and that this blogger, like others described in this book, is doomed to cry in the wilderness. But "On Lesotho" plays a significant role in promoting auto-emancipation among Africans, as it not only points to difficulties but also to the range of options open to those willing to do something about their condition.

Self-reliance is conditioned by having an independent voice. In an article on "The Rock Star's Burden," Paul Theroux complained about rock stars like "Bono" whose exclusive focus is on money to be poured into the African continent. As Theroux puts it, "It seems to have been Africa's fate to become a theater of empty talk and public gestures. But the impression that Africa is fatally troubled and can be saved only by outside help—not to mention celebrities and charity concerts—is a destructive and misleading conceit."[4] Africa, he believes, has no shortage of capable people, even of money, and Africans have proven to be resilient, something they never receive credit for. The patronizing attention of donors, he writes, has done violence to Africa's belief in itself.

This is where blogging as a way of expressing an independent voice may have a truly emancipating role. Fanon's writings came to represent the thoughts of the "black man," that is, a universalized model of millions of black-skinned men and women seeking liberation from colonialism. Here, one black man voices his concerns about poverty, AIDS, violence, corruption, and discrimination, as well as about the beauty of his native land, and other matters, in ways that are often reminiscent of Fanon yet depart from him in an important sense: the personification of the issues and thus their treatment in greater complexity. The complexity does not allow simple solutions such as all-out revolution of the black man, nor treatment of blacks as a helpless herd. The blog is written by someone who, as a result of his personal touch and independence of mind, resorts to self-reliance rather than reliance on the ideologies of the past or the rock concerts of the present.

Rethabile, who describes in detail the devastation of his family during a political strife in Lesotho, does not propose one dimensional answers, based on psychopathology, to the hard questions facing contemporary Africa but rather shares with us a whole array of thoughts on language, life, and politics in this tormented continent. Writing from the perspective of one exile in France, he is of course representing nobody, but neither was Fanon. The individual who is looking at the many facets of his life, including their ambiguities, may actually provide us with a more instructive picture of the black man's plight today, and the options available to resolve that plight, than can be found in twentieth century ideologues.

On Lesotho

Lesotho, formerly Basutoland, is a small mountainous enclave of South Africa populated by less than two million people, most of them Basotho. The Basotho nation was consolidated in the early nineteenth century by King Moshoeshoe I. In 1868, Basutoland was placed under British protection and in the 1950s it gradually gained independence from Britain, with an elected council formed in 1959, general elections held in 1965, and the founding of an independent constitutional monarchy in 1966. The blogger, who often refers to the country's history with special pride in the greatness of King Moshoeshoe I, lays out the story of its foundation with a combination of love and irony: "How did he do it? Well, he simply gathered refugees fleeing regional wars (Lifaqane), fed them; asked cannibals (more hungry refugees) to join his clan, fed them, and there, you have it: Lesotho was born" (18.6.03).

The light tone changes when the tale of the country after independence is being told. In 1970, the ruling party BNP lost an election and Prime Minister Leabua Jonathan refused to step down, called a state of emergency, dissolved parliament and suspended the constitution. This led to continuous strife, culminating in a military take-over in 1986. "Bingo! That is where we fucked up," Rethabile writes. "As far as I can remember, we were on this nice, hopeful path toward country-hood when WHAM! A lot of people were suddenly arrested because they voiced disagreement with a dictator. Many more were tortured. And some were later assassinated or nearly assassinated" (3.4.04).

Among those tortured and assassinated were members of his close family.

The arrest of the father is told from the perspective of the high school kid he was at the time:

> They came in Land-Rovers...It was late in the afternoon and it was a smoky or foggy day, Saturday or Sunday or a bank holiday, since ntate and 'mè were home. There were no fights, no arguments, nothing of the sort. I don't even re-member anyone crying, although 'mè might have, right after the jailers' depar-ture. I was in fact proud that they had hauled ntate away, because it meant our family was important, too. *Kids*. Little did I know what was in store for us. (20.5.04)

The blog provides a first hand view of what is at store for those enduring civil war in Africa:

> I had a taste of that kind of life when my father was thrown in jail in 1970. Our existence changed and we lost most priviledges we had come to take for granted. In order to survive, under an openly hostile government, 'mè struck deals with people who had fields. She provided the seed and the fertilizer, I think, and they provided the land. We shared the harvest. I can remember win-ter dinners of *papa* (corn bread) and canned peaches. Of course 'mè canned them herself. She also ran a grocery store which hardly made any profit, since it was also the family food-stock and we, the children, pillaged it mercilessly. (11.5.04)

The circumstances surrounding the assassination of his brother are not elaborated, partly because Rethabile is not sure of them. He does not know whether a pistol was held to his forehead, whether his wrists were cut with a sharpened knife, or whether he was tortured before he was killed. This is where we get a glance at another aspect of the African civil wars: the human agony stemming from lack of knowledge about the fate of one's loved ones. This urge is apparent in many references to the Truth and Reconciliation Commission (TRC) in South Africa, and similar organs in Kenya and elsewhere. "I would like to know what happened to my brother, Khotsofalang Reaboka Masilo, who was killed by his own countrymen apparently for political gain" (2.12.03). His concern is less with the knowledge of what happened to his brother than with where his bones are, so he might be properly buried.

Desmond Tutu's logic in founding the TRC as a way to come to terms with the past by finding out what happened rather than by succumbing to the instinct of revenge, is echoed here from one person's perspective.

> I want to see 'people' who have the answers squirming in the hot seat, in front of a legitimate committee, not for my pleasure, but because I think that's the only way we'll ever get to find Khotsofalang. And the day I find my brother's body is the day I start cleaning out the darkest corners of my mind. And taking full advantage of my life today, with my lovely wife and wonderful children. And that day means some sort of Truth and Reconciliation Commission, Leso-tho style. (2.12.03)

The difficult questions raised by the concept of the TRC have not been resolved in people's minds, and the blog provides an arena for their contemplation. The concept suits Rethabile's moderate attitude to politics and he fully realizes its function in establishing a more peaceful Africa. A truth commission would find out the reasons for the madness, get neighbors torn apart by civil war to forgive each other, punish those who cannot be forgiven, and perhaps enable him to find his brother's remains. He is also aware, however, how difficult it is to provide immunity to notorious criminals, as the TRC did, even for the sake of the truth. If President Robert Mugabe of Zimbabwe were to step down, he asks, would it be possible to wipe off years of misrule, embezzlement, and other crimes?

What these conjectures lead to are mainly more questions that no inquisitive person can avoid:

> Why did this Mosotho or Basotho kill Khotsofalang? And most important, what is this Mosotho or Basotho thinking today? Do they look at themselves in the mirror every morning and feel like shit—or are they proud for having done this devastating deed? Or have they already forgotten about it ('It was all in a day's work')? If this Mosotho or Basotho are reading this, what would they like to tell me, I wonder, and my two other brothers and my two sisters and my parents? (3.11.03)

The circumstances in which Rethabile left the country are not elaborated. He describes himself as a black man living with his white wife and two children in France, longing for his native Lesotho which, since the early 1990s, has more or less stabilized as a constitutional monarchy with working democratic institutions. Although he spent many years in exile, his heart is still in Lesotho: "That's where I first met hope, felt the joy of belonging, faced desperation, knew fear, and touched compassion" (1.3.04).

Rethabile's interest in language is related to his status as an exile; like other exiles, language provides him with a connection to the new world he lives in and with a link to the world he has left but not abandoned. "I like English. It's a fun language. Through it I'm able to talk to millions (precisely what I'm trying to do at this very moment), but I like Sesotho more. (it's more fun and it sounds better and tones), and it is all mine! (6.1.04).

The educated blogger who turned from biology to linguistics is aware of the need for exiles to speak like the incumbents of their host countries, as part of their attempt to be accepted. He is also aware, however, that when he speaks French or English, his pronounciation singles him out. Sesotho remains his natural form of expression: "[W]hen I speak Sesotho, I feel whole and on a par with anybody else" (6.1.04). Speaking in his native tongue is not without its problems; during the colonial era pupils were discouraged from speaking Sesotho in school and when he was growing up he mainly spoke English. He notes the repercussions of the process in which people are dissociated from their mother tongue. One of these repercussions is the inferiority complex identified in *Black Skin White Masks*: "You're doing your darndest to speak someone else's language, but you'll always be a step or two behind in a meeting, at the restaurant during a heated discussion, at the job interview, and so on. And you know it. The crunch comes when you realise that you don't really master your mother tongue either" (6.1.04).

The cultural difficulties of the black exile in France frequently arise in the blog. Rethabile tries not to stretch the racism motif but cannot avoid it. Consider the incident when the black poet comes to a store to buy a job advert magazine and the shopkeeper hands him one that lists only manual and blue collar jobs. When he asks for an upscale magazine, the vendor admits he has it in the store but did not think it would be relevant as it lists only management jobs. The reaction:

> Son of a bitch. The first magazine he mentions usually has manual and other blue-collar job offers. But how does one react, in general, to such behaviour? My usual reaction is no reaction at all...go on as if nothing had happened...and hope that perhaps that in itself suffices to sow some doubt in the racist's mind. Like, *What? He didn't whip out a razor blade and slit my throat?* I also get regular comments in supermarkets, whereby I'm asked where the potatoes or the onions are. The speaker has already concluded that, one, I work at the supermarket, but also that, two, I'm in the produce section. (9.5.04)

On another occasion, he sees three black people sweeping the street, and another one sweeping the pavement near a supermarket, which raises the question why is it almost exclusively black people who are doing such jobs. Is it because they are black? The blogger does not accept statements that explain the condition of blacks in Europe, or for that matter in Lesotho, as racism. He assumes these people do manual work because they are unqualified to do other work, and discusses the causes, with racism being only one such. He then evaluates the pros and cons of affirmative action, looking for practical solutions rather than for parties to blame.

This non radical approach to race relations does not diminish his pride as a Basotho. When, for instance, he notices that many African men and women in Europe are having their hair straightened, a phenomenon he relates to an inferiority complex vis a vis whites, he voices his objection:

> The issue is the same wherever one people oppresses another, and manages to blatantly or subconsciously convince the oppressed party that it is ugly. In Lesotho's case, it was a blatant declaration related to both colonial and South-African racism, and subconscious by way of adverts, barbie and the sight of all the rich, glamorous, white folks in hotels and casinos. So we set about scouring our skins and sizzling our hair. (20.7.04)

The attempt to adjust one's language, pronunciation, life style, and even the shape of the hair to standards set by colonizers or former colonizers bothers him. He feels political liberation demands liberation of the soul and devotes several entries to the changes of consciousness African people must go through in order to acquire true freedom. He begins with self-criticism. One of his childhood heroes was a local Lesotho footballer, Mochini Matete, whom he compares to Maradona. Although African and European or South American teams are not held to the same standards, and Matete never played in the world cup, he remains Rethabile's uncontested hero. What he criticizes is the notion prevailing in his mind according to which global is beautiful while local is second rate. His football world always consisted of a pyramid of teams with Brazil the most admired, then Liverpool, then Cameroon and at the bottom—his local teams. This pyramid, he feels, must be turned on its head: "The Inverted Pyramid Syndrome is a scourge that must be fought, just like poverty and hunger and AIDS and corruption and discrimination" (23.1.04).

Auto-Emancipation

Most of the blog is devoted to the fight against poverty, hunger, AIDS, corruption and discrimination. These issues are treated within the frame of reference noted before; the blogger refuses to adopt a "post-colonial" approach according to which the ills of Africa can be attributed exclusively to the colonial experience. His discourse on Africa is marked by the language of pragmatism. Rather than blaming others for poverty and other disasters in Lesotho, he searches for the profound reasons underlying them, as well as for the points of intervention that could elevate the situation. In this, he differs from both the colonialists and post colonialist who share the patronizing attitude according to which the problems of Africa are not likely to be solved by African policy makers themselves.

Moreover, Rethabile does not consider the problems of Africa to be a chronic disease with no possibility of a cure. He resorts time and again to the glorious past of Lesotho under the rule of King Moshoeshoe I, in order to demonstrate that the people have the potential to flourish. But in order to flourish, they must first ask where they themselves went wrong. This is a recurrent motive in the blog:

> We had a king who had *Peace* for a sister. A born negotiator who forgave the folks who had eaten his grand-daddy, then convinced them to join his nation in the making. A guy who immediately saw how three Froggies wandering around southern Africa could be helpful. And boy, were they! Moshoeshoe did everything possible to preserve the sovereignty of Basutoland, later Lesotho, and he won--against all odds he won. Today there's a speck of a country called Lesotho, within but not part the mightier South Africa, because of Moshoeshoe's actions and wisdom. What happened after independence in 1966? How did we screw up? That's one hell of a question whose reply eludes me. The guy had cultivated the food, harvested the food, cooked the food and chewed it for us—and we weren't able to swallow it. (19.5.04)

In one of his first entries, he posts the country's anthem in Sesotho and in English. The anthem includes the lines "Lesotho, land of our Fathers, / Among countries you are the most beautiful," which makes the blogger comment that no country, city, village or home becomes beautiful if nobody is doing anything to render it beautiful. This is the first of many entries in which he objects to empty patriotic gestures, calling instead for civil and political commitment. *"Let's start by LIVING IN THE COUNTRY if we can. Let's start by supporting home businesses. Let's start by voting when there are elections. Let's start by planting trees (you know, on that day that is set aside for tree-planting). Do we love Lesotho? Do we? Do you?"* (23.6.03).

While Africa is rarely treated as a ground for the development of civil associations, as Eastern Europe is for instance, Rethabile sees the potential for civil society. The people of Lesotho speak the same language and share the same customs, which is no good reason for butchering one another.

Civil and political commitment begins with a non-passive, non-deterministic attitude. The blogger enhances such an attitude by arguing that famine, for instance, is not a God-given necessity. He highlights the similarities between Lesotho and Belgium, refusing to accept Belgium's richness vis à vis Lesotho's poverty as inevitable. If half of the population of Lesotho lives below the poverty line the reasons cannot be attributed only to objective circumstances such as Belgium's more fertile land, he writes, for Lesotho has plentiful supplies of water from the mountains. The reasons lie in human behavior: "We must have messed up somewhere in the course of our road to independence, or right after Independence" (26.6.03).

The blogger proposes practical solutions whose implementation depends on the citizens themselves. He calls upon these citizens to support local businesses and local produce in order to help the Lesotho economy, to assist their neighbors, to pester their village chiefs and their representatives in parliament with evidence of starving people, in the form of letters, phone calls, and personal representations, and to engage in charity:

> Do not think you were meant to have enough food and that others were not. Think you are bloody lucky, because that's what you are. Poor or rich, we're all the same, Jack. See that *Lehlanya* at the OK shopping complex? Why don't you slip him a cigarette next time? How about a sandwich? Or better yet, talk to the man for five minutes. What's his name? Where does he come from? Begin your conversation with: Lumela, ntate. When you finish, say Sala hantle, ntate. I think ntate Moshoeshoe I would have liked it that way. (26.6.03)

While having had a privileged childhood and presently living in an affluent society, Rethabile is voicing the plight of those who have no food, clothing, education, decent housing or hygiene. As in other third world countries, while much of the population walks around hungry and unclothed, a small minority flourishes. Again, the issue is brought up as an item for a civil and political agenda, with special emphasis on voting. "**Vote**, and vote well. Don't vote for your cousin or your pal, vote for the candidate who looks like they mean business. We're tired of all these fat-cat lackeys who are hungering for power. Tell your employees to go and vote or they're fired (Don't tell them who to vote for, though)" (10.1103).

It may not be customary to talk about African politics in terms of a public sphere of the kind attributed by Jürgen Habermas to bourgeois Europe. From the perspective of this blog, however, the formation of a public sphere, in which individuals and groups engage in talk about constitutional matters, is a necessary condition for Lesotho. Many of the blogger's suggestions concern talks among the yet unactivated citizens of the new constitutional monarchy, and between them and the government.

> Read the constitution, so that you can better choose who to vote for, and so that you can better know what Basotho are supposed to be getting, so that you can better fight to improve the system. Talk freely about the constitution and about human rights...dare the government to match you. Talk to somebody high up there somewhere in the government. If you are not important enough to be accorded an audience, convince an important citizen who is and go with them. Get the government to send one Mosotho to school (fees, books, clothes, food) for every Mosotho child you send. Fight and refuse to take no for an answer. The general effect would be to double the number of children who go to school, insread of running after goats all day long. (10.11.03)

The demand for engagement in civil and political activities, stemming from a pragmatic approach to politics, is not devoid of vision. The blogger has a dream. At one point he spells out the need to set up visionary goals which, he admits, is not easy in view of the present conditions in Africa.

> How many of us do dream today?, I mean, truly dream. What is dreaming, anyway? It's when the odds and more are all stacked up against you and you go ahead and want to accomplish something nonetheless. Dreaming is something that occurs while we are asleep, and it is usually something unattainable that we dream about. You may dream you're taking the taxi and going to work, that's not the dream. The dream is the sexy woman/man who shares the taxi with you and invites you upstairs to her/his pad with a wow! wink, just before your spouse elbows you and tells you to stop snoring. (8.12.03)

The awareness that visionary goals are hard to accomplish and require great effort makes him skeptical of visionary declarations by the government that do not seem to stem from a true commitment to change. When the government declares Lesotho will be a stable, democratic, united, prosperous nation at peace with itself and its neighbors by 2020, the blogger comments: "Great! Grrrreat! That's a dream, a nice dream at that, the stuff sweet dreams are made of" (8.12.03). But the important question for him is what it will take for the dream to come true in a country tnat has been mishandled and mismanaged for so long.

The answer lies in the sphere of pragmatic public action: send an E-mail to government officials or see your village chief daily, be a model citizen (e.g., recycle waste and plant trees), and—most importantly—develop the self-consciousness of a citizen in a national state. As he puts it:

> be a nation—yes be a nation, which we're not. We're each individually proud

of our country, but together we remain several groups. Catholics and Protestants, or BCP and LCD, or LCD and BNP. It's amazing how divisible 2.5 million people can be. We really discredit that old adage, 'United we stand, divided we fall.' (8.12.03)

In contrast to the skepticism displayed toward public authority that prevails in many countries, here the government is seen as a source of hope in spite of many instances of mismanagement and corruption. In one entry, portraits of the king and his government are posted under the title "team" taken from the football culture:

> Ladies and gentlemen, here is The Government of Lesotho. It is our team against misery and fear. We chose it! For the first time ever, Lesotho's team against misery was chosen by the people *and* is seemingly liked by the people and appears to me to be a winner. Of course, when things go awry we always single out and punish somebody, usually the coach. Or the goal-keeper. Or hooligans. Yes, the fans or supporters are part of the team. That makes you and I and other people who like Lesotho part of the team. Hooligans! Uh-huh. Not us. We're not hooligans, we work with the team. (24.12.03)

These declarations have echoes of speeches made by the founders of democracy in earlier centuries, as if a new beginning can now be expected in an African nation that has managed to restore a constitutional monarchy and is trusted to take its fate in its own hands. One can only share in the blogger's faith that his team will not let him down. "you are it. Our A-team. The proverbial buck stops with you. We're looking at you. We chose you. You will not let us down. And you will do everything in your power to fulfill the promise, as it is embodied in the National Vision, that you made to the Basotho people" (24.12.03).

The blogger is aware that the restoration of a constitutional monarchy after a decade of military rule is no guarantee of a viable democracy. There is still traditional lore and established ways that must be overcome but he is hopeful they will be overcome because Africa did have democratic political cultures before colonialism. In Lesotho, he tells us, King Moshoeshoe I always made his decisions after consulting his advisors. The main difficulty he sees is the lack of a civil tradition in which people consider their rulers to be accessible. Time and again he resorts to the need to approach the ruling team with demands and concerns, for civil and political action has no substitute and without it, Africa will fall into stagnation. "we are faced with a simple choice between keeping abreast with civilisation and progress on the one hand or embracing decadence, stagnation and regression on the other ... we have to make a deliberate choice between survival or extinction as a nation" (23.1.04).

Blogging and Emancipation

The civil approach to problem solving in Africa emerging from this blog is no trivial matter, especially in view of the widely accepted claim that only through violence can Africa be liberated and a new civilization emerge. Where does this civil approach stem from? One influence on Rethabile's intellectual development was the political education he received in Peka High School in Lesotho. He emphasizes his encounter with South African refugee children who escaped the Soweto riots of 1976 and ended up in his school, bringing with them a unique political message.

Rather than being bitter and full of hate they expressed their deep conviction that South Africa belongs to all who live in it, black and white. Being aware of the fact (emphasized in Desmond Tutu's presentation of the TRC's findings in 1998) that South Africa's apartheid regime had its foundation in a culture of lies, an important component of which was the distortion of the country's history, the students' message to their Lesotho friends was to study history extensively. In the contemporary world, in which history is often a neglected subject bounded to reconstruction, it is amazing to read of black South African kids in the 1970s whose main message to their peers across the border is to engage in their history lessons.

The study of history taught the young Lesotho man that the world is more complex than the grand ideologies of the twentieth century claimed. He discovered, for instance, that there are good and bad people among both blacks and whites. While it is impossible to assess how many Africans share the views expressed in this blog, a new African voice is definitely emerging here. Recalling with nostalgia the Soweto refugee kids in his high school, Rethabile writes:

> Thank them for instilling in me (Mum had already done the ground work) the fact that people are people, and hate has no business in our heads, and that no, the first thing you do is not to kill your enemy but to find out why you differ then try to win them over if you think they're dead wrong, or meet them half-way if you're not sure. Today that's one of the basic tenets of my life. And it is fuelled by my personal experience (having my brother and my nephew taken away by violent political death), my mother's teachings (which have never been teachings, really, but observations, what I learned from studying her), and my own beliefs (my faith in God, in Jesus Christ and in the goodness of humans). (18.3.04)

The new African voice emerging here is strongly connected to the blogging revolution. The blog seems immanent to the civil message conveyed here just as the pamphlet or the poster were immanent to the ideological messages of the past. Rethabile demonstrates this point when he speaks of his blogging activity:

> This activity, which does take a lot of time, has otherwise given me a mega-phone to the world. But it is not a megaphone for SHOUTING OUT MY THOUGHTS. It is rather a megaphone that lets me get heard along with the other megaphones, because the one who doesn't have one is sunk. There shouldn't be any shouting about any aspect of blogging. I try to be firm and truthful, even where I'm clearly not being objective. I think there's a difference

between fibbing and being subjective, and I think I can remain subjective but truthful. (9.2.04)

The blogger explains this uncommon wedding of subjectivity and truth by the example of his own autobiography. On the one hand he feels a deep dislike for the political party that murdered his brother and nephew, threw his father in jail, tortured and killed many Basotho and squandered the country's scant. On the other hand, he feels he has acquired the power, partly through the medium of blogging, to bring all that up in a truthful manner, which has a healing effect on him: "Blogging has helped me, together with poetry and my family, to remain cool and to get rid of the damned demons that just kept nagging and nagging and tugging at my soul. I was able to remain sane. I can't forget. I can forgive" (9.2.04).

Blogging is an important dimension of Rethabile's life. As an exile whose heart is in Africa while his information sources are mainly Western, he relies on blogs for information about his native country. He complains about Lesotho's news providers who are constantly off line and do not update their sites regularly. Even "AllAfrica," the largest electronic distributor of African news worldwide, is not satisfying his need for detailed and relevant information. Interestingly, this consumer of news, who wants to know how a constituency did in an election, how a city council handles its tasks, what plans and policies a government makes, etc., feels the need to turn to personal Weblogs rather than to established media outlets, in spite of the subjective nature of blogging.

Rethabile becomes gradually aware of the function his own blog fulfills as a news source about Lesotho:

Although *On Lesotho* is a personal weblog, initially with personal objectives and run by personal effort and conviction, although the initial format was based on taking a contentious or important issue and commenting on it, with a large dose of objectivity and a smaller one of subjectivity, although these were the initial intentions, I've recently watched myself publish news without commenting on it, simply because it was important for Lesotho and the world would have a hard time finding it out" (9.4.04).

But the blog satisfies a deeper need than the desire for updated news. In an entry devoted to the psychology of blogging, Rethabile posts a paragraph from a pioneering article by John Grohol, which stresses the role of the blogger as a storyteller. While admitting that most Weblogs are drivel and banal, providing little insight into anything, he refers the readers to abandoned or forgotten sites produced by genuinely interesting personalities. "They are storytellers. They understand the need for a beginning, a middle, and an ending. They draw together like-minded links into themes for the day, for the week, for a lifetime."[5]

The function of blogging to provide narratives in an intellectual environment which has blurred them may be the most important function of this medium. The first blog, as Grohol wrote, was published out of need. Before the introduction of search engines, people needed a way of exchanging links with one another so as to know what new sites were coming onto the Web. But even after the introduction of search engines, perhaps because of their introduction, people found themselves in want of an orderly story.

The contemporary mass media—the press, radio, television, the Internet—bombard us with information on events occurring in the world, with little connectedness between them. In the past, ideological dogmas served as ordering devices. "Post colonialism," for instance, allowed us to make sense of the multitude of occurrences in Lesotho, providing a frame of reference to sort out the information and evaluate it. The doctrine told us who was to be praised or blamed, where things stood and even what the future held.

The demise of ideological doctrines left us uncertain; the information we get simply does not fall into place. And while blogging, as we have seen in some of the instances studied here, often contributes to the turbulence, some blogs, like the one discussed in this chapter, are helpful in assembling information, sorting it out, and providing guidelines for its interpretation. No wonder Rethabile rejoices whenever a new African blog appears in cyberspace. To him, a new blog means a new tale to consider, another opportunity for someone to be "black, loud and proud!" (9.3.04). Within the drivel of blogosphere, stories and testimonies emerge that are mostly useless yet sometimes organize reality for us, as *On Lesotho* does when it reveals another voice on Africa, the voice of emancipation.

Notes

1. <http://lesotho.blogspot.com/>
2. Frantz Fanon, *Black Skin White Masks* (New York: Grove Weidenfeld, 1967).
3. Franz Fanon, *The Wretched of the Earth* (New York: Grove, 1963). P. 73.
4. Paul Theroux, "The Rock Star Burden." *New York Times*, December 15, 2005.
5. John M. Grohol, "Psychology of Weblogs: 1998." Psych Central. <http://www.psychcentral.com/blogs/blog.htm>

Chapter 11

The New Political Arena

Since 2003, when I began this study into what promised to become a media revolution and political emancipation, several things have changed. Many people who at that time had not heard of blogs are now familiar with the term; some bloggers have become household names in the news and entertainment industries; and political parties, corporations, news media, and other enterprises have made use of blogs and of the blog format to advance their interests. As the *Financial Times* put it: "To blog, or not to blog? That is the question vexing marketing managers and public relations executives as they struggle to get to grips with the soaring popularity of weblogs, the online journals that are redefining the way millions of people around the world get news and entertainment on the internet."[1]

While millions of people have been attracted to the free, light-minded, unconventional medium of blogs, its champions, like those of many revolutions in history, have been sidelined. Those individuals who at the turn of the twenty-first century had begun to express themselves through life writing have been defeated or co-opted by the forces of the *ancien régime*. Iranian girl was literally defeated by a regime, which as I write, is becoming even more brutal; Jason Kottke's blog was transformed into a commercial enterprise along with those of other bloggers who joined media groups sponsored by corporations, political parties, publishing houses, and the like; And Pamie and her like were defeated by their drive to become a part of popular culture, which demands some accommodation to its jargon and rules of conduct.

Some bloggers receive a lot of media attention. Their opinions are reproduced in newspapers, and television stations call attention to their writings. This attention points at the cooptation of what has been seen as a blogging revolution by the mainstream media. Once a revolution is hailed by the forces it is out to destroy, it ceases to be a revolution. As Jason Gallo notes, it is more realistic to speak of a convergence between the blogosphere and mainstream media, which, he argues, is already beginning to take place as bloggers sign contracts with media outfits, as media outlets publish blogs on their official Web sites, and as employed journalists privately publish Weblogs in their own time.[2]

This convergence occurs also in the economic sphere for example through corporations advertising in blogs or bloggers turning their blogs into commercial enterprises. This changes the nature of the discourse on blogging, which takes on the excessiveness characterizing the twenty-first century consumer society. For example, the promotion of a new technology allowing bloggers to guide viewers through sights captured on their cell phone cameras announces the coming of a "blog-olution."[3] Advertisements like this oriented toward the consumer in the Christmas shopping season, assure that the new technology will be anything but revolutionary; it will definitely not overthrow existing consumption and advertising practices.

In 2005, Hugh Hewitt, blogger and *New York Times* best selling author, published *Blog*, whose cover carried the promise that readers would be instructed about "how the blogosphere is smashing the old media monopoly and giving individuals power in the marketplace of ideas." This is a good example of how a potentially emancipating medium allowing individuals to negotiate their identity, search for sanity, and bring private concerns into the public sphere, can be captured by a self-proclaimed revolutionary vanguard, thereby turning it into a consumer product.

In this book, directed at executives, the author announces a revolution that will expand to all corners of the world. Through the medium of blogging, Hewitt writes, everyone is potentially a journalist, "including your executive assistant and the messenger bike boy."[4] He assures his readers that, unlike television viewers, most visitors to his site are attracted because they believe he is offering something that is unique: trust. As none of us has time to understand everything, he writes, we have to trust surrogates. And who are the surrogates? Not the old media, which he accuses of having a leftist bias, but bloggers, which he compares with the sixteenth century Reformers:

> The old guard of old media is in a situation very similar to the Roman Catholic Church's situation when Luther arose to challenge the pope's authority. Once Luther's spark set the fire, the availability of editions of the Bible made the collapse of the Church's authority inevitable, though the struggle was long and often bloody.[5]

In case the Reformation is not sufficiently bloody to serve as an analogy for the blogging revolution, Hewitt draws on historical analogies from seventh century Muslim domination and the thirteenth century Mongol uprising, to Erwin Rommel and Norman Schwarzkopf. These analogies point to the melancholic nature of the discourse. As long as one launches a *blitzkrieg* (to use the author's term) in cyberspace, there is no limit to the power one can attribute to oneself. Hewitt imagines himself and his fellow bloggers as swarming across the world and hence as being worthy of the attention of "senior and mid-level executives in business, government, the arts, the church, and especially in politics,"[6] Throughout the book he emphasizes the destructive power of blogs, and their ability to mock and shame the mainstream media; he declares war on the media in the best tradition of Cervantes's Don Quixote:

> Swarming is a seemingly amorphous but carefully structured, coordinated way to strike from all directions at a particular point or points, by means of sustainable 'pulsing' of force and/or fire, close-in as well as from stand-off positions.

It will work best-perhaps it will only work-if it is designed mainly around the deployment of myriad small, dispersed, networked maneuver units. The aim is to coalesce rapidly and stealthily on a target, attack it, then dissever and redisperse, immediately ready to recombine for a new pulse.[7]

There is nothing more melancholic, Cervantes teaches us, than a revolutionary without a revolution, a warrior without a war. There were many flaws in seventeenth century Spain, and Don Quixote was right to try to seek for a cure; but what made him the prototype of the melancholic was his excessiveness, his defining of his cause as a war against imaginary knights. Hewitt's excess occurs not only in the rhetoric—comparing blogosphere to the big bang and claiming it began with the ancient priests of Sumer around 3000 BC, but in the reconstruction of the urge to publish online diaries as a mythological war between the children of light and the children of darkness. By such a reconstruction, the elite of blogosphere, as Hewitt calls it, transforms blogging from a civil emancipation into a social force steered by that elite and functional to its commercial and political ambitions. The online diaries written by individuals turn into "the modern, internet-equivalent of the ancient signal fires that would pass word from hilltop to hilltop of the approach of the enemy."[8]

All too frequently civil activities have been impounded by elites, and all too often these elites have been composed of people whose initial social marginality and lack of political power led them to fantasize about overcoming the forces ruling the world. The less power one has, the more powerful the forces ruling the world appear to be and the more intense the fantasy of one's victory over them. Citizens engaged in civil activity, for instance a town meeting over a local school board's policies, are mostly aware of the extent of theirs and others' powers, while those on the margins are not. What is striking in Hewitt's writing is the pervasiveness of the fantasies about takeover and revenge among people who cannot be classified as marginal. Hugh Hewitt who hints at the universal takeover of the public sphere by bloggers in reminding us that Luther's impact was not limited to the Vatican is showing himself to be a person of great credentials: radio host, best-selling author, and professor of law.

What we find here is melancholic behavior among people who otherwise seem as champions of a new emancipation. This epitomizes above all failed emancipation, not just as a result of the huge political, corporate, or cultural forces suppressing it, although their role cannot be overlooked, but as a result of the failure of early twenty-first century individuals to engage in civil dialogue free of commercial interests, and political domination towards their fellow individuals. Blogosphere is a global political arena that ostensibly frees individuals, allowing them a voice in the public sphere, and in many instances yet what we find is not the sublimation of the citizen but the excessiveness of the melancholic.

Melancholy was defined in Chapter 1 by two variables: solitude and political helplessness. It is hard to tell whether it is these variables that attract millions of people to the blog medium or whether it is the medium itself that encourages solitude and political helplessness. I would argue however that these two components of melancholy are signifiers both of blogosphere, the culmination of millions of online diaries, and the political world of which blogosphere becomes an immanent part.

Solitude

Enlightenment theorists of the eighteenth century placed high value on emancipation of the individual. The individual they envisaged existed within well-defined limits of political discourse and behavior. The assumption that individuals are capable of sublimation and hence cooperation allowed their endowment with inalienable rights to life, liberty and the pursuit of happiness. But eighteenth century enlightenment theory, neither in its European nor in its American versions, did not develop a satisfactory response to the lack of sublimation found in some nineteenth and twentieth century writings, or in blogosphere. By lack of sublimation I refer to the abandonment of civil dialogue for the sake of what Christopher Lasch calls a "culture of narcissism,"[9] a culture that has given up hope of improving human life through politics, turning instead to psychic self-improvement wrapped in the rhetoric of authenticity and awareness.

One could imagine that had America's founding fathers Internet access in their graves, they would have been turning over when in 2002 blogger "N.Z. Bear" began to propose his reinterpretations of the Declaration of Independence of July 4, 1776. Calling his blog "The Truth Laid Bear," and hinting at his strong urge to hibernate, he contends that moral codes are tricky and dangerous things, which after a few generations or so of interpretation have a tendency to spin wildly out of control. He offers to examine some of the prevailing moral codes in the planet and to propose a new moral code, seeing this as an easy task: "what if the idea of a packaged system doesn't appeal? Not a problem: roll your own."[10]

In the process of rolling his own moral code, "N.Z. Bear" registers his reservations about the norm of happiness, which lacks an objective measure. "It's a mess," "N.Z. Bear" complains, because most people do not stand a chance of assessing their own happiness—let alone judging what makes other people happy. He then launches into lengthy deliberations over the difficulty of disseminating a common norm of happiness. These deliberations are taken up by other bloggers, including Jack Adams who finds them "dumb," "Kiwi" who writes that "this is the most solipsistic, self-congratulating, masturbatory pile of crack that I have had the misfortune to encounter!" and "zzyzx" who calls upon the community to be nice to the bear for "it takes guts to take a stab at a question like this. And there's no time like now to be taking a fresh look at the truths we hold to be self-evident."[11]

This last point is worthy of some consideration. We live in a postmodern world in which no truth is held to be self-evident and in which everything is open to individual deliberation. Blogging allows authentic voices, such as that of "N.Z. Bear" to embark on a stream of consciousness in relation to the formerly self-evident truths devised by eighteenth century gentlemen and to define their own conceptions of life, liberty, and the pursuit of happiness.

This authenticity, however, has its drawbacks, as discussed in Richard Sennett's *The Fall of Public Man*.[12] Sennett claims that most citizens in the second half of the twentieth century approach their dealings with the state in a spirit of resigned acquiescence. Manners and ritual interchanges with strangers are looked on as threatening, while the psyche is treated as though it had an inner life of its own. Sennett argues that this leads not only to the demise of a public culture, but to the loss of individualism because the more privatized the psyche, the less it is stimulated, and the more difficult it is for people to feel or to express feelings.

In *The Ethics of Authenticity*, Charles Taylor discusses the notion, an offshoot of modern individualism, that all people have the right to develop their own way of life grounded on their own sense of what is really important or of value. Taylor spells this out: people being called upon to be true to themselves and to seek their own self-fulfillment. He agrees with Alan Bloom and other critics of this notion that the culture of self-fulfillment has taken trivialized and self-indulgent forms (which in turn may result in new modes of conformity), although he also notes that there is a powerful moral ideal at work here, debased and travestied as its expression might be.

Taylor makes us realize the moral force of authenticity and claims it should be taken seriously as a moral ideal rather than as a mistaken departure from standards rooted in human nature. At the same time he stresses the dialogical condition of authenticity; the development of our unique identity requires dialogue with significant others. He could be referring to bloggers who confuse their idiosyncratic reporting with having a unique identity, when he writes:

> I may be the only person with exactly 3,732 hairs on my head, or be exactly the same height as some tree on the Siberian plain, but so what? If I begin to say that I define myself by my ability to articulate important truths, or play the Hammerklavier like no one else, or revive the tradition of my ancestors, then we are in the domain of recognizable self-definitions.[13]

Taylor warns against suppressing or denying the horizons against which things take on significance. As he puts it:

> I can define my identity only against the background of things that matter. But to bracket out history, nature, society, the demands of solidarity, everything but what I find in myself, would be to eliminate all candidates for what matters. Only if I exist in a world in which history, or the demand of nature, or the need of my fellow human beings, or the duties of citizenship, or the call of God, or something else of this order *matters* crucially, can I define an identity for myself that is not trivial.[14]

The triviality in blogosphere stems not from a lack of reference to things that matter crucially but from excessive reference to them. History, nature, human solidarity, and God are all taking part in the online celebration of solitude. In my three years of research on blogging I encountered many important ideas but rarely have they been expressed in a fashion reminiscent of dialogue. Celebrity bloggers, and those aspiring to become celebrities, sound equally solipsistic. Even when presenting their life as meaningless, the unique combination of solitude and publicity in which the presentation is made turns it into a self-assured contention rather than a conversation. To converse, whether online or offline, is to engage in cooperation rather than laying the truth bare. The test of a conversation lies in the participants' attentiveness, something that the blogging medium does not encourage. Blogging, like other forms of autobiography, is done in solitude.

This is not to undermine the value of solitude. In a book titled *The Value of Solitude*, John Barbour shows that the condition of solitude can provoke the most serene, profound, or exhilarating moments in life. Being alone, he writes, may provide the necessary setting for people's spiritual search, their attempt to understand life's meaning and to be related to the ultimate sources of goodness and power.[15] But how many bloggers can be seen as engaged in a spiritual search? One could argue, of course, that reporting on one's ordinary life in itself comprises a spiritual journey. This argument is made in Christina Baldwin's book of the know-how of journal writing when she states that "The spiritual journey is what the soul is up to while we attend to daily living. The spiritual journey is the soul's life commingling with ordinary life."[16]

But a spiritual journey requires some reflective withdrawal, while blogosphere is marked by imminence and immediacy. Baldwin promises prospective journal writers too easy a journey: "The spiritual journey doesn't require a grand tour. There are no bon voyage parties for the beginning of a quest. We don't even know when it began, we are simply aware one day that we are underway."[17] Yet not every expression of ordinary life involves a spiritual quest. The reporting on a trip to the supermarket does not turn it into a life journey unless a *bon voyage* party is given, in the sense of developing and sharing a degree of consciousness over its meaning. But blogosphere, as the example of "N.Z. Bear" so nicely demonstrates, often prides itself for the lack of shared meaning. It may thus be seen as the same old arena as the world at large, in which millions of individuals are wandering without meaning and purpose, yet being desperate enough about their solitude to allow the definition of their wandering as a spiritual journey.

Political Helplessness

That millions of individuals surf the net in solitude in search of life stories written by strangers, or write such stories themselves, cannot be attributed only to the availability of the technology but seems to reflect a deep frustration with the prevailing systems of political communication.

In this study, we have observed a handful of online diaries whose common denominator is the dissatisfaction expressed by the writers over social control and manipulation by powerful political, corporate, and media forces, and a large degree of deceit in their respective countries.

Blogging may be seen as an attempt to restore a degree of authenticity, expressing some inner truth in a world in which the boundaries between truth and untruth have been blurred. In a *New York Times* article, Frank Rich traced the current culture of deceit back to Orson Wells's famous 1938 radio program on a Martian invasion. Wells, he writes, unwittingly set up the path toward the utter destabilization of reality coming to bear today in such instances as the fakery with which the war in Iraq has been sold to the world or the freak show performed by Tom Cruise by jumping on a couch in a popular television show as an alleged expression of love to a young actress. Cruise's romance, Rich notes, proved less credible to Americans in 2005 than did the announcement of a Martian invasion in 1938, because the boundary between reality and fiction has been blurred by show business, news business, and the government.[18]

People who lived under the totalitarian regimes of the twentieth century knew the government was lying and developed mechanisms to read between the lines and maintain their civil connections. These mechanisms, however, become ineffectual when the deceit is not being generated by identifiable political authorities but is becoming a way of life. Individuals today are being subjected to media spins such as the vindictive disclosure of the CIA agent Valerie Plame's name to divert attention from her husband's critique of the Bush administration; people are manipulated by best-selling authors who present their fiction as real life stories, as has been alleged in the cases of Norma Khouri's *Forbidden Love* and James Frei's *A Million Little Pieces*; and they are surrounded by dubious scientific and statistical information in stock market reports, health and nutrition data, public opinion polls, and the like.

Elements of the culture of deceit can be found not only in an authoritarian country like Iran where the regime exercises extensive control over public information, but also in the democratic countries discussed in this study. Consider the Katrina disaster of August 2005 in the US. In the past, American citizens, even those living in low-income neighborhoods, could be confident of being rescued during or following a hurricane. The shattering of these expectations has come about as a result not only of the inefficiency of public institutions but also the untruthfulness prevailing within them. The sense of responsibility that provoked some people to come to the rescue of others, has fallen prey to the familiar bureaucratic concern for shifting the responsibility elsewhere.

Canada is also experiencing deceit: there is a wide gap between the public image of Canadians as peaceful people enjoying a good quality of life, and the growing crime rate, urban decay, ethnic strife, decrease in services and substantial political corruption that is the reality.

Israelis are suffering from the delusion that they are engaging in a "peace process" which has never taken off. A series of well-orchestrated photo opportunities in which Middle East leaders have shaken hands has had little impact in reality.

India conveys the public image of a country on the road to modernization, measured by such indicators as the number of high tech professionals the country employs or exports, while much of that modernization is illusory. Not only is modern India suffering from many of the ills of modernity, but the conditions in many parts of the country are worsening dramatically as a result of the processes of globalization.

The greatest deceit concerns Africa where millions are dying of malnutrition, AIDS, malaria, and war while the world indulges in the apparent attention being given to the continent, especially by rock musicians, with minimal results.

No wonder individuals in these and other parts of the world aspire to break away from the networks of public information. Blogosphere provides an escape in that government, business, and media lies are exposed and civil concerns can be freely expressed without manipulation from above. As blogosphere becomes more salient, it provides bloggers with a sense of victory of truth over untruth, of good over evil.

The problem is that blogosphere does not have a monopoly over the truth and its power to do good and refrain from evil is limited. In a summary of the year 2005 *Time* includes several references to bloggers who brought to public attention matters the mainstream media initially ignored and who provided elaborate coverage of important issues, such as the Terri Schiavo affair. This affair demonstrates both the degree of bloggers' involvement in public life and the limits to that involvement.

Terri, a twenty-six-year old woman, in 1990 suffered a cardiac arrest and went into a coma, which left her in a vegetative state. In the mid 1990s she became the subject of a legal struggle between her husband, who ordered the removal of her feeding tube, and Terri's parents who had managed to overrule all removal orders until 2005. The case became a rallying point for pro-life and pro-choice politicians and advocacy groups who turned it into what *Time* calls a "circus."[19]

In that circus, bloggers played the parts of acrobats, clowns, and elephant trainers. Not only were specific blogs set up, such as "The Terri Schiavo Blog" or "Blogs for Terri," but millions of blogs from "kottke.org" to "Blogs for Bush" made reference to the case. A report by the Associated Press on the way the affair was played out in blogosphere pointed at its uncivilized nature. While some bloggers had a related agenda, such as support for the rights of the disabled or opposition to euthanasia, and lawyers provided legal commentary in their blogs, many bloggers simply entered the arena in order to be heard. Some blogs carried unproven accusations that Terri's husband had caused the injury that put his wife in a vegetative state; others speculated about the financial motives of the two sides in the dispute. One blog was dedicated to exposing the lies of the media, judges, and elected officials who were allegedly trying to cover up the attempted murder of Terri. Other blogs launched attacks against pollsters whose findings did not match their convictions, accusing them of fraud. "There is a distinct mistrust of authority in the Schiavo blogosphere," the report concluded.[20]

Although on occasion bloggers can be right when the authorities and the mainstream media, innocently or basely, are wrong, there is little guarantee that discourse in blogosphere will enhance a culture of truthfulness in society. Not every fanciful possibility that surfaces in a blog turns out to be the truth. Nor does the sum of millions of views expressed in solitude become a marketplace of ideas. As Howard Rheingold showed in *Smart Mobs*, although modern technologies provide new opportunities for citizens who resist powerful institutions to band together, the discourse has a high probability to go astray:

> Some people proclaim opinions that are so abhorrent or boring, use such foul language, or are such bad communicators that they sour discussions that would otherwise be valuable to the majority of participants. Some people have a voracious need for attention and don't care whether it is negative attention. Other people use the shield of anonymity to unleash their aggressions, bigotry, and sadistic impulses.[21]

Blogosphere is an arena in which many people disappointed by the culture of deceit propose a cure by expressing their inner truth, or what they choose to present as such. However, blogosphere has its share of aggressors, bigots, and sadists who make sure that a medium providing for the emancipation of the individual, and virtual cooperation among the emancipated, continues to resemble the world at large. As in the real world, bloggers are helpless vis à vis the evil they experience or observe, and their helplessness is only marginally relieved by the sense of community that is emerging online.

Various studies have shown that Internet communities may be quite effective. Katz and Rice surveyed ethnographic studies claiming that rich and fertile, diverse and expanded interactions are possible through the Internet and that impassioned members of many online groups provide emotional and other resources to each other.[22] J. Macgregor Wise argued that in a post-modern world in which the social cohesion has been lost, the Internet has come to our rescue. As a non-centralized, non-hierarchical network it allows people to reconnect and have a voice "in the grand debate that is society."[23]

Yet society is not a "grand debate" but a concrete network of relations steered by political elites, bureaucratic routines, economic interests, and cultural industries. None of these is significantly affected by online or offline discourse. Judging by the blogs studied here, feelings such as fear of oppression, resentment toward authority and vulnerability vis à vis real or imagined systems are not easily reduced by online life writing. While having an outlet for one's frustrations, the online diarist cannot even expect a sympathetic ear, such as might be found in the psychiatrist's couch. The online outpourings bloggers get in response to their posts can put the death of an aging cat on the same emotional level as the earthquake in Pakistan, which leaves one lonely and helpless.

I want to conclude by arguing that the solitude and helplessness detected in blogosphere are variables of significant explanatory power for some of the political forces operating in the world; a strong correlation exists between the melancholic withdrawal in cyberspace and in the "real world." Both in blogopshere and in the global political arena of the early twenty-first century, Paul McCartney's words in *Eleanor Rigby* seem more than ever relevant: "All the lonely people/ Where do they all come from?/ All the lonely people/ Where do they all belong?"

Judging by the present study, they come from government, business, industry, journalism, academia, the arts, high school, home, the hospital, the asylum, the street—the list is endless. If they have access to a computer and free time they may belong to the community of bloggers telling life stories, commenting on public affairs, expressing opinions on anything under the sun and producing billions of words on their keyboards. This community is situated in a zone between emancipation and melancholy. Its incumbents are to an extent liberated and acquire a voice while their social and political impact is limited, largely because of the virtual nature of the endeavor.

But those who do not write blogs are situated in the same zone. Many citizens resent the public communication networks surrounding them and are aware of their deceitful nature but see no escape, because no alternate system of truth is available. Practices such as letters to the editor, talkbacks, talk radio, and the reading on television of viewers' emails create a false sense of access to decision centers at a time when public institutions are becoming less accessible and responsive.

Disenchanted citizens resort to a variety of attitudes and behaviors including apathy toward political affairs, resistance to the global processes deemed responsible for their powerlessness, quest for redemption through religious fundamentalism and, in some cases, terrorism. No wonder some bloggers like to compare themselves to terrorists, the ultimate rebels against mainstream society. "Like al-Quaeda," Tim Cavanaugh writes in an article on blogs of war, "the war bloggers are a loosely structured network, a shadowy underground whose flexibility and impulsive log-rolling make them as cost-effective as they are deadly."[24]

Although the comparison is stretched, the two endeavors have something in common. Terrorists, like bloggers, are not necessarily from the margins of society yet they operate within a framework of solitude and helplessness and attempt to break away from it by changing the rules of the game. And while the methods advocated by the two groups are obviously very different, they both represent a similar trend in the present world, one of diversion of respected but disenchanted citizens from the norms of civil society to a fantasy world in which the excessive use of words—or bombs—would make everybody listen.

In both cases, that of individuals expressing their helplessness vis à vis the systems of the modern world through terror and that of individuals combating those systems by forming an alternate system of public communication, I suspect the efforts have little chance of success, for no political goals are achievable without a degree of civil cooperation. Political, economic, and media structures may be disrupted by acts of violence, or by millions of blogs, but never defeated or replaced by the actual or virtual assembly of all the lonely people who, as

Eleanor Rigby reminds us, are doomed to "writing the words of a sermon that no one will hear."

Notes

1. Kevin Allison, "Who is Afraid of the Big Bad Blog?" *FT.com Financial Times*, 3.11.2005. <http://news.ft.com/cms/s/5bf3007c-4c98-11da-89df-0000779e2340.html>
2. Jason Gallo, "Weblog Journalism: Between Infiltration and Integration." *Into the Blogosphere*. <http://blog.lib.umn.edu/blogosphere/weblog_journalism.html>
3. Sarah Staples, "B.C. Firm Predicts Webcast Software Will Be Beginning of Blog-olution." *Calgary Herald*, 17.12.05.
4. Hugh Hewitt, *Blog; Understanding the Information Reformation that's Changing our World* (Nashville, Tennessee: Nelson, 2005), X.
5. Hugh Hewitt , 2005, XVII.
6. Hugh Hewitt, 2005, XIX.
7. Hugh Hewitt, 2005, 4.
8. Hugh Hewitt, 2005, 45.
9. Christopher Lasch, *The Culture of Narcissism: American Life in an Age of Diminishing Expectations* (New York: Norton, 1978).
10. "The Truth Laid Bear." 21.4.03. <http://www.truthlaidbear.com/archi.../life_liberty_and_the_pursuit_of_happiness.ph>
11. "The Truth Laid Bear." 21.4.03.
12. Richard Sennett, *The Fall of Public Man* (New York: Knopf, 1977).
13. Charles Taylor, *The Ethics of Authenticity* (Cambridge, MA: Harvard University Press, 1991), 36.
14. Charles Taylor, 40-41.
15. John D. Barbour, *The Value of Solitude: The Ethics and Spirituality of Aloneness in Autobiography* (Charlottesville, VA: University of Virginia Press, 2004).
16. Christina Baldwin, *Life's Companion: Journal Writing as a Spiritual Quest* (New York: Bantam, 1990), 5.
17. Christina Baldwin, 1990, 7.
18. Frank Rich, "Two Top Guns Shoot Blanks." *New York Times*, 19.6.05.
19. "Fight to the Finish." *Time: The Year In Review* (2005), 73.
20. "Terri Schiavo Case Fuels Blogging Storm." *The Associated Press*, 23.3.05. (MSNBC.Com.) <http://www.msnbc.com/id/7277674/1098>
21. Howard Rheingold, *Smart Mobs: The Next Social Revolution* (Cambridge, MA: Perseus, 2002), 121.
22. James E. Katz and Ronald E. Rice, *Social Consequences of Internet Use: Access, Involvement, and Interaction* (Cambridge, MA: The MIT Press, 2002).
23. J. Macgregor Wise, "Community, Affect, and the Virtual: The Politics of Cyberspace." In *Virtual Publics: Policy and Community in an Electronic Age*, Beth E. Kolko ed. (New York: Columbia University Press, 2003).
24. Tim Cavanaugh, "Let Slip the Blogs of War." In *We've Got Blog: How Weblogs are Changing our Culture* (Cambridge, MA: Perseus, 2002), 189.

Bibliography

Alavi, Nasrin. *We Are Iran*. New York: Soft Sull Press, 2005.

Anderson, Benedict. *Imagined Communities: Reflections on the Origin and Spread of Nationalism*. London: Verso, 1991.

Axthelm, Peter M. *The Modern Confessional Novel*. New Haven, CT: Yale University Press, 1967.

Baldwin, Christina. *Life's Companion: Journal Writing as a Spiritual Quest*. New York: Bantam, 1990.

————*Storycatcher: Making Sense of Our Lives through the Power and Practice of Story*. Novato, Cal.: New World Library, 2005.

Barbour, John D. *The Value of Solitude: The Ethics and Spirituality of Aloneness in Autobiography*. Charlottesville, VA: University of Virginia Press, 2004.

Barker, Hannah, and Simon Burrows. *Press, Politics and the Public Sphere in Europe and North America 1760-1820*. Cambridge: Cambridge University Press, 2002.

Bartman, Sandra, and Annabelle Sreberny-Mohammadi. *Globalization, Communication and Transnational Civil Society*. Cresskill, NJ: Hampton Press, 1996.

Bausch, Paul, Matthew Haughey, and Meg Hourihan. *We Blog: Publishing Online with Weblogs*. Indianapolis, IN: Wiley, 2002.

Beiner, Ronald. *Liberalism, Nartionalism, Citizenship: Essays on the Problem of Political Community*. Vancouver, BC: UBC Press, 2003.

Ben-Zeev, Aaron. *Love Online: Emotions on the Internet*. Cambridge: Cambridge University Press, 2004.

Bimber, Bruce, and Richard Davis. *Campaigning Online: The Internet in U.S. Elections*. New York: Oxford University Press, 2003.

Blood, Rebecca. *The Weblog Handbook: Practical Advice on Creating and Maintaining Your Blog*. Cambridge, MA: Perseus 2002.

Brown, Wendy. "Resisting Left Melancholy." Boundary *2* 26 (Fall 1999): 19-27.

Clarke, Bruce, and Linda Darlymple Henderson. *From Energy to Information: Representation in Science and Technology, Art, and Literature*. Stanford, Cal.: Stanford University Press, 2002.

Colas, Dominique. *Civil Society and Fanaticism: Conjoined Histories*. Stanford, Cal.: Stanford University Press, 1997.

Dahlberg, Lincoln. "The Internet and Democratic Discourse: Exploring the Prospects of Online Deliberative Forums Extending the Public Sphere." *Information, Communication & Society* 4 (2001): 615-633.

Deuze, Mark. "The Web and its Journalisms: Considering the Consequences of Different Types of News Media Online." *New Media and Society* 5 (2003): 203-230.

Dostoevsky, Fyodor. *Notes from Underground and The Grand Inquisitor.* New York: Dutton, 1960.

Edel, Leon. *Writing Lives: Principia Biographia. New York:* W.W. Norton, 1987.

Egan, Susanna. *Mirror Talk: Genres of Crisis in Contemporary Autobiography.* Chapel Hill, NC: University of North Carolina Press.

Enterline, Lynn. *The Tears of Narcissus: Melancholia and Masculinity in Early Modern Writing.* Stanford, CA: Stanford University Press, 1995.

Evans, Andrew. *The Virtual Life: Escapism and Simulation in Our Media World.* London: Fusion, 2001.

Forter, Greg. "Against Melancholia: Contemporary Mourning Theory, Fitzgerald's The Great Gatsby, and the Politics of Unfinished Grief." *A Journal of Feminist Cultural Studies* 14 (Summer 2003): 134-170.

Freud, Sigmund. "Civilization and its Discontents." In *Civilization, Society and Religion,* translated by James Strachey. London: Penguin, 1985.

————"Mourning and Melancholia." In *Collected Papers,* translated by Joan Riviere. London: Hogarth, 1971.

Fulford, Robert. *The Triumph of Narrative: Storytelling in the Age of Mass Culture.* Toronto: Anansi, 1999.

Fulton, Katherine. "A Tour of Our Uncertain Future." *Columbia Journalism Review* 34 (March/April 1996): 19-27.

Gamson, William A. *Talking Politics.* Cambridge: Cambridge University Press, 1992.

Godwin, Mike. *Cyber Rights: Defending Free Speech in the Digital Age.* Cambridge, MA: MIT Press, 2003.

Goldfarb, Jeffrey C. *Civility and Subversion: The Intellectual in Democratic Society.* Cambridge: Cambridge University Press, 1998.

Habermas, Jürgen. *The Structural Transformation of the Public Sphere: An Inquiry into a Category of Bourgeois Society.* Cambridge, MA: MIT Press.

Hanen, Marsha P., Alex Barber, and David Cassels, eds. *Community Values in an Age of Globalization.* Victoria, BC: The Sheldon M. Chumir Foundation, 2002.

Hartman, Geoffrey. *Scars of the Spirit: The Struggle Against Inauthenticity.* New York: Palgrave Macmillan, 2002.

Hewitt, Hugh. *Blog: Understanding the Information Reformation that's Changing our World.* Nashville, TN: Nelson, 2005.

Jenkins, Henry, and David Thorburn, eds. *Democracy and the New Media.* Cambridge, MA.: MIT Press, 2003.

Kahn, Richard, and Douglas Kellner. "New Media and Internet Activism: From the 'Battle of Seattle' to Blogging." *New Media and Society* 6 (2004): 87-95.

Katz, James E., and Ronald E. Rice. *Social Consequences of Internet Use: Access, Involvement, and Interaction.* Cambridge, MA: The MIT Press, 2002.

Kennedy, Helen. "Technobiography: Researching Lives, Online and Off. *Biography* 26. (Winter 2003): 120-139.

Kendall, Lori. *Hanging Out in the Virtual Pub: Masculinities and Relationships Online.* Berkeley, CA: University of California Press, 2002.

Keren, Michael. *The Citizen's Voice: Politics and Literature in the Twentieth Century.* Calgary, AB: University of Calgary Press, 2003.

———*The Pen and the Sword: Israeli Intellectuals and the Making of the Nation-State.* Boulder, Col.: Westview 1989.

Killoran, John B. "The Gnome in the Front Yard and Other Public Figurations: Genres of Self-Presentation on Personal Home Pages." *Biography* 26 (Winter 2003): 66-83.

Kitzmann, Andreas. "That Different Place: Documenting the Self within Online Environments." *Biography* 26 (Winter 2003): 48-65.

Kolko, Beth E., ed. *Virtual Publics: Politics and Community in an Electronic Age.* New York: Columbia University Press 2003.

Lasch, Christopher. *The Culture of Narcissism: American Life in an Age of Diminishing Expectations.* New York: Norton, 1978.

Lash, Scott. "Being after Time: Towards a Politics of Melancholy." *Cultural Values* 2 (April 1998): 305- 320.

———*Critique of Information.* London: Sage, 2002.

Lila, Mark. *The Reckless Mind: Intellectuals in Politics.* New York: NYRB, 2001.

Matheson, Donald. "Weblogs and the Epistemology of the News: Some Trends in Online Journalism." *New Media and Society* 6 (2004): 443-468.

Mccaughey, Martha, and Michael D. Aters, eds. *Cyberactivism: Online Activism in Theory and Practice.* New York: Routledge, 2003.

Mcneill, Laurie. "Teaching an Old Genre New Tricks: The Diary on the Internet." *Biography* 26 (Winter 2003): 24-47.

Meikle, Graham. *Future Active: Media Activism and the Internet.* New York: Routledge, 2002.

Mortenses, Torill, and Jill Walker. "Blogging Thoughts: Personal Publication as an Online Research Tool." Pp. 249-272 in *Researching ICTs in Context*, edited by Andrew Morrison. Oslo: InterMedia Report, 2002.

Mutz, Diana C., and Byron Reeves. "The New Videomalaise: Effects of Televised Incivility on Political Trust." *American Political Science Review* 99 (February 2005): 1-27.

Nafisi, Azar. *Reading Lolita in Tehran.* New York: Random House, 2003.

Orgad, Shani. *Storytelling Online: Talking Breast Cancer on the Internet.* New York: Peter Lang, 2005.

Pax, Salam. *Salam Pax: The Clandestine Diary of an Ordinary Iraqi.* New York: Grove, 2003.

Pensky, Max. *Melancholy Dialectics: Walter Benjamin and the Play of Mourning.* Amherst, MA.: University of Massachusetts Press, 1993.

Rainer, Tristine. *Your Life as Story: Discovering the 'New Autobiography' and Writing Memoir as Literature.* New York: Putnam, 1998.

Rheingold, Howard. *Smart Mobs: The Next Social Revolution.* Cambridge, MA.: Perseus, 2002.

————*The Virtual Community: Homesteading on the Electronic Frontier.* Cambridge, MA.: MIT Press 2002.

Riesman, David. *The Lonely Crowd: A Study of the Changing American Character.* New Haven, CT: Yale University Press, 1950.

Rodríguez, Juana María. "Scripting autobiographical Subjectivity Online: Confessions of a Latina Cyber-Slut." *A/b: Auto/Biography Studies* 15 (Winter 2000): 223-247.

Rowland, Wade. *The Spirit of the Web: The Age of Information from Telegraph to Internet.* Toronto: Key Porter, 1999.

Scarry, Elaine. *Resisting Representation.* New York: Oxford University Press, 1994.

Schneider, Barbara. "Mothers Talk about their Children with Schizophrenia: A Performance Autobiography." *Journal of Psychiatric and Mental Health Nursing* 12 (2005): 333-340.

Seidman, Steven. *Social Theory in the Postmodern Era.* Malden, MA.: Blackwell, 1998.

Sennett, Richard. *The Fall of Public Man.* New York: Knopf, 1977.

Smith, Sidonie. *Subjectivity, Identity, and the Body: Women's Autobiographical Practices in the Twentieth Century.* Bloomington: IN: University Press, 1993.

Smith, Sidonie, and Julia Watson, eds. *Interfaces: Women Autobiography Image Performance.* Ann Arbor, MI: University of Michigan Press, 2005.

Sorapure, Madeleine. "Screening Moments, Scrolling Lives: Diary Writing on the Web." *Biography* 26 (Winter 2003): 1-23.

Soufas, Teresa Scott. *Melancholy and the Secular Mind in Spanish Golden Age Literature.* Columbia, MO: University of Missouri Press, 1990.

Starr, Paul. *The Creation of the Media: Political Origins of Modern Communications.* New York: Perseus, 2004.

Stevenson, Nick. *The Transformation of the Media: Globalization, Morality and Ethics.* London: Longman, 1999.

Taylor, Charles. *Sources of the Self: The Making of the Modern Identity.* Cambridge, MA: Harvard University Press, 1989.

————*The Ethics of Authenticity.* Cambridge, MA.: Harvard University Press, 1991.

Taras, David, Fritz Pannekoek, and Maria Bakardjieva, eds. *How Canadians Communicate.* Calgary, AB.: University of Calgary Press, 2003.

Théberge, Paul. "Everyday Fandom: Fan Clubs, Blogging, and the Quotidian Rhythms of the Internet." *Canadian Journal of Communication* 30 (2005): 485-502.

Traverso, Enzo. "Intellectuals and Anti-Fascism: For a Critical Historization." *New Politics* 9 (Winter 2004): 91-101.

Tridgell, Susan. *Understanding Our Selves: The Dangerous Art of Biography.* Oxford: Peter Lang, 2004.

Vatimo, Gianni. *The Transparent Society.* Baltimore, MD: The Johns Hopkins

University Press, 1992.

Vogt, Christina, and Peiying Chen. "Feminism and the Internet." *Peace Review* 13 (2001): 371-374.

Zalis, Elaine. "At Home in Cyberspace: Staging Autobiographical Scenes." *Biography* 26 (Winter 2003): 84-119.

Zuern, John. "Online Lives: Introduction." *Biography* 26 (Winter 2003): v-xxv.

Index

About the Author

Professor Michael Keren, an Israeli political scientist specializing in political communication and philosophy, holds a Canada Research Chair in Communication, Culture and Civil Society at the University of Calgary. His publications include the following books: *Ben Gurion and the Intellectuals: Power, Knowledge and Charisma* (1983); *The Pen and the Sword: Israeli Intellectuals and the Making of the Nation-State* (1989); *Professionals against Populism: The Peres Government and Democracy* (1995); *The Concentration of Media Ownership and Freedom of the Press* (1996); *History of Political Ideas* (2001); *International Intervention: Sovereignty vs. Responsibility* (with Don Sylvan, 2002), *Zichroni v. State of Israel: The Biography of a Civil Rights Lawyer* (2002); *The Citizen's Voice: Twentieth Century Politics and Literature* (2003); *Reality and Fiction at the turn of the Millennium* (2006).